# Cruising the Dead River

# *Cruising the Dead River*

## David Wojnarowicz and New York's Ruined Waterfront

FIONA ANDERSON

The University of Chicago Press
Chicago and London

The University of Chicago Press, Chicago 60637
The University of Chicago Press, Ltd., London

Published 2019
Printed in the United States of America

28 27 26 25 24 23 22 21 20 19    1 2 3 4 5

ISBN-13: 978-0-226-60361-2 (cloth)
ISBN-13: 978-0-226-60375-9 (paper)
ISBN-13: 978-0-226-60389-6 (e-book)
DOI: https://doi.org/10.7208/chicago/9780226603896.001.0001

Library of Congress Cataloging-in-Publication Data

Names: Anderson, Fiona, 1985– author.
Title: Cruising the dead river : David Wojnarowicz and New York's ruined waterfront / Fiona Anderson.
Description: Chicago : The University of Chicago Press, 2019. | Includes bibliographical references and index.
Identifiers: LCCN 2018058853 | ISBN 9780226603612 (cloth : alk. paper) | ISBN 9780226603759 (pbk. : alk. paper) | ISBN 9780226603896 (e-book)
Subjects: LCSH: Wojnarowicz, David. | Cruising (Sexual behavior)—New York (State)—New York. | Sexual minority community—New York (State)—New York. | Waterfronts—Social aspects—New York (State)—New York. | New York (N.Y.)—In art. | Ruins in art. | Waterfronts in art.
Classification: LCC N6537.W63 A53 2019 | DDC 709.2—dc23
LC record available at https://lccn.loc.gov/2018058853

♾ This paper meets the requirements of ANSI/NISO Z39.48-1992 (Permanence of Paper).

*For Douglas Crimp*

# *Contents*

INTRODUCTION

# Queer at the Water's Edge

In February 1977, while living in Brooklyn's Red Hook neighborhood near the New York Naval Shipyard, the young writer and aspiring artist David Wojnarowicz produced a short poem titled "Circulating drunk to midnight music." By the water's edge, at the "bridges [*sic*] base," he wrote, wandered "monks of the dead river" and "ancient heretics, those that / proposition your image." Bodies moved snakelike through "river stone and storm pipage," by "street corners" and "alleyways," "weary," "bent and blood-stained." Wojnarowicz's poem evokes the disused Brooklyn harbor of the late 1970s as a bleak and dangerous place, desolate, dystopian, and highly erotic. Monks and heretics shift "into delirium . . . and curse softly when bodies are set into motion." "Pumping organs" bring about an orgasmic "flash of holiness."[1]

What monks were these? Of what queer religion? Playing with the abstinence implicit in his metaphor, Wojnarowicz alludes to the rich imaginative potential emptiness permits. The navy yard had been decommissioned in the mid-1960s and was economically functionless. Derelict, the empty warehouses and dark industrial avenues by the East River played host to a diverse cruising culture. Since the mid-nineteenth century, Red Hook, Vinegar Hill, nearby Sands Street, and, later, the navy yard had been appropriated as gay cruising spaces. Wojnarowicz cruised the waterfront in the late 1970s, his "image" propositioned by "ancient heretics," just as the poet Hart Crane had stood, waiting, cruising, "under the shadows by the piers" by the Brooklyn Bridge in the 1920s. "Only in darkness," Crane wrote, "is thy shadow clear."[2] The novelist Edmund White described the piers on Manhattan's Lower West Side, also a cruising site, in similarly sacral terms, as "a ruined cathedral" where "the wind said incantations."[3] Cruising for anonymous sex in the abandoned spaces along the city's fringe in the late 1970s, White wrote, "we were isolated men at prayer, that man by the font (rainwater stagnant in the lid of a barrel), and this one in a side chapel (the damp vault), that pair of celebrants holding up a flame near the dome."[4]

A long history of corrupt unions and gangsters, brotherhoods of stevedores and itinerant sailors, echoes in this cloistral symbolism. In economic decline since federal crackdowns on the harbor's extensive Mafia networks in the mid-1950s, the rise of air transportation and white-collar urban labor in New York in the 1960s, and subsequent "white flight," the once-bustling Lower West Side Manhattan waterfront sat, ostensibly empty, and fell into ruin (figure 0.1). Its abandonment coincided with a crackdown on gay male cruising in the borough's public parks, restrooms, and subway stations in the years leading up to the 1964–1965 New York World's Fair. Its emptiness drew men toward the water. For a time, empty haulage vehicles that were parked unlocked overnight along the West Side Highway provided spaces for anonymous sexual encounters. But as these trucks disappeared, along with the shipping companies that owned them, men moved further out, cruising the vast crumbling structures of the formerly industrial riverside. Their migration highlights the complex political dynamics governing public and private sexual association in the dense urban environment of Manhattan, careful management of which was essential to police regulation of homosexual behavior in the 1960s. Systemic municipal and industrial neglect had rendered the waterfront's piers and warehouses a no-man's land. No longer economically viable, they were effectively outside any civic or private proprietary jurisdiction.

In the following decade, the piers and warehouses along the Hudson River fell further into ruin. Following the collapse of a portion of the West Side Highway in December 1973, parts of the harbor were cut off from the main body of Manhattan, accessibly only on foot or by bicycle. Through the 1970s, the stone piers on the West Side functioned as makeshift parks, where neighbors sunbathed and men cruised, sex workers hustled for business, and workers from the nearby Meatpacking District ate lunch. With the city near bankruptcy, thorough redevelopment was unfeasible. Robert F. Wagner Jr., serving as deputy mayor for policy, noted in a study on waterfront development in 1980, that the "least desirable activities were assigned to the waterfront. . . . [It] suffered serious neglect, to the point where an observer approaching many parts of it today would think the nation's leading port a South Bronx-by-the-Sea," alluding to the legendary dilapidation of New York's northernmost borough.[5] The author of a later *New York Times* article complained that the underutilized riverside left the island of Manhattan like "an unhemmed dress."[6] Largely unpoliced, these littoral frontiers permitted a diverse range of queer sexual uses. They appeared to hold spectral traces of their prior uses, latent

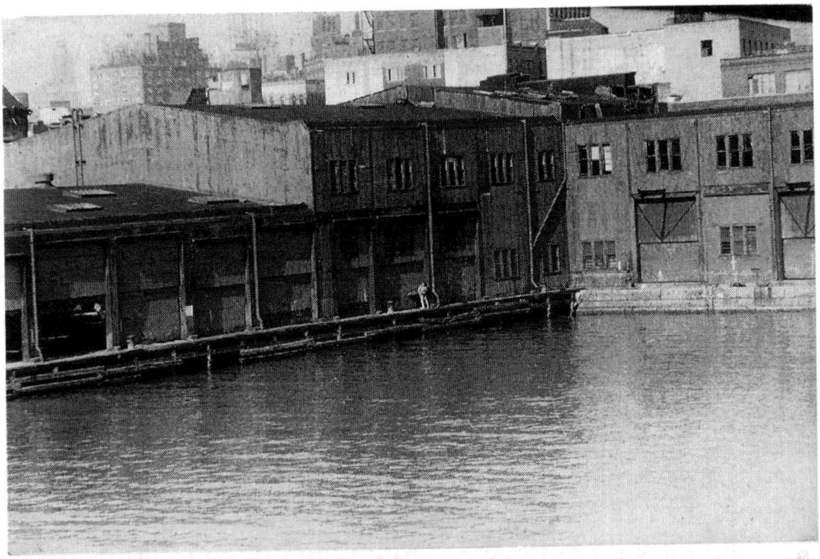

FIGURE 0.1. Alvin Baltrop, *Piers with Figures*, n.d. (1975–1986). Silver gelatin print. Photograph courtesy of the Alvin Baltrop Trust. 

stories of Manhattan's maritime past. When the ruined warehouses "became silhouetted at a certain point of the day," Wojnarowicz told the curator Barry Blinderman, "I could dream myself—project myself—all around the world in my imagination by looking at those qualities of light, and by looking at those structures."[7] As he cruised there, Wojnarowicz was reminded "of sailors, of distant ports," that, even as maritime trade declined and disappeared, cast a long erotic shadow on the waterfront.[8]

Many of the gay leather bars and sex clubs in nearby Greenwich Village and the Meatpacking District were located in former longshoremen's saloons that had lost their original clientele as the shipping industry declined.[9] From these frequently raided venues, an abundant after-hours cruising culture spilled out to the ruined piers. With no entry fees, membership restrictions, or dress codes, and more cursory policing, the piers offered a complicated hybrid of private and public space for erotic and social relations. Muggings and homophobic attacks were commonplace, as were accidents in the steadily decaying warehouses. Seemingly outside the purview of police, Wojnarowicz observed, cruising men often "had their throats cut by thieves, were shot and dumped into the river."[10] "Packs of gaunt young marauders also prowl these areas for 'queers,'" the novelist John Rechy noted, carrying "sticks, slashed bottles, knives, guns, crowbars."[11] A place of pleasure and of danger, the cruising

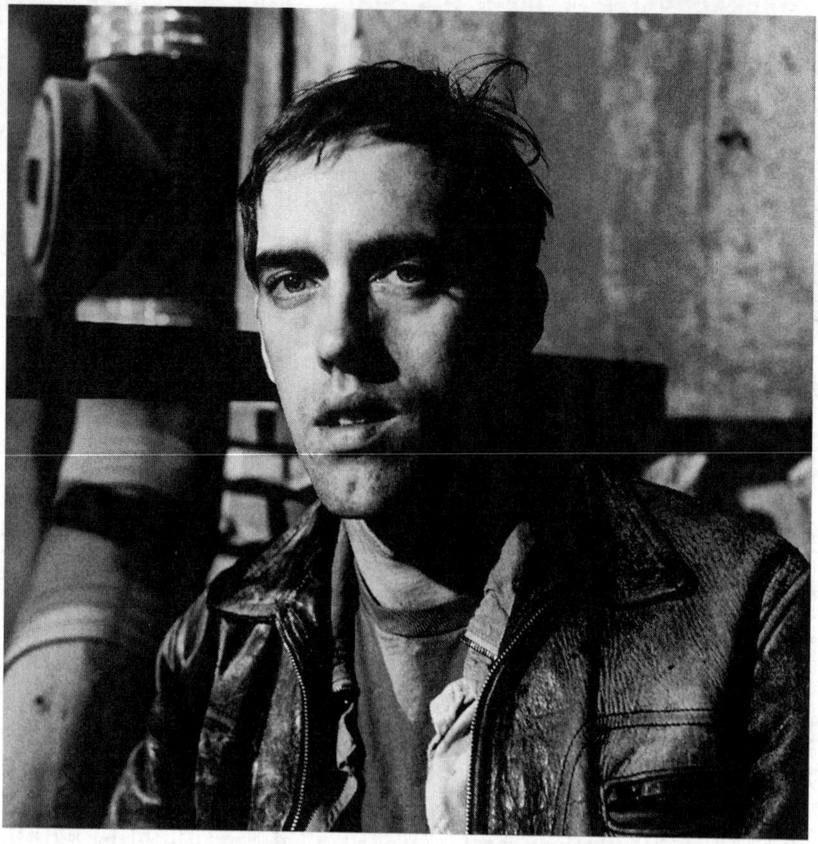

FIGURE 0.2. Peter Hujar, *David Wojnarowicz, Manhattan, Night*, 1985. © The Peter Hujar Archive.

ground of the abandoned waterfront appealed, in erotic and aesthetic terms, to a range of writers, artists, filmmakers, and amateur photographers. The piers were, the novelist Andrew Holleran wrote, a space of "peculiar magic."[12]

This book examines the combined erotic and aesthetic pull of the abandoned waterfront, exploring the queer appropriations of its piers and warehouses in the late 1970s and early 1980s. While it takes as its point of departure the art and writing of David Wojnarowicz, following the multiplicitous literary allusions, visual references, and erotic visions that characterize his work, slipping between past and present in a nonlinear fashion as he did, it is not so much a book about Wojnarowicz as it is a book around him. It takes his work as a guide to the erotic and creative reuses of the piers by queer New Yorkers in the years that preceded the HIV/AIDS epidemic. Its approach is thematic, rather than chronological. This stems, in part, from a desire to follow the disjointed, discontinuous, experimental approach of Wojnarowicz's own writing, and to reflect the fragmentary material form of the ruin itself, as artists like Paul Thek, Peter Hujar, and Gordon Matta-Clark did in their own work. In the ruin, the relation between past and present becomes difficult to ascertain. In 1911 Georg Simmel argued that the ruin is appealing precisely because it is at once physical and metaphysical—the past persists not only in the material form of the ruin but in the imaginative potential sparked by its fragmentation and the processes of ruination.[13] In writing this book, I have found the dissolute character of the ruin, and the partial, ephemeral traces of the cruising cultures of the late 1970s it retains, to be a liberating force.

In chapter 1, "Nostalgia for the Mud: Cruising in Ruins," I trace a material history of the waterfront area as a cruising ground, from historic bathhouses and empty trucks in the 1960s to warehouses and piers in the 1970s, examining David Wojnarowicz's art and writing alongside that of the photographers Leonard Fink and Alvin Baltrop, and writers such as Andrew Holleran, John Rechy, Edmund White, and Tim Dlugos. In much of this work, the ruined buildings on the waterfront appear as props and theatrical sets in the sexual encounters that took place there, as cruising men fantasized about their former uses by sailors and longshoremen. The structural decay that made the warehouses so dangerous rendered them more appealing as cruising spaces. Drawing on journal entries, poetry, photographs, and archival ephemera, I use Wojnarowicz's experiences as a lens through which to view the waterfront cruising cultures before HIV/AIDS and the peculiar eroticism of ruins. The sociologist Laud Humphreys, in *Tearoom Trade* (1970), his groundbreaking study of male cruising in public toilets in the late 1960s, posited that "these men seem to acquire stronger sentimental attachments to the buildings in which they meet for sex than to the persons with whom they engage in it."[14] Taking Humphreys at his word, and engaging with Tim Dean's notion of the queer character of the cruising archive, I examine how and why the ruined buildings that dominated this landscape assumed such a powerful erotic role in the cruising that took place there in the late 1970s and, sifting through the traces that remain, offer an embodied archival history of the pier's erotic uses in the pre–HIV/AIDS era.

Chapter 2, "The Whole World and the Cemetery: The Queer Visual Culture of Ruins," explores how Wojnarowicz and other New York artists, including Peter Hujar and Paul Thek, engaged with ruins visually in their artwork from the 1950s through to the early 1980s. Hujar, for example, documented the ruined piers in a series of photographs that recall his work in industrial junkyards in New Jersey in the 1970s. In the spring of 1983, Wojnarowicz and the downtown performance artist and painter Mike Bidlo invited hundreds of friends to join them in staging an illegal artistic repossession of the dilapidated Pier 34, the former Ward Line pier. They filled its vast space with painted murals, stencil graffiti, sculptures, and performances. The warehouse was demolished later in the year and the artworks destroyed, but this chapter is accompanied by documentary photographs, most previously unpublished, by the German photographer Andreas Sterzing. Sterzing's images are an unparalleled record of this artistic appropriation and depict many of the artists involved inside the pier, alongside their work. In this chapter, I am concerned with how and why what might be called a visual culture of ruins developed with such fervor in the late 1970s and early 1980s, and how artists manipulated the city's very real dilapidation to their creative advantage. I trace the development of a queer visual culture that focused on ruins as both subject matter and medium, and its relation to a critical aesthetic interest in urban processes of abandonment, ruination, and renewal. I also consider this visual culture of ruins in relation to site-specific art practices and cultures of display, an interest in "crummy" spaces that had been gaining momentum in Manhattan from the time of the waterfront's abandonment in the early 1960s, looking at work by Joan Jonas, Vito Acconci, and Gordon Matta-Clark. I am interested in how this work might appear, achronologically, different from the erotic vantage point of cruising, itself a queer way of looking in the city and a visual culture interested in ruins and in the places where the city's heteronormative fabric falls apart.

In chapter 3, "Cruising Ghosts: David Wojnarowicz's Queer Antecedents," I extend the notions of cumulative erotic architectural and material histories explored in the first chapter and lend Jacques Derrida's theory of "hauntological" time and spectral presence to the temporally problematic cruising spaces of the abandoned waterfront. As Wojnarowicz's waterfront writing developed in the late 1970s, he looked for new ways to represent the strange temporality of this ruined place. The figure of the ghost became the ideal symbol with which to articulate the experience of cruising there. The anonymous "toughs" he cruised on the piers were reimagined in his journals in ghostly terms as writers he admired, as Jean Genet or Vladimir Mayakovsky. He produced the photographic series *Arthur Rimbaud in New York*, placing the nineteenth-century French poet in sites that Wojnarowicz himself frequented, including the derelict piers and warehouses of the waterfront. In his writing, Wojnarowicz took up cross-temporal invitations of connection and erotic communion found in the work of writers such as Walt Whitman and William S. Burroughs. Accordingly, I explore the development of Wojnarowicz's ghostly idiolect in the late 1970s and early 1980s through a hauntological investigation of my own, examining the erotic possibilities it offered him and the queer new personal temporalities he generated through it. Through close reading of the work of Wojnarowicz, Rimbaud, Burroughs, and others, I trace a cross-generational history of literature in ruins and by the sea that positions Wojnarowicz's waterfront writing within a broader social and cultural context, effecting a rich, interdisciplinary interpretation of his multitemporal creative practice and his resistance to teleological narratives of himself and his influences, as well as exploring his own influence on contemporary artists like Emily Roysdon.

Returning to the politically fraught landscape of New York in the late 1970s, the fourth chapter, "Protest and Preservation on the Waterfront," examines the relation between the oppressive effects of homophobic municipal and federal legislation in New York in the 1970s and early 1980s and the rapid escalation of the gentrification of downtown Manhattan in the same period, a relation in which a false homogenizing public narrative of the abandoned waterfront as rotten and empty played a key role. A study of the gentrification of the waterfront in this period provides a vantage point from which to consider the city's long-standing disinclination to archive itself, evident in its promotion of urban developments that resist the renewal of existing buildings and landmarks, and to explore the commitment of queer writers, artists, and filmmakers to preserving the ruined waterfront in the face of initiatives that tend to erase minority histories. Cruising, as an illicit appropriative occupation of the city's derelict spaces, was itself a form of preserving them as noncommercial spaces and places for queer association. This chapter brings to the fore queer appropriations of the New York waterfront and nearby bars, its identity as a gay men's cruising space, as a place that facilitated the political organizing of gay men and lesbians, as a site for sex work, and as a home for displaced and at-risk trans people.

In addition, here I explore the complex activist politics of the queer cruising and bar scene in and around the waterfront—the appearance of political graffiti at the piers, the establishment of bar owners' organizations to protect managers and customers from continued police raids, and the close connections between activist groups, bars, and sex clubs—which have often been obfuscated and homogenized by singular narratives of the waterfront's abandonment that aim to bring about regeneration quickly and smoothly. These histories exist instead in archival paraphernalia, in films, and in photographs. In this final chapter, by focusing on the complex, confusing, and sometimes contradictory archival traces that remain and on visual records of the queer appropriations of the city's piers, I examine the civic battleground of the city's historic waterfront from the perspective of those who were absent from mainstream accounts of its use, exploring the "complex realities" of activism, preservationism, and protest that have been obscured by the gentrification of both the waterfront and its queer history.[15]

My interest in presenting this history in an achronological and thematic manner is also an effort to refuse any moralistic suggestion of a causal relation between the diverse cruising cultures of the late 1970s and the advent of HIV/AIDS in the early 1980s. I am keen to rid this period of the sense of viral momentum that often accompanies popular, or at least heteronormative, narratives of gay life in the late 1970s, as I explore in this book's conclusion. It can, of course, be difficult for us as contemporary readers and viewers to conceive of a time before HIV/AIDS, so monumental is its impact on queer identity and experience. While *Cruising the Dead River* is, at times, a nostalgic book, as it wanders through now-demolished piers and warehouses and recalls abandoned bars and absent city spaces, it is not a book that longs for a return to a supposed golden age of pier cruising. I am not looking back wistfully to a bareback utopia, though I recognize that there is pleasure and power in doing so. Instead, I am interested in how New York's gay cruising cultures in the late 1970s are remembered and how they have been historicized. I ask whether cruising in ruins itself might be figured as a model for tracing the discontinuous, fragmentary, and ephemeral erotic and social histories of this queer moment. Might it offer us an erotic means to conceive of the past queerly, outside heteronormative historical or genealogical markers, with what Christopher Reed and Christopher Castiglia have termed "a de-generational remembering"?[16] Writing on the groundbreaking gay porn films *L.A. Plays Itself* (1972) and *Boys in the Sand* (1971) in 2014, Cindy Patton reflected on the temporal complexities of viewing condomless sex from the pre-AIDS era in the present and urged readers to consider the 1970s on its own terms. The value of returning to the queer time of the pre-AIDS era is not that it offers us a vision of sex without risk but, rather, that it helps us envision the experimental erotic, social, and political relations that were threatened, lost, or abandoned with the appearance of HIV/AIDS in the early 1980s.

For Max Page, Manhattan's landscape has been shaped across the past two centuries by abandonment and loss, a pattern he terms "creative destruction." Through the late nineteenth and early twentieth centuries, Page argues, as modern building projects expanded across the city to accommodate its burgeoning industries and a growing population, "New Yorkers learned to see the cycle of destruction and rebuilding as 'second nature'—self-evident, unquestionable, and inevitable." For the novelist Henry James, New York was "nothing more than a provisional city," a place of "restless renewals," an always temporary construction "that will be replaced by another city."[17] Page's theory recasts Michel de Certeau's observation in *The Practice of Everyday*

*Life* that New York is a "city composed of paroxysmal places in monumental relief," that it "invents itself, hour by hour, in the act of throwing away its previous accomplishments and challenging the future."[18] The liminal, transitory qualities of the waterfront, as the domain of ships and of peripatetic sailors and temporary laborers, were augmented by the incompleteness of the city that it fringes and its proclivity for "restless" redevelopment.[19]

It was this tendency toward totalizing renewal and the replacement of existing buildings with new ones that Jane Jacobs resisted in her third condition for urban diversity in *The Death and Life of Great American Cities*: "the district must mingle buildings that vary in age and condition, including a good proportion of old ones." The latter should not be limited to "museum-piece old buildings," Jacobs argued, "but also a good lot of plain, ordinary, low-value old buildings, including some rundown old buildings." "New ideas," she posited, contrary to mainstream municipal building policy at the time, "must use old buildings."[20] Jacobs's preservationism is not about preserving the past in stasis. It is, rather, about creating spaces of opportunity for multiple social and economic communities to exist in the city simultaneously. Intriguingly for my purposes, she noted that as "time makes certain structures obsolete for some purposes, . . . they become available for others."[21]

While Jacobs does not discuss cruising (though there was an active cruising scene in the parks and at the trucks in her Greenwich Village neighborhood at the time), and her focus is very often on heterosexual families, apparently ideal citizens of the living city, I have sought in this book to approach the waterfront's past in a comparable way, creating space for multiple histories and queer appropriations of the harbor to coalesce. In a similar way, Sarah Schulman, in *The Gentrification of the Mind*, argues that the urban process of "gentrification literally replaces mix with homogeneity, it enforces itself through the repression of diverse expression." "Key to the gentrification mentality," she writes, "is the replacement of complex realities with simplistic ones."[22] In light of Schulman's theory of the gentrification of the mind, there is a clear and urgent political drive to my interest in documenting the queer life of New York's abandoned waterfront in the 1970s. These stories of the harbor's queer appropriations and its value for queer community building in the past run the risk of being lost as the area is rigorously redeveloped in the present under the Hudson River Park Act, explored in chapter 4. These historical narratives are obscured by the exclusionary development policies of one mayoral administration after another.

As I have researched and written this book, I have often returned to a passage in Wojnarowicz's journals in which he writes about the affective weight and radicalizing potential of attending many, many memorials for friends and lovers who had died from AIDS. "IT IS IMPORTANT," he wrote, "TO MARK THAT TIME OR MOMENT OF DEATH. IT'S HEALTHY TO MAKE THE PRIVATE PUBLIC." But, he continues, the spaces we provide for mourning and memorialization, the chapel and the home, are unnecessarily divisive and atomizing. They separate us from each other in our time of need. "ONE SIMPLE STEP," he writes, "CAN BRING IT OUT INTO A MORE PUBLIC SPACE. DON'T GIVE ME A MEMORIAL IF I DIE. GIVE ME A DEMONSTRATION."[23] This avowal has shaped my experience of writing about Wojnarowicz and of making that writing public. The act of writing this book, of cruising the archive and walking the gentrified pathways of the West Side waterfront, has been an effort to preserve and make this history available in a mode that corresponds to Wojnarowicz's powerful belief in the fundamental value of public disclosure and of truly public space. As I explore the diverse erotic and political histories of the abandoned waterfront in the 1970s that have slipped from view or have not been historicized publicly at all, ruination and the complex and achronological histories that it points to, as it resonates with Wojnarowicz's own belief in the politics of nonlinear time, offers a queer model for thinking about the recent past in a city known as much for its queer pleasures as for its "restless renewals." About, for, and with Wojnarowicz, *Cruising the Dead River* isn't a memorial; it is a demonstration.

# 1

# Nostalgia for the Mud: Cruising in Ruins

Detailed descriptions of sex at the West Side piers appear in David Wojnarowicz's personal journals from the summer of 1977. Walking "through Soho and over to Christopher Street" that September, he found himself in the dilapidated districts he had spent time in as a hustling teenager, by "the big pier past the old truck lines and the Silver Dollar Café/Restaurant."[1] There, he wrote, "away from the blatant exhibitionist energies of the NYC music scenes gay scenes," he felt "uncontrollably sane."[2] In journal entries, poetry, memoir essays, photographs, short films, and drawings, he depicted the derelict piers of the pre–HIV/AIDS era as busy "sexual hunting grounds," and the ruined waterfront as a liminal space "as far away from civilization as I could walk."[3] In an interview with the curator Barry Blinderman in 1990, years after many of the dilapidated structures had been torn down, Wojnarowicz recalled the pull of these "extraordinary warehouses where a lot of sexual activity occurred, where a lot of homosexual men would roam the hundreds of rooms of those abandoned shipping structures and engage in open sex."[4] The gargantuan buildings were, he wrote,

> like some kind of museum with vast numbers of tourists rolling in off the streets in crowds—gliding through the hallways and rooms, picking their way over trash and fire charred heaps. Upstairs they filled every room, half the ceiling fallen in and they stopped carefully around charred beams and rusted metal and glass—a guy here or there with shorts down around ankles playing with his hard cock or getting fucked by someone else.[5]

In Wojnarowicz's writing from the late 1970s, as in that of Edmund White, Andrew Holleran, and John Rechy, the decaying form and dangerous character of the warehouses and piers assume an erotic role in the cruising that takes place there. The ruined piers are rendered in fleshy, bodily terms. John Rechy, in the opening chapter of his novel *Rushes* (1979), wrote of "haunted male figures lurk[ing] for nightsex in the burnt-out rooms, among the rubble of cinder, wood, clawing cans, broken metal pipes, tangled wire like dry veins."[6] Decay was both mourned and celebrated, in what Holleran characterized as a "nostalgia for the mud."[7] There were "slight traces" in the warehouses, Wojnarowicz observed, of "déja-vu, filled with old senses of desire," with erotic remnants of the harbor's maritime history.[8] In a journal entry from June 1979 he wrote of "the semblance of memory and the associations" invoked as he cruised the West Side piers, reminded "of oceans, of sailors, of distant ports and the discreet sense of self among them, unknown and coasting."[9]

In *The Power of Place*, Dolores Hayden argues for a history of place focused on the "traces of time embedded in the urban landscape in every city," for they "offer opportunities for reconnecting fragments of the American urban story." The recording of history in the urban context, she asserts, should be a collaborative, multitemporal process that "engages social, historical, and aesthetic imagination to locate where narratives of cultural history" are "embedded in the historic urban landscape."[10]

In a similar way, "restless walks" through Manhattan to the West Side piers left Wojnarowicz "filled with coasting images of sights and sounds . . . like some secret earphone connecting [him] to the creakings of the living city" and the erotic traces "embedded" therein.[11] The waterfront was filled with traces of his own youthful experiences as a street hustler, as well as, in more general terms, its earlier sexual appropriations by sailors and stevedores when New York's harbor was still an active port. In a later essay, "Losing the Form in Darkness," he wrote of the industrial paraphernalia that littered the warehouses: "paper from old shipping lines scattered all around like bomb blasts among wrecked piece of furniture; three-legged desks, a naugahyde couch of mint-green turned upside down." In the same essay, he reflected on "the sense of age" in this "familiar place":

> The streets were familiar more because of the faraway past than the recent past—streets that I walked in those odd times when in the company of deaf mutes and times square pederasts. These streets are seen through the same eyes but each time with periods of time separating it: each time belonging to yet an older boy until the body smooths out and lines are etched until it is a young man recalling the movements of a complicated past.[12]

Wojnarowicz's nostalgic cruising sensibility, his sense of these "traces" of cruising pasts rooted in the derelict warehouses of the waterfront, of a "secret earphone," offers a point of entry into an alternate history of Manhattan's queer fringes and its erotic former uses that, through his conflation of the waterfront's erotic pasts and present, reflects the complex, multilayered relations between the cruising cultures of the trucks, the bathhouses, the piers, and the men who cruised there.

In *Backward Glances*, Mark Turner traces a history of urban cruising that begins with the Industrial Revolution and the development of the modern metropolis in the mid- to late nineteenth century. Cruising in both New York and London was and is, he writes, "an act of mutual recognition amid the otherwise alienating effects of the anonymous crowd." It is, he argues, "a practice that exploits the fluidity and multiplicity of the modern city to its advantage," a "process of counter movement" that "necessarily resists totalizing ways" of narrating the temporal and spatial character of cruising. Cruising is, Turner emphasizes, "the stuff of fleeting, ephemeral moments not intended to be captured."[13] Tim Dean offers a similar account in *Unlimited Intimacy*, his book on contemporary barebacking cultures. "Since cruising is a practice of the ephemeral and the contingent," Dean argues, echoing Charles Baudelaire's paradigmatic definition of the experience of modernity, and Turner's evocation of it in *Backward Glances*, "it is all the more remarkable that it has given rise to such a voluminous archive."[14]

Cruising, then, even as it exploits urban anonymity and is structurally dependent on movement and ephemerality, has a queer historical orientation that is both imaginative and material, as is perceptible in the erotic use of ruined buildings along the Manhattan waterfront in the late 1970s. In this chapter, focusing on Wojnarowicz's early written work and his sense of the waterfront as an imaginative space, embedded with vestiges of its erotic uses, I trace a material history of the waterfront area as a cruising ground, from historic bathhouses and empty trucks in the 1960s to warehouses and piers in the 1970s, rooting through archival ephemera and photographic traces of rusted metal and rotting wood.

## From the trucks to the baths

In Manhattan in the early 1960s, underneath the elevated West Side Highway, commercial haulage vehicles were frequently parked overnight, waiting to load or unload goods at the warehouses on the nearby waterfront. In and between the trucks, men cruised for anonymous sex with other men. Since drivers routinely left the trucks "unattended, with the backs unlocked," it was notoriously difficult for police to arrest cruisers on grounds of trespassing.[15] Samuel Delany, in *The Motion of Light in Water* (1988), his memoir of 1960s West Village life as a black, queer writer (during the early years of his marriage to the poet Marilyn Hacker), describes moving through a labyrinthine landscape of "waist-high tires," the parked trucks forming "van-walled alleys" in the darkness.[16] The labyrinth, as Ira Tattelman has observed, was a common spatial trope in urban areas appropriated for cruising during the 1960s, sites that offered means of evading exposure, arrest, and homophobic violence. "To participate in sex that was prohibited in both private and public spaces," he wrote,

> gay men found out-of-the-way places in which to engage in sexual relations. Wooded parks, often called meat racks, became a web of passageways and meeting rooms. . . . Darkened alleys and dead-ends were disrupted by the watchful eyes of seemingly aloof but ultimately eager partners.[17]

The trucks beneath the highway became renowned as "a place to go at night for instant sex." Delany remembers "between thirty-five and a hundred fifty (on weekends) men . . . slipping through and between and out of the trailers, some to watch, but most to participate in, numberless silent sexual acts." On his first visit, he "stayed for six hours" and "had sex seven or eight times."[18] He describes "a hugely ordered, highly social, attentive, silent . . . community" of men of between the trucks, where, at times, a state of what he terms "libidinal saturation" would be achieved:

> cock passed from mouth to mouth to hand to ass to mouth without ever breaking contact with other flesh for more than seconds; mouth, hand, ass, passed over whatever you held out to them, sans interstice.[19]

Delany's account suggests a diverse community, in terms of class, age, and race. During one predawn visit, he notices "a tall black guy, in jeans and a red T-shirt, about thirty, whom I'd seen there every night I'd ever come," then makes it with slightly balding "white guy in his late twenties, early thirties" in "workman's greens, short sleeves rolled up over muscular arms," who "looked like a driver from one of the trucks," and then "a black guy who'd stepped up to watch us." Exhausted, the men leave the truck as "the sky was getting light"; the nighttime river, he writes, "had taken a blue glaze" and "the water shook and shimmered with the cobalt reflection."[20]

The expansion of the cruising scene at the trucks coincided with "a massive campaign of police harassment against homosexuals" across Manhattan under Mayor Robert Wagner, which peaked in 1963 "as the city began a concerted drive to make homosexuals invisible in time for the 1964–1965 World's Fair."[21] This echoed an earlier crackdown, ordered by Mayor Fiorello La Guardia in preparation for the 1939 world's fair. But, as Burton Peretti has observed, while police then made a number of highly public arrests of "transvestites" and closed down numerous popular and publicly visible gay venues, "the city raised little objection . . . when gangsters began to underwrite a new network of clandestine and unpretentious gay bars."[22] These bars, throughout Greenwich Village and Harlem, provided Mafiosi a means to evade tax and sell contraband liquor after the repeal of the Eighteenth Amendment in late 1933 brought Prohibition to an end. The institutional homophobia of the State Liquor Authority (SLA), the post-Prohibition agency "authorized to issue liquor licenses and . . . expected to revoke the licenses of establishments that served homosexuals and other groups considered disreputable, such as prostitutes and gamblers," bolstered the association, forcing bar owners to "resort to police payoffs and protection from organized crime to avoid the common fate of license revocation."[23] In their salacious midcentury city guide *New York: Confidential!*, Jack Lait and Lee Mortimer note matter-of-factly that "all fairy night clubs and gathering places are illegal, and operate only through pay-offs to the authorities. They are organized into a national circuit, controlled by the Mafia."[24] An increase in police raids on gay bars in Greenwich Village in the mid- to late 1960s was accompanied by increased Mafia involvement in the area's nightlife. In 1966 younger members of the Genovese family, which allegedly controlled much of the New Jersey shore as Manhattan port activity declined in the 1950s, "put up $3,500 to reopen the Stonewall [Inn] as a gay club," running it successfully without a liquor license.[25]

In the years preceding the June 1969 riots at the Stonewall Inn, where protests erupted after a routine police raid, as "steady progress on court rulings . . . continually ate away at the SLA's ability to revoke or withhold liquor licences from gay bars," waterfront cruising at the trucks continued.[26] As its visibility along the thoroughfares by the river increased by the late 1960s, "so did harassment and violence" by representatives of other city authorities, including the Transit Police.[27] The Gay Liberation Front (GLF), founded in New York in 1969, began handing out flyers at the trucks, encouraging men cruising there to attend strategy meetings and support GLF demonstrations. In 1968 an off-duty transit cop, Colin Kelly, killed two gay men at the trucks near the waterfront, and, David Carter noted, "the circumstances of the killings and subsequent police conduct caused the Mattachine Society to suspect that the men had been murdered."[28] Following Kelly's release without charges in early 1969, the New York chapter of the Mattachine Society ran an article in its monthly newsletter titled "Docks, Darkness and Danger," warning cruising men to exercise caution at the waterfront, or to avoid it altogether:

> The area has become a mecca for uptight hoodlums looking for a "queer" to beat up. One of the favorite games is to shove a homosexual into the cesspool known as the Hudson River. . . . At least four people have drowned in the filth after hitting their heads on pier footings.[29]

Those who cruised the waterfront in the years preceding its industrial abandonment and municipal neglect were also threatened with abuse from antagonistic private policemen and detectives, hired by waterfront businesses to protect vehicles and warehouse stock. As Carter notes, "some of the private detectives shook down the gay men" who cruised the area, but on the whole New York City police turned a blind eye.[30]

The Mattachine Society urged its members to seek anonymous pleasure instead in the city's gay bathhouses. In contrast to the postindustrial antiglamour of the trucks, many of the bathhouses of the 1960s modeled themselves on the sexual decadence and imagined luxury of the ancient world. The Continental Baths, located in the basement of the Ansonia Hotel, uptown at West Seventy-Fourth Street, boasted an Olympic-size pool, steam room, sauna, restaurant, and overnight accommodation. Washroom facilities set the bathhouses apart from the cruising scene at the trucks. As the writer Perry Brass has noted, venereal diseases were another concern down at the waterfront. With no place to wash up after sex, men were at greater risk of catching sexually transmitted diseases "like penile gonorrhoea."[31] Stephen Ostrow, the founder of the bathhouse at the Ansonia, wanted to open a facility "that would be safe and clean and would treat homosexuals with dignity."[32] Indeed, in an interview for *New York* magazine in 1998, Larry Kramer remembered, "Everybody there was walking around half-naked and having fun. It was clean. It was a party. . . . The Continental Baths were like ancient Greece."[33] However, the distinction between dangerous cruising at the trucks and safe sexual association at the bathhouses was not as clear-cut as the Mattachine article suggested. Twenty-two patrons were arrested in a raid at the Continental Baths in February 1969, having been identified by an undercover policeman. The owners reported that the raid took place after they neglected a police pay-off.[34]

John Rechy, in his first novel, *City of Night*, published in the United States in 1963, at the apogee of Mayor Wagner's crackdown, depicts cruising in 1960s New York as dangerous and furtive, a practice of the "exiled," but intimate, a collective erotic endeavour. Police raids frame the novel's early descriptions of cruising: "At the beginning of the warm days," Rechy writes, "the corps of newyork cops feels the impending surge of street-activity, and for a few days the newspapers are full of reports of raids: UNDESIRABLES NABBED." In the "sweltering intensity" of the New York summer, however, the police soon "relent," "bogged down by the heat."[35] The novel's narrator, a young hustler, observes men cruising on summer afternoons in Central Park, away from the bars and bathhouses:

> Sundays especially, a parade of hunters prowled that area—or they would sit and lie in the grass waiting for that day's contact. Even in the brilliant white blaze of newyork sun, it was possible to make it, right there, in the treesecluded areas.

After dark, the scene is transformed. Unlike most of the city's bathhouses, which required payment upon entry, "hobos" and "homosexuals" shared the same space:

> At night they sat along the benches, in the fringe of the park. Or they strolled with their leashed dogs along the walks. . . . The more courageous ones penetrated the park, around the lake, near a little hill: hoods, hobos, hustlers, homosexuals. Hunting. Young teenage gangs lurk threatening among the trees. Occasionally the cops come by, almost timidly, in pairs, flashing their lights; and the rustling of bushes precedes the quick scurrying of feet along the paths.
>
> Unexpectedly at night you may come upon scenes of crushed intimacy along the dark twisting lanes. In the eery mottled light of a distant lamp, a shadow lies on his stomach on the grass-patched ground, another straddles him: ignoring the danger of detection in the last moments of exiled excitement.[36]

Rechy's attitude to Manhattan and Los Angeles cruising cultures in *City of Night* is complex and reflects the queer experience of oppressed gay desire in early 1960s America. The "World of the Gay Bars" in Los Angeles is, he writes, a "shadowed world of dim bars characterized by nervous gestures, furtive looks, masked Loneliness." Similarly, the descriptions of park cruising in New York move from erotic voyeurism to somber recollection:

> once, on night in that park, aware of an unbearable exploding excitement within me mixed with an unexplainable sudden panic, I stood against a tree and in frantic succession let seven night figures go down on me. And when, finally, the rain came pouring, I walked in it, soaked, as if the water would wash away whatever had cause the desperate night-experience.[37]

Intentionally, queerly ambivalent, Rechy's characterization of the "exiled excitement" of sex in Central Park and the "desperate night-experience" of cruising reflects, in stark terms, the dangerous, necessarily clandestine sexual culture of 1960s New York and the persistent erotic appeal of its "crushed intimacy," a tension between secrecy and exposure.[38] Like the perpetual threat of violence inherent in the decaying piers and warehouses on the waterfront, cruising in the late 1960s was marked, according to Rechy, by a dialectical energy of despair and "frantic" pleasure. This dialectic is what Rechy later termed, in reference to the cruising culture of the piers, "the pornography of implied violence," a complex and violent eroticism that resonates in the multiplicitous uses made of the abandoned piers and warehouses of the waterfront in the following decade.[39]

### From the baths to the bars

By the early 1970s, after a series of protests against the frequent raids on New York gay bars by city police, including the "Sip-In" at Julius' bar in April 1966, the riots at the Stonewall Inn in June 1969, and New York's first Gay Liberation Day march in June 1970, the terms of this dualistic dynamic had shifted. Bathhouse development and membership across the United States increased, and New York's gay bar scene expanded. Dotted along West Street and Twelfth and Eleventh Avenues, many of the gay bars, bathhouses, and sex clubs that appeared on the Lower West Side in the 1970s were saloons once frequented by longshoremen. Like the outhouses built by city authorities in Manhattan in the late nineteenth and early twentieth centuries, municipal bathhouses were designed to encourage greater personal hygiene; they provided a location for tenement dwellers to relieve themselves and to socialize outside of downtown saloons, away from alcohol and its accompanying erotic temptations.[40] Historically, New York bathhouses had served as social centers supporting the customs and native cultures of the city's Russian and Turkish immigrant population. Both were appropriated as locations for mostly clandestine homosexual encounters by the early 1900s. As Allan Bérubé notes in his important essay "The History of Gay Bathhouses," presented to the California Supreme Court in defense of bathhouses in 1985, a professor visiting from Denver in 1914 observed on his visits to the baths that "among the many Turkish baths in New York, one is frequently visited by homosexuals in the afternoon and one in the evening. . . . The Turkish baths of America are generally a very safe place for homosexuals."[41]

By 1971 the Club Baths chain of exclusively gay bathhouses had opened fourteen branches across the country. By the mid-1970s clubs and bars were charging expensive memberships fees. The Flamingo, for example, located in an empty warehouse on Houston Street, charged seventy-five dollars for an annual membership. In his queer American travelogue *States of Desire* (1980), Edmund White described the bar scene that developed in downtown Manhattan in the early 1970s as "a completely new beginning."[42] Returning to the United States after ten months in Rome, an old friend took White down to Christopher's End, a bar in the West Village, where,

> a go-go boy with a pretty body and bad skin stripped down to his jockey shorts and then peeled those off and tossed them at us. A burly man in the

> audience clambered up onto the dais and tried to fuck the performer but was, apparently, too drunk to get an erection.

Later, the pair drifted into the back room, which was overwhelming dark, White recalled:

> I never received a sense of its dimensions, though I do remember standing on a platform and staring through the slowly revolving blades of a fan into a cubbyhole where one naked man was fucking another. A flickering candle illuminated them. It was never clear whether they were customers or hired entertainment; the fan gave them the look of actors in a silent movie. All this was new.[43]

The appearance of the spaces had also changed. Rather than aping the grandeur of ancient Greece or appropriating the tight-knit, coded homosocial culture of a Turkish bath, many of the new bathhouses and clubs appeared to mimic the dilapidation of the trucks by the waterfront. Larry Kramer wrote of the Everard Baths on West Twenty-Eighth Street ("*the* bath") that, in contrast to the pristine neo-Grecian interior of the Continental Baths in the pre-Stonewall era, the Everard "was hideous, like Kafka. There were wire-mesh walls, and the floors were filthy and stank."[44] In his novel *Faggots* (1978), Kramer wrote that "the Everhard" was "rancid and ratty," marked by the "distinct odors of poppers, dope, spit, shit, piss, and a bevy of lubricants. Hundreds of assorted bodies paraded through refuse and puddle-spotted floors, barefoot, bare-chested."[45]

In his study of the Mineshaft, a gay club that opened in 1976 at Washington and West Twelfth Streets in the Meatpacking District, Ira Tattelman noted that while the new homosexual bathhouses were "located in neglected urban spaces such as warehouses and factories," nonresidential areas, similar to the desolate backdrop of the waterfront trucks, "recreating these dark, raunchy city spaces became a commercial enticement, reminiscent of previously clandestine encounters now safely celebrated inside."[46] In the mid-1970s, a hollow truck was installed on the top floor of the Fifteenth Street bathhouse Man's Country, in an effort to evoke the dark, "van-walled alleys" of the harborside trucks.[47] A gay club on Perry Street took the name the Ruins.[48] "The look of jail cells, auto repair shops, and army barracks," Tattelman recalled, "were inserted into bars, enticing the fantasies of their patrons."[49] In Kramer's viciously satirical depiction of the Village sex scene, one waterfront-adjacent bar, the "Lusitania Lounge," appropriates a ruined maritime aesthetic, "all fitted out most smartly with the gleanings from a sunken Cunard liner."[50] Clubs "enhanced a sense of place" through labyrinthine layouts that catalyzed erotic appropriative queer spatial narratives, "choreographing a series of encounters and narratives" that recalled former cruising spaces, in parks and among the trucks.[51] In an earlier article, "The Meaning at the Wall: Tracing the Gay Bathhouse," Tattelman noted that these strategic devices and the ruinous, labyrinthine layout of the West Village clubs and bathhouses "fostered an environment of anonymity," evoking the wandering of the sexual hunt, but did so strictly within the circumscribed erotic space of the fee-paying, specifically and intentionally gay bathhouse.[52] The clubs were, as Tattelman later argued, "alternative sites *inserted into* the city," rather than appropriated or reclaimed. Distinct from the erotic culture active in the trucks along the waterfront, these were "places of containment and consumption."[53]

Though they were spaces that "allowed men the opportunity to break rules and express what is ordinarily denied," where "men pushed their eroticism in multiple directions," there were extensive rules, enforced through strict membership codes.[54] In a pamphlet celebrating the fifth anniversary of the opening of the Mineshaft in 1981, the club's management affirmed the establishment's strict dress code:

> those items not approved are those which do not fit into a man's club where visions of leather, cowboys, uniforms, and jocks are a reality and not just sugar plums at Christmas. . . . So buy it, don't defy it!

The pamphlet reiterated the exclusive nature of the club by stressing its unique character and its appeal to a "raunchy gay male minority": "it is truly a place where many a gay man would never come because it is surely not a place for everyone." At times, dress codes and membership fees served as subtle means of ensuring members of the public did not enter the bar unwittingly. In 1980 the management at Alex in Wonderland, a gay bar on Tenth Avenue near Thirteenth Street, a location they termed "New York City. Dockstrip," distributed a flyer describing the bar as "a social disco" that "intends to facilitate the fantasy world that the name suggests, and help every patron feel like a STAR!" "To prevent offenses to the sensibilities of persons inadvertently seeking entrance to this basement-level scene," the flyer continued, "a dress code will be strictly enforced beginning 1 January 1981 (then, the door man will assume 'you are what you wear'!)"[55]

Though membership rules had a clear protective function, supporting the development of gay bars and sex clubs as safe spaces as raids and legislative harassment by the State Liquor Authority and the New York Police Department's Public Morals Division continued throughout the 1970s, they also enabled thinly veiled discriminatory entry policies. The Monster, a gay bar on Grove Street in Greenwich Village, was subject to boycotts and pickets in the early 1980s, with activists reporting that the bar "discriminates against women and blacks at the door," and suggesting that former patrons report the bar to the SLA. In a letter to the bar's management in December 1984, Jim Jordan Smith complained about the racist and sexist overtones of their door policy:

> I do not think there is room within the "gay community" to practice discrimination of any kind (except of course, to keep out rowdy, drunken troublemakers who interfere with the pleasure of others who wish to have a pleasant time) which reflects prejudices of gender, race, or sexual orientation.[56]

In an article on the Duchess, a lesbian bar on Grove Street that was shut down by the Public Morals Division of the NYPD in September 1982, the *Village Voice* noted that the bar, "like some bars for gay men, has itself been picketed for discriminating against blacks and Hispanics."[57]

In his essay "Is the Rectum a Grave?," written in 1987 as HIV-seroconversion rates in New York increased almost exponentially, Leo Bersani similarly recalled Manhattan's bathhouses of the late 1970s and early 1980s as "ruthless ranked, hierarchized, and competitive," institutions whose selective clientele mirrored "racist and phobic social relations from outside," as their entry fees and strict membership requirements suggest.[58] Keller's Bar, on the ground floor of the old Keller Hotel at the corner of Barrow and West Streets, close to the Christopher Street pier, was a notable exception: a long-running gay men's leather bar with a largely African-American clientele. In *City Boy*, Edmund White describes Keller's as "a gay black bar" at which the photographer Robert Mapplethorpe, who "went nearly every night" "was one of the few white men to be found."[59] In *No More Tomorrows*, his novel about love and loss as a black gay man in the midst of the AIDS crisis, Rodney Lofton recalls that at Keller's in the 1970s and into the 1980s, "depending on the night, there were wall-to-wall black gay men—all ages, all shapes and sizes, all colors of a black rainbow, if there was such a thing."[60]

Bersani's interpretation of gay bathhouse culture as commodifying or fetishizing discrimination and racist exclusion stands out within academic discourse on bathhouse sex, in which participant-writers often employ metaphors of collective, amorphous pleasure, what Dennis Altman called "a Whitmanesque democracy."[61] For the art historian John Paul Ricco, the baths are "the placeless place of erotics," where

> individuals forfeit their subjective selves and are reconstituted as parts of a collective assemblage in which personal identities are exchanged for a multiplicity of desiring bodies.[62]

These characterizations resonate in descriptions of New York's bathhouses in the early twentieth century, recounted by Bérubé as sites of "democracy and camaraderie":

> refuges from society's prejudice against homosexuals, as oases of freedom and homosexual camaraderie. The clientele was primarily homosexual and from a variety of occupations and classes, temporarily "democratic" in their nakedness. Members of the staff, too, were sometimes homosexual, making these early baths one of the first identifiably gay social and sexual institutions.[63]

Bersani's critique stands in sharp contrast to Aaron Betsky's analysis, in *Queer Space* (1997), of the "counter-space" of the modern city bathhouse. Betsky considers the modern gay bathhouse a site "centered on middle-class white men," but one which, through sex and erotic imagination, "wipes out at least for a moment, class distinctions just as surely as it allows the middle-class city to dissolve." Invoking Michel Foucault's theory of the heterotopia, he explores the cruising spaces of the postindustrial metropolis. Betsky characterizes queer space as facilitated by "an awareness of the emptiness within the city that does not defeat but animates one's self to always go searching."[64] In the same way, Foucault's example of the mirror is both utopian and heterotopic: "It makes this place that I occupy at the moment when I look at myself in the glass at once absolutely real, connected with all the space that surrounds it, and absolutely unreal, since in order to be perceived it has to pass through the virtual point which is over there."[65]

Within this framework, New York's abandoned riverside warehouses represented an ideal heterotopia and, thus, an ideal cruising ground, which as Betsky argues, "unerringly occur at the places where the supposed rationale of the urban structure falls apart because it is not functional."[66] However, as Dianne Chisholm has argued, in eulogizing the bathhouse and the piers as "classless" places, Betsky "forfeits history entirely to fetish spatiality." He views, she writes, all spatial "appropriation as aestheticisation," failing to consider the socioeconomic, cultural, and political factors behind the waterfront's use as a cruising space, and the interplay of this queer space with the many gay bars, bathhouses, and sex clubs active at the same time in the surrounding area.[67] Erotics, for Wojnarowicz and so many other men who cruised the waterfront in the late 1970s, was never "placeless" and never classless, as their experiences on the piers demonstrate.[68]

## From the bars to the piers

Though the clubs and bars in Greenwich Village and along West Street were culturally distinct from the cruising space of the piers and warehouses, the populations that used them were not mutually exclusive. Their location on the fringes of Manhattan rendered them a kind of queer thoroughfare between the then-abandoned, dangerous waterfront and the increasingly commercial gay bar and club scene of the West Village and the Meatpacking District. John Rechy, in the opening chapter of *Rushes* (1979), described West Side bar country as a "battered landscape"[69] of "implied violence" on the edge of "civilized" Manhattan:

> blocks and blocks populated by men roaming or waiting—blocks and blocks populated only by men, homosexual men; only men, hundreds, more, many more, most in the costumes of leather and Western "masculinity," . . . men standing mutely on corners or pressed against buildings darker gray than the sky, or, others, torsos stripped, leaning out of windows, or shoved in clusters against shaded doorways along the crooked streets; men gathered in laughing groups outside tough male-crammed bars, or slouching against motorcycles or on the steps of apartment buildings; men connecting openly or waiting to connect: a vista charged with a dark sexuality which rushes from the streets into the waterfront bars, to the abandoned piers, into the dank warehouses and toward the edge of the water, the end of the land.[70]

In contrast to the aggressive environment "choreographed" inside many of the rules-bound West Street bars and clubs, cruising the abandoned warehouses and side streets along the waterfront, even those between the bars, represented a genuine risk to personal safety, owing particularly to the conception of the area by civic authorities as a marginal jurisdiction, largely ignored by law enforcement agencies. David Wojnarowicz notes in his "Biographical Dateline" that "people in the warehouses had their throats cut by thieves, were shot and dumped into the river, etc."[71] The harbor's appropriation as a queer space made it a target for homophobic attacks and muggings. In his 2009 memoir *City Boy*, Edmund White recalls hearing "of bodies discovered floating down the river, of horrible mutilations, of drive-by murders" along West Street.[72] What Rechy calls the "implied violence" of the piers was also structural. The warehouses were in a state of dangerous disrepair: collapsed floorboards led directly to the Hudson River, and fires sparked by stray cigarettes were not uncommon. In "Close Them, Seal Them Up, or Tear Them Down," an article about the piers for Manhattan newspaper *Our Town* in November 1975, the journalist John Turcott described the structural decay of the warehouses, having visited, he made clear in an interview with a newsletter published by Jim Ryan, solely "to take pictures for this article." There he witnessed

> a scene straight from a horror movie: broken glass scattered everywhere, rats the size of small dogs, holes in the floor with the Hudson River and all the debris in it floating by; sagging walls; broken stairs; charred sections from several arson jobs, and shaky landings.[73]

Peter Hujar's photographs of the Canal Street pier in the early 1980s, such as *Pier—Four Doors* (1981; figure 1.1), revel in the ruinous aesthetic of the waterfront warehouses, playing with their functionlessness. The multiplicitous doors offer no spatial or temporal direction. They encourage wandering, visual cruising. They face the edges of the picture plane and, in their ineffectuality, direct our gaze toward the peeling animation of the rotting walls. Accidental orifices have developed on almost every surface, revealing the underlying structure of the warehouse or only darkness. Light pours in from above—we might imagine, a burned or windblown hole in the room's ceiling—illuminating graffitoed texts encouraging contemporary visitors and latter-day viewers to "CELEBRATE" something. Waterfront buildings stripped of their original purpose, lacking the prescriptive spatial narratives that well-maintained architectural spaces produce, were the ideal location for anonymous sexual encounters, since they encouraged the projection of phantasy, distinct from the quotidian urban time-space of places of work, public transport, apartment buildings, and the street.

Unpoliced and largely unlit, the warehouses and piers often acted as an extended back room after closing time. There, the strict rules and membership codes of the West Street bars held little sway. As photographs by the amateur photographer Leonard Fink and the artist Alvin Baltrop make clear, while many of the men who cruised the piers wandered there from the adjacent bars, others were those intentionally excluded from such spaces. Many of them were homeless, overweight, disabled, older, poor. Many were African-American or Latinx. In February 2008 *Artforum* published a series of ten black-and-white photographs from Baltrop's vast archive, accompanied by a short essay by Douglas Crimp. The photographs, he wrote,

> constitute rare and indispensable evidence of the proximity and simultaneity of artistic and sexual experimentation in the declining industrial spaces of Manhattan during the 1970s, a time of particularly creative ferment for both scenes.[74]

Baltrop's photographs capture the grandeur of the nineteenth- and early twentieth-century piers, their vast hallways and broad corrugated walls, and the play of light through metal beams and open doorways. And they demonstrate that waterfront cruising, like the cruising scene in Central Park in the 1960s, was not only a nighttime activity, as numerous couples and groups dot the sides of the piers in the bright daylight of summer. Men are pictured cruising in Pier 52, the site of Gordon Matta-Clark's vast cutting work *Day's End*, in the summer of 1975 (figure 1.2). The men Baltrop depicts are white, African-American, Latinx, and of various ages (figure 1.3). Sex is not always

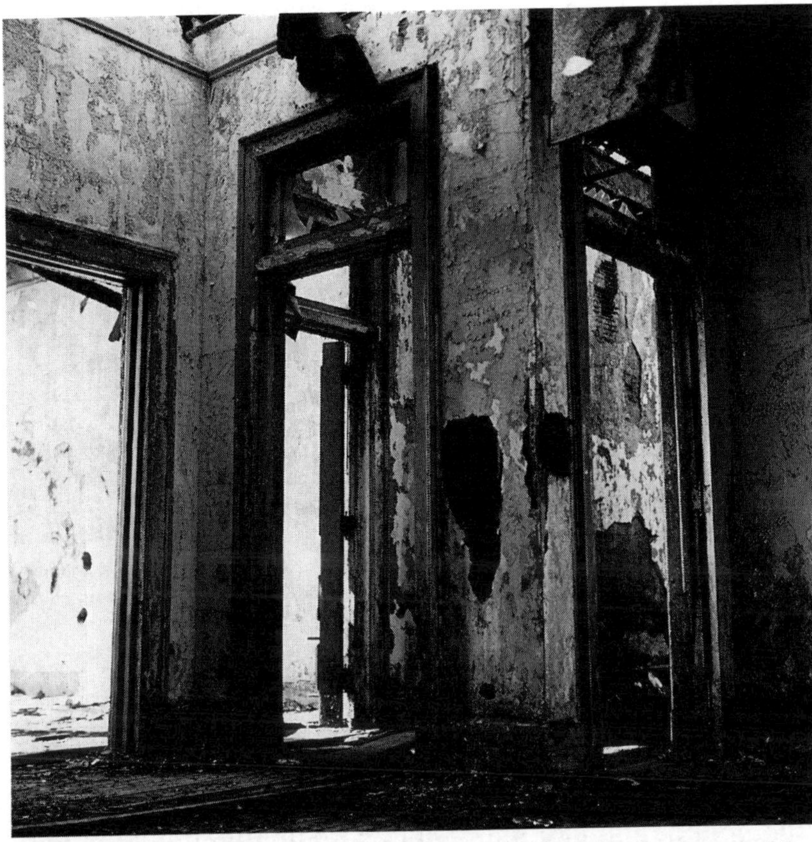

FIGURE 1.1. Peter Hujar, *Pier—Four Doors*, 1981. © 1987 The Peter Hujar Archive. Courtesy of Pace/MacGill Gallery, New York; Fraenkel Gallery, San Francisco.

immediately discernible. We have to cruise the images for clues. In some, pairs or groups of men are partially obscured behind steel frames or warehouse walls, the photographer's gaze paralleling the stealth of the cruising act (figure 1.4). An image of a shirtless young man peering through a gaping hole in a warehouse wall plays with the notion of the frame and, again, of voyeurism (on the wall is a drawing by the graffiti artist Tava; figure 1.5). As we, the viewers, observe this young man from behind, scouring the frame for the erotic action that he appears to be seeking, we become involved in a kind of cruising ourselves. Sometimes this inquisitive, eroticized looking uncovers social encounters that are not sexual; the life on the piers documented in Baltrop's photographs is sometimes solitary. The artist Emily Roysdon remarked in 2011 on being struck that Baltrop "has hundreds of pictures of people sitting out on the piers alone reading. There were all kinds of things going on

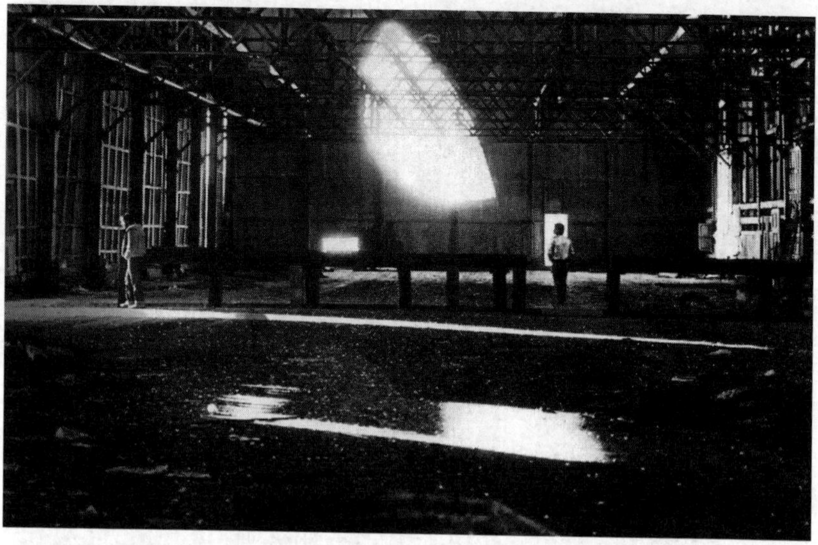

FIGURE 1.2. Alvin Baltrop, *Pier 52 (Gordon Matta-Clark's "Day's End" building cuts with two people)*, n.d. (1975–1986). Photograph courtesy of the Alvin Baltrop Trust. © 2010 Third Streaming, NY; Galerie Buchholz, Berlin/Cologne/New York. All rights reserved.

there and I am more broadly interested in the fact that queers chose, and it was a choice, to go there."[75]

Other photographs offer seemingly impossible vantage points on the warehouses' most dangerously ruined interior spaces, fantasy visions of sex from above or of erotic encounters on adjacent, more ruined warehouses and piers (figure 1.7). Baltrop went to great lengths to work from such perspectives, often attaching himself to the ceiling of a warehouse on a makeshift harness, "watching and waiting for hours to record the lives that these people led (friends, acquaintances, and strangers), and the unfortunate ends that they sometimes met."[76] Baltrop also documents the violence that punctuated the life of this sexual playground. In one photograph, three policemen stand before a damp, lacerated body, just pulled from the river.

Other, contemporaneous photographs suggest that Baltrop's images accurately represent the diversity and sociosexual character of the waterfront of the late 1970s. Leonard Fink, whose amateur photographs were donated to the Lesbian, Gay, Bisexual and Transgender Community Center in New York after his death in 1993, also recorded the bodily variety and racial diversity that the waterfront, as an unregulated, noncommercial space, permitted. Fink worked as an attorney for the New York City Transit Authority, defending it against employees who sued for unfair dismissal. On evenings and at

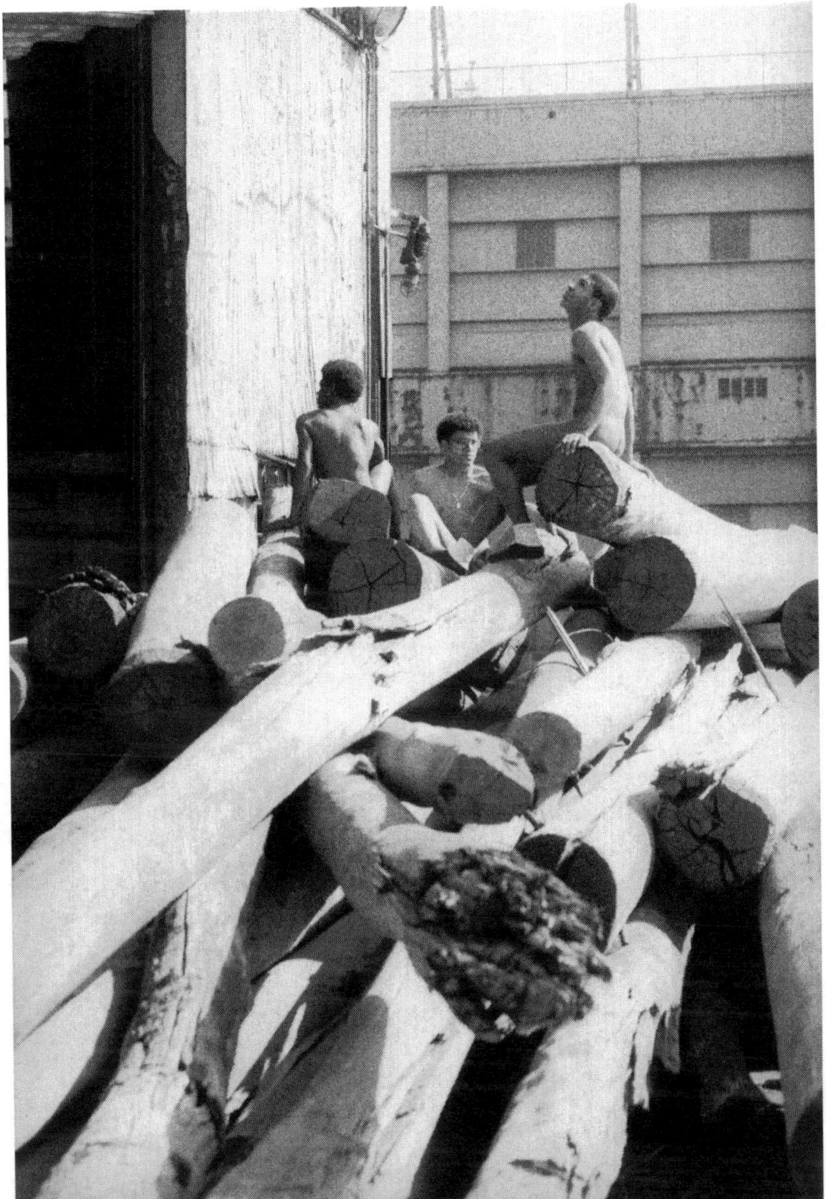

FIGURE 1.3. Alvin Baltrop, *River Rats II*, n.d. (1975–1986). Photograph courtesy of the Alvin Baltrop Trust. © 2010 Third Streaming, NY; Galerie Buchholz, Berlin/Cologne/New York. All rights reserved.

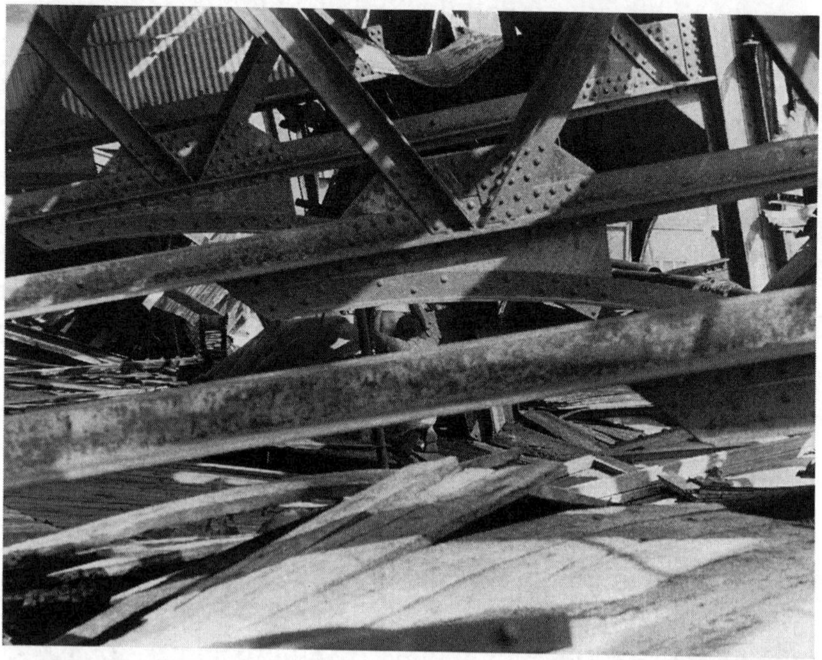

FIGURE 1.4. Alvin Baltrop, *The Piers (blowjob)*, n.d. (1975–1986). Silver gelatin print. Photograph courtesy of the Alvin Baltrop Trust. © 2010 Third Streaming, NY; Galerie Buchholz, Berlin/Cologne/New York. All rights reserved.

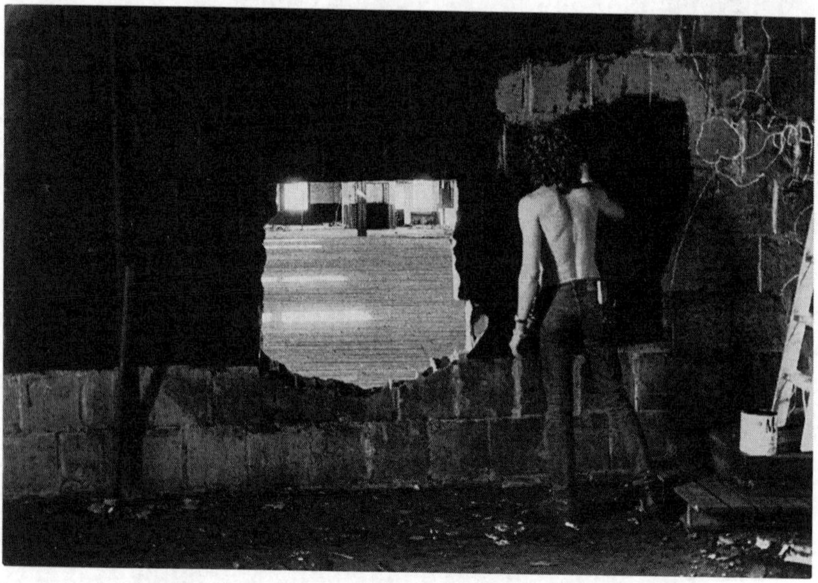

FIGURE 1.5. Alvin Baltrop, *The Piers (featuring Tava)*, n.d. (1975–1986). Silver gelatin print. Photograph courtesy of the Alvin Baltrop Trust. © 2010 Third Streaming, NY; Galerie Buchholz, Berlin/Cologne/New York. All rights reserved.

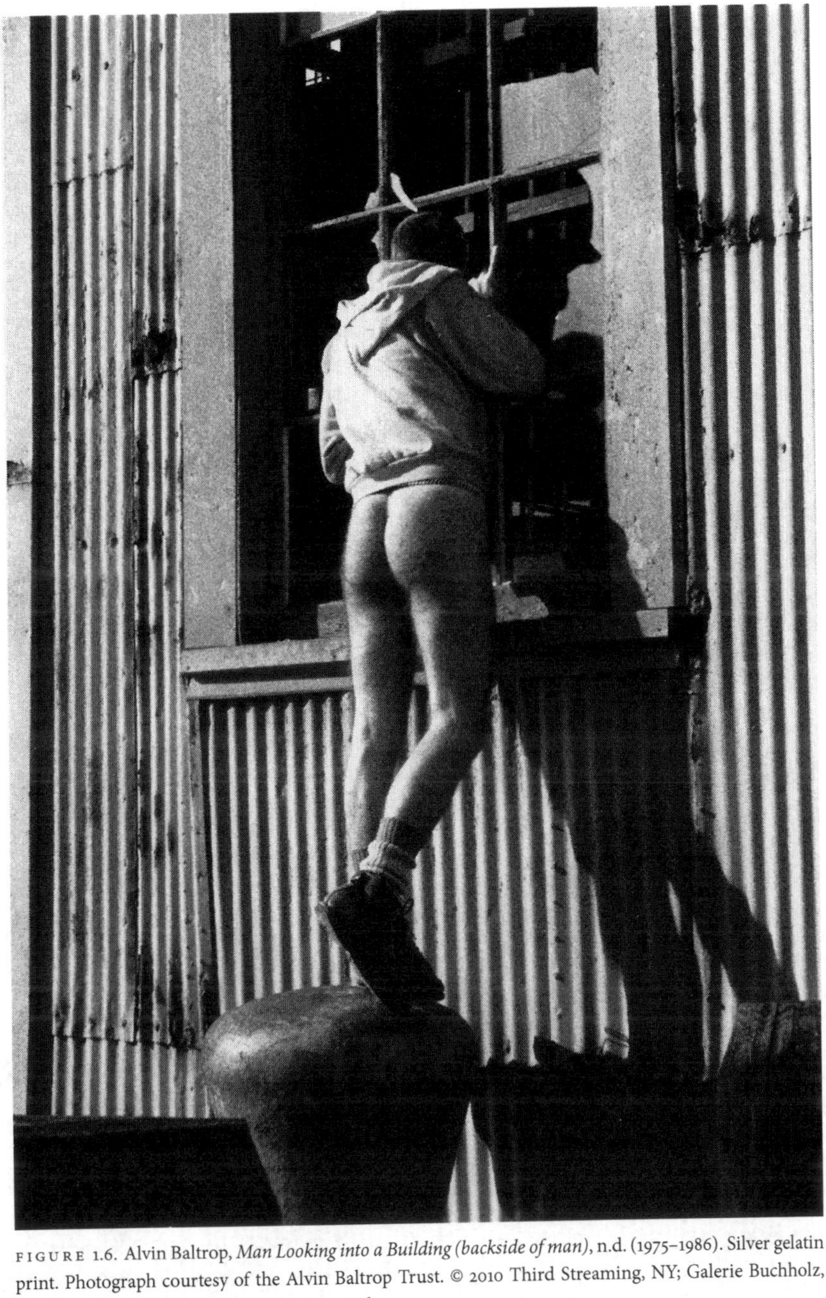

FIGURE 1.6. Alvin Baltrop, *Man Looking into a Building (backside of man)*, n.d. (1975–1986). Silver gelatin print. Photograph courtesy of the Alvin Baltrop Trust. 

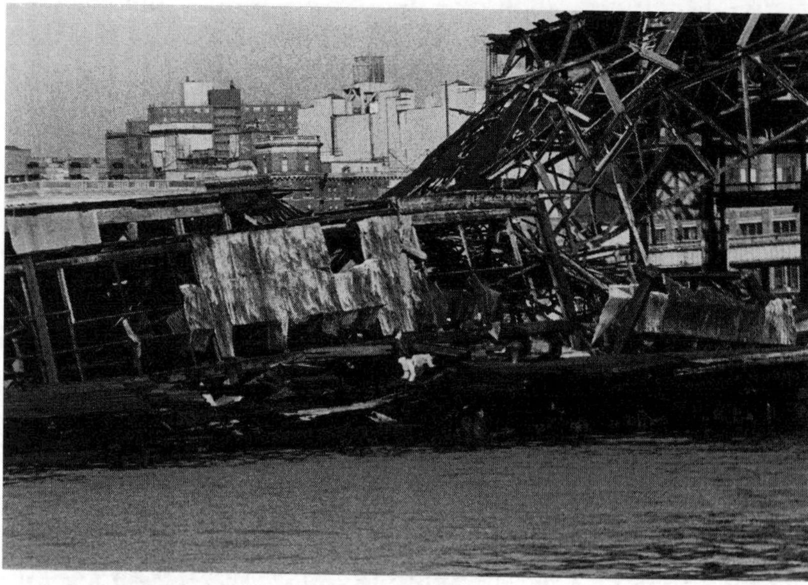

FIGURE 1.7. Alvin Baltrop, *Piers (couple having sex)*, n.d. (1975–1986). Silver gelatin print. Photograph courtesy of the Alvin Baltrop Trust. © 2010 Third Streaming, NY; Galerie Buchholz, Berlin/Cologne/New York. All rights reserved.

weekends he wove through the streets of Greenwich Village in denim cutoffs and roller skates, photographing the patrons of the Eagle and the Ramrod, former longshoremen's saloons turned leather and Western bars. His photographs of waterfront and warehouse cruising chronicle a rich sexual community by the river, made up of white, African-American, and Latinx men of various ages and physical types, as extensively as does Baltrop's work. Some of Fink's photographs show men and women workers from the nearby Meatpacking and Financial Districts sitting on the stone piers enjoying sandwiches on lunch breaks from work. Others are more explicit and depict sexual contact from a few feet away.

Fink's work is more straightforwardly documentary than Baltrop's, and his photographs do not display the same interest in perspective, composition, and the architectural qualities of the warehouses. Fink's work is playful, and his personal and erotic engagement in the cruising scene at the piers is very much apparent in his close connections with many of his subjects. In one shot, a man in sneakers and shorts leaps in a balletic pose for Fink's camera. In another, a man lies reading on Pier 42, acknowledging the photographer's presence with a wry, inviting smile. In yet another, an older man in a peaked leather cap sits with three other shirtless men, one of whom is overweight and seated in a wheelchair (figure 1.8). Though some are dressed in the leather gear of the clone, a mainstay of downtown gay bar life, these are not the molded, muscular bodies of the "dancing machines" who patronized downtown disco clubs like the Flamingo, where, as Douglas Crimp wrote later, the "sculpted pectoral muscles [that] had become one of the main attributes of gay male desirability" was "institutionalized."[77] The same men appear, smiling and laughing, in a number of Fink's other photographs. Fink's photographs of noticeably older men, some overweight, some visibly disabled—like

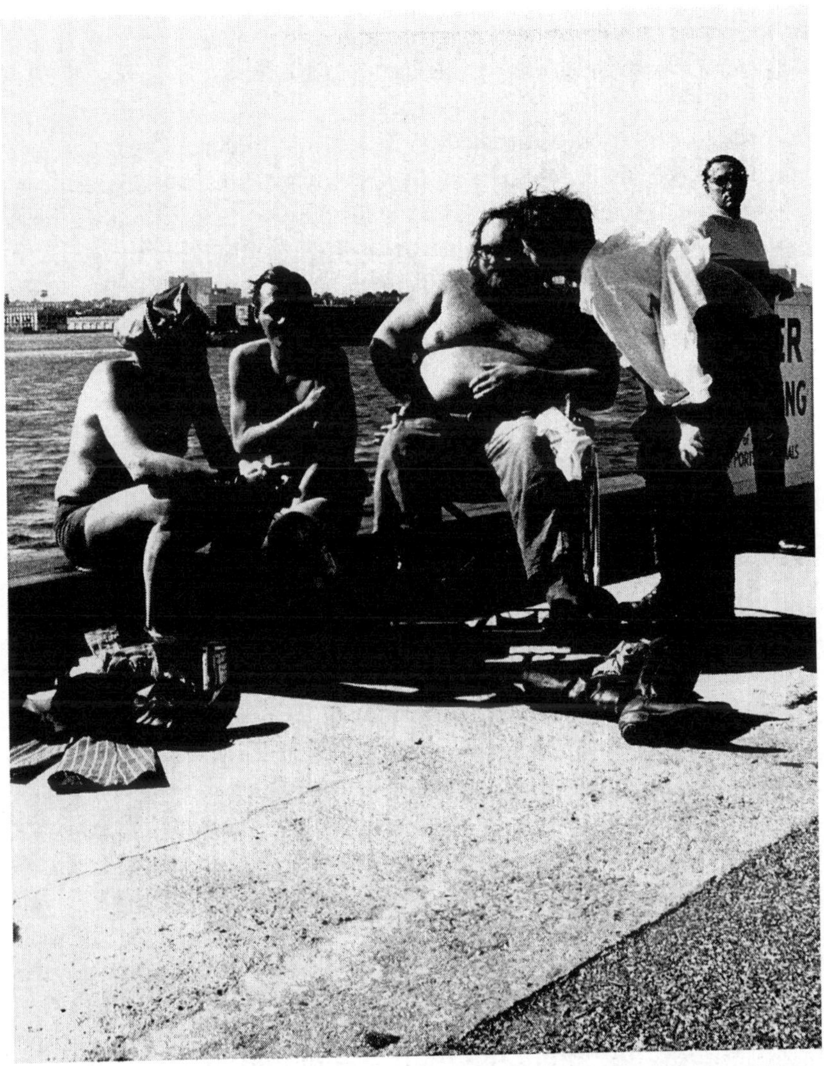

FIGURE 1.8. Photograph by Leonard Fink, 1974–1975. © The LGBT Community Center National History Archive.

the photographs of Alvin Baltrop and Peter Hujar showing cruising men of color—document the diversity and playfulness of the libidinal queer community of the piers. Seen alongside Fink's earlier photographs of queues of young, white, muscular patrons of the Mineshaft and the Ramrod, they simultaneously mark the absence of such bodies from many downtown gay establishments.

## "If these floorboards could talk . . ."

In one of Leonard Fink's more overtly erotic photographs of the sex scene at the piers, a man in a jockstrap stands holding a leather belt on an open level of a dilapidated warehouse. He is poised to strike a semiclothed partner who lies strapped to a sheet of corrugated iron, fallen in from the ceiling (figure 1.9). In a photograph of a pier cruiser by Stanley Stellar, *Red*, a solitary man penetrates a metal grate and, with a knowing look, offers himself simultaneously to the photographer and, to us, the viewer (figure 1.10). Both images recall the climax of Arch Brown's pornographic film *Pier Groups* (1979), set at the West Side piers, in which an unsuspecting construction worker, asked to inspect a riverside warehouse prior to demolition, stumbles upon an afternoon orgy centered upon a male figure tied to girders in the ceiling of the dilapidated building. The degeneration that made the warehouses structurally precarious also rendered them more appealing as cruising spaces: long corridors facilitated wandering, office partitions formed private cubicles, hidden rooms provided peepholes, and cracked windows and broken floorboards created glory holes.

For Rechy and Wojnarowicz, too, the derelict condition of the waterfront architecture was part of its erotic appeal. Both writers saw the warehouses and piers as animated by an erogenous charge that exceeded its appropriation by cruising men and its proximity to the leather and Western sexual cultures of the bars. This charge seemed to emanate from the physical form of the harbor, from the ruined buildings themselves. "Collapsing piers and warehouses," Wojnarowicz wrote in a journal entry from June 1980, "brought back images that smelled young and cleared the world of its weariness." These were lustful ruins. In an unpublished poem from 1979, "Dream of Federico Fellini/Pasolini," Wojnarowicz wrote of men "curving their bodies along" the walls of a Roman coliseum and of the warehouses and piers as "late night walkways where history strolls." In "End Street," cruising men "among the loading docks of shipyards" are likened to "pillars," like the rotting pier footings that punctuated the Hudson shore.[78]

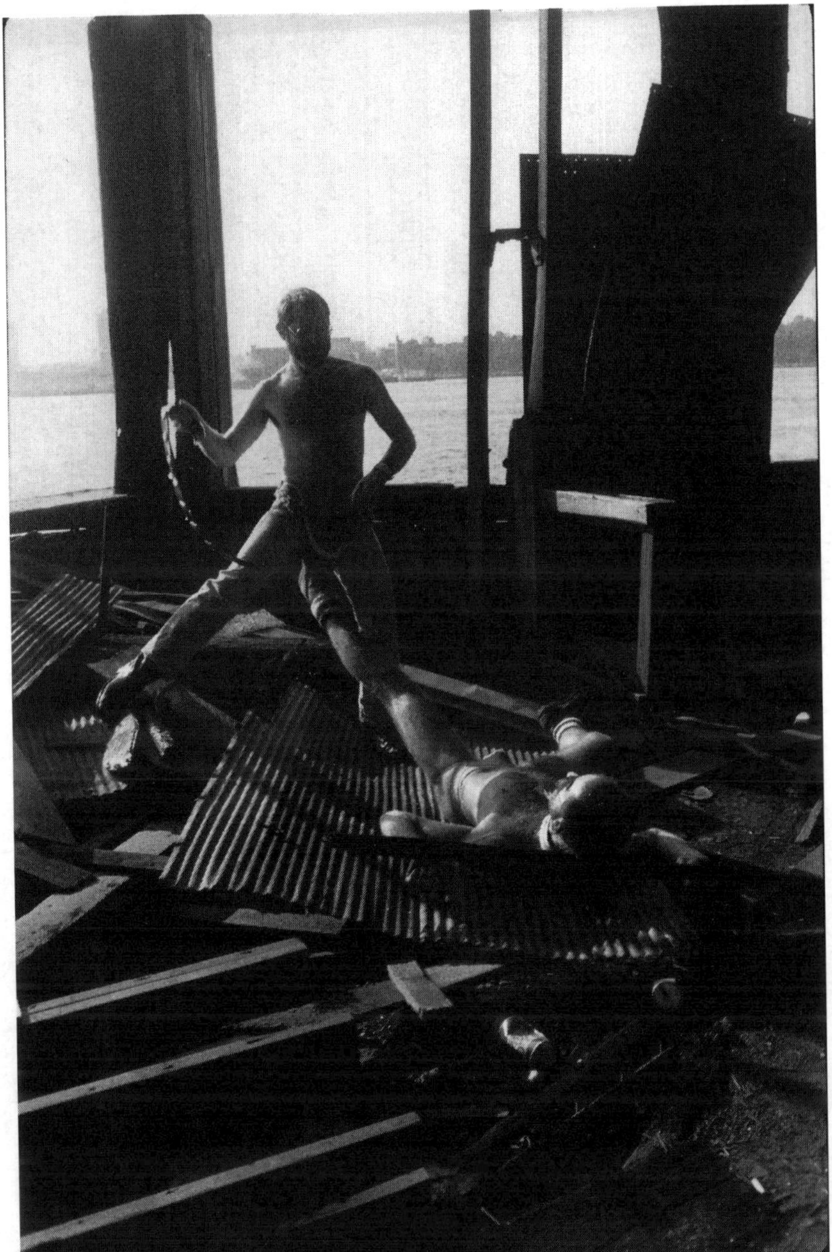

FIGURE 1.9. Photograph by Leonard Fink, 1974–1975. © The LGBT Community Center National History Archive.

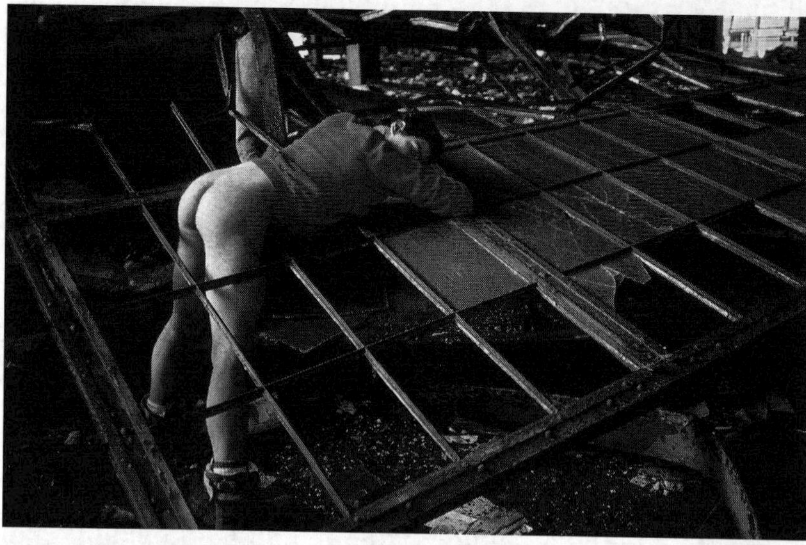

FIGURE 1.10. Stanley Stellar, *Red*, 1984. © Stanley Stellar.

These poetic visions were made possible by the ruination of the buildings themselves, generating peculiar images as they slipped into obsolescence and disappeared. In Rechy's *Rushes*, sexually charged glances at fellow cruisers produce what he calls a unique "sextime" in which men appear as "young ghosts haunting the streets" and the city presents itself, in bodily terms, as a "cadaver," the piers its "rotted gut." In his fictive descriptions, traveling through the labyrinthine warehouses parallels the repeated thrusts of the sexual act, and he makes explicit the role of the crumbling waterfront architecture as a prop in the sexual encounters that take place there. As Endore, the central character, cruises the riverside, he focuses not on other men but on "the giant buildings stabbing at the sky." Cruising men and cruising spaces appear indivisible:

> Iron, steel, cement, the buildings—at times they crush him tiny; other times he searches the sharp angles of light and dark they create, shoving himself in and out of them to become a part of their ordered patterns.[79]

In *The Pleasure of Ruins*, the English writer Rose Macaulay similarly limns the strange appeal of the ruin, "*ruinenlust*," in active, anthropomorphic terms. "New ruins," she writes, "are for a time stark and bare, vegetationless and creatureless; blackened and torn, they smell of fire and mortality." But not for long. "Very soon," she reflects, "trees will be *thrusting* through the empty window *sockets*, the rose-bay and fennel blossoming within the broken walls, the brambles tangling outside them." The pleasure of the ruin increases as it becomes “enjungled,” “engulfed” by nature. Yet traces of the ruin’s former uses persist: “We stumble among stone foundations and fragments of cellar walls, among the ghosts of the exiled merchants and publicans who there carried on their gainful trades.” So too do hints of its earlier inhabitants, offering “a catastrophic tipsy chaos, a bizarre new charm.”[80]

In a journal entry from March 1980, Wojnarowicz detailed a sexual encounter with an anonymous cruiser in an abandoned warehouse that captures the erotic appeal of the piers, their labyrinthine layout, and the charge they evoked. His use of anthropomorphic language and metaphor demonstrates the importance of coexistent temporalities and architectural memory, his sense of the “traces of times embedded” in ruined places,[81] motifs that appear throughout his waterfront writing:

> Later, after dark, down at the river, a man emerged from the darkness and sounds of the waterfront, waves turning slightly, raising sounds beneath the wheels of the highway traffic. The guy was large, a strapping laborer’s or weight lifter’s frame, his hair cropped close to his skull, growing in recently from having been shaved.
>
> I turned on my heel with no hesitation; he turned down by the brick wall that bordered the walkway leading to the crushed sides of the covered pier. Hesitating he muttered something that sounded like a cross between a low whistle and a statement. I followed him as he turned the brick corner and disappeared in the direction of the warehouse.[82]

In Wojnarowicz’s description, his psychic investment in this anonymous sex is distributed equally between the cruised man and the cruising space, a fire-damaged warehouse, cracks in which throw light from passing cars onto the shadowy pair:

> Stepping over rigging irons and broken pipes I followed his retreating back covered by a black leather jacket that shone softly in the darkness, like shining shoes beneath a surface of water. Stooping beneath the half-raised doorway (loading doors) I saw him walk further into the darkness and then turn suddenly and squat down, motioning me towards him with a single wave of his large hands. Rubbing my palms around the base of his neck over and over, feeling the bristle of his shaved skull against the sensitive undersides of my wrists, movements like birds in a stationary flexing of wings, my hands riding his forehead, smoothing along his jacket, over his hard shoulders and muscles. . . .

“Stepping over rigging irons and broken pipes” in the dilapidated warehouse space is cast as a kind of foreplay. The structural decay of the building is sketched in as much detail as the physical characteristics of the man himself.

Wojnarowicz is keen to uncover personal information that might, however briefly, lend a physical intimacy to his partner similar to what he finds embedded in the "broken" interior of the abandoned warehouse. "To be confronted by space," he writes, to be met with anonymity in darkness, "is to fill it like a vessel with whatever designs one carries."[83] As he seeks to generate an erotic connection between body and building in this cruising encounter, Wojnarowicz looks for material correlations between himself, his partner, and the warehouse in which they are fucking; he creates an embodied material genealogy:

> Feeling something soft and foreign, I realized he had a couple large feathers hanging from one shoulder by a piece of string, some decoration that perplexed yet gladdened me for it threw meaning into his image, as if it were a tribal gift, a sense of mysterious beauty placed within the projections I had put upon his sturdy shoulders of who he was and what distances he had traveled. . . . I wrapped my hands around his body, my arms pressing against his sides, the wind moving closer and the lights of turning cars spreading beneath the slight cracks in the wall where it joined the concrete floor. . . .
>
> When I came he stood up and whipped out a white rag from his pocket and smoothed it over his forehead and mouth and laughed: Jesus, and I said, Yeah, whew. And he said, the fire really took this place apart, but man if these floorboards could talk . . .[84]

When the warehouses "became silhouetted at a certain point of the day," Wojnarowicz told Barry Blinderman in an interview in 1990,

> I could dream myself—project myself—all around the world in my imagination by looking at those qualities of light, and by looking at those structures. Those qualities of light, of sound, of pieces of tin rattling in the breeze way off in some other part of the building.[85]

As he did with the warehouses, stripped to only traces of their original usage and ripe for erotic historical revisions, Wojnarowicz projected multiple prior lives, functions, identities onto the men he cruised there. He took his partner's metaphorical aside literally, reflectively anthropomorphizing the warehouse in which they stood and considering the pasts embedded within its rotting wooden floor:

> Yeah if these floorboards could talk, if those streets could talk, if the huge path this body has traveled—roads, motel rooms, hillsides, cliffs, subways, rivers, planes, trucks—if any of them could speak, what would they remember most about me? What motions would they unravel within their words . . . ?[86]

Wojnarowicz approaches the queer space of the waterfront as a kind of ancestral site, suggesting that he, and the man with the "tribal" feathers and "black leather jacket that shone softly in the darkness," and the rotting floorboards are connected by an orgiastic relation outside of time, enabled and sustained by these ruins by the river.

One finds unexpected precedents for Wojnarowicz's writing on the queer appeal of ruins and his use of anthropomorphic language to describe the experience of cruising ruins. "If the site of a ruin seems perilous, I shudder," wrote Denis Diderot, in a review of the Paris Salon of 1767. "If I feel safe and secure there, I'm freer, more alone, more myself, closer to myself." For Diderot, the temporal character of the ruin, suspended "between two eternities," seemed to permit a kind of reflective intimacy, a homosociality not possible in more populated, active spaces:

> It's there that I call out to my friend, it's there that I miss my friend; it's there that we enjoy ourselves without anxiety, without witnesses, without intruders, without those jealous of us. It's there that I probe my own heart; it's there that I interrogate his.[87]

In a drawing from one of Wojnarowicz's journals, given the tentative title *Thug Obscured*, a stubble-faced man stands in a waterfront setting, pier pilings darkly visible over one shoulder and beside him, though across the river, a factory spewing smoke, most likely on the New Jersey waterfront (figure 1.11).[88] His face is "obscured" by black scribbles that evokes the smoke from the factory. Importantly, these appear as later additions to the work, like the mental image of a face fading from memory. The "thug' "s blue shirt blends into the blue of the water; he returns to the river or, perhaps, has emerged from it. In the unrealized "Waterfront Thug" series, studies for which appear in the same journal, Wojnarowicz removed the figure's face entirely.[89] His notes for the work indicate that drawings of a more visible, muscular torso were to sit atop photographs of buildings on the waterfront—images of the piers rather than the men who cruised there—which would extend into the crotch of the depicted "thug," explicitly heightening the erotic, anthropomorphic charge of the harbor's architecture.

In these drawings, the factory chimneys on the shoreline become abundantly phallic, a connection that the German director Rainer Werner Fassbinder also made in his 1982 film *Querelle*, an adaptation of Jean Genet's homoerotic novel *Querelle de Brest* (1947), about murderous sailors in the northern French port town of Brest. In Fassbinder's filmic vision of Brest, harborside factory chimneys take on the thick, fleshy proportions of erect phalluses. In Wojnarowicz's drawing, the thug's musculature draws on the bodies of men he met at the waterfront and wrote of extensively in his published and unpublished journals. He recalls the form of their bodies from phantasmic

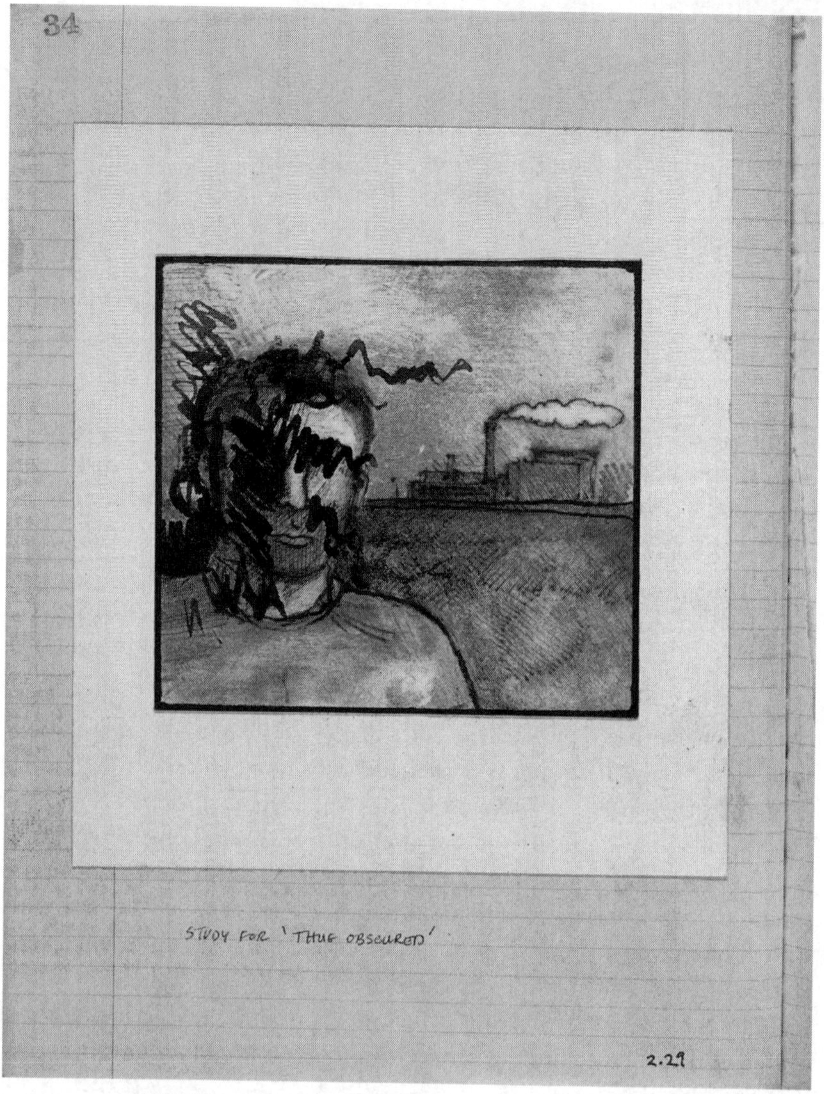


FIGURE 1.11. David Wojnarowicz, study for *Thug Obscured*, 1980. Courtesy of the Estate of David Wojnarowicz; P•P•O•W, New York. © David Wojnarowicz.

memory. In an unpublished note from an early journal, written in preparation for an imagined film set in the riverside warehouses, Wojnarowicz notes his attraction to men he described as "sailor looking . . . all of them tattoos and bodies hard like you get from a harbor rather than a gym."[90] This muscular aesthetic was informed also by Lewis Hine's photographs from the

1930s of workmen, including longshoremen, which Wojnarowicz glued into the same journal. By pairing Hine's intimate images of laborers with images of the cruised buildings of the ruined harbor, Wojnarowicz activated their contemporary homoerotic value. The importance of these maritime fantasies for Wojnarowicz is underscored by his playful working of the homonymic and homoerotic possibilities of the word "seamen," comparable to his play with the material and metaphoric possibilities of the ruin. In a journal entry from August 1980, he describes an orgasm as producing "a lightness in the base of my skull in my neck, legs shaking and [weak] and the image of the seaman."[91]

In *Cruising Modernism* (2003), Michael Trask examines Hine's photographs of longshoremen as indicative of the queer kinds of physical intimacy that developed among men living and working at sea, away from family, or by the shoreline, in casual labor arrangements, outside of normative temporal and social markers. The social and cultural standing of the longshoreman, Trask observes, was "historically ambiguous," as their peripatetic lifestyle "did not correspond to any recognizable pattern of domestic regularity."[92] Similarly, in *In A Queer Time and Place* (2005), Jack Halberstam argued that queer subcultures, such as cruising cultures, "produce alternative temporalities by allowing their participants to believe that their futures can be imagined according to logics that lie outside of those paradigmatic markers of lived experience."[93] What Wojnarowicz describes as the erotically charged "continual motion" of thugs and toughs in the illicit space of the abandoned waterfront, like the "unknown and coasting" figure of the sailor,[94] Trask analyzes as "a fantasy of plural and public sex outside the insulated precincts of domesticity" and pertaining to an imagined link between irregular harbor work and sex that recalls the ephemerality of the cruising encounter: "both the labor and the desire attached to these bodies are discontinuous, casual rather than purposive, impermanent rather than sustained."[95]

In a journal entry from June 1979, Wojnarowicz explicitly links his interest in the sexual charge of buildings with the architectural eroticism of Genet's sole film work, *Un Chant d'Amour* (*A Song of Love*, 1950). In the film, two prisoners in adjacent cells create fantasies about the other, which they play out through inventive, semi-onanistic gestures such as sharing a cigarette through a crack in the wall between them. A prison guard patrols the cells, peering through the bars like a latter-day cruiser at the piers, watching other men cruise through a smashed window. Wojnarowicz makes an imaginative connection between Genet's work and his own after going home with a man he met in "the shadows of the night pier" who looks like the French writer. In the anonymous man's apartment, Wojnarowicz finds himself in darkness, struggling to see.

The room, like the two men, is "receding into distances"; they are "embraced by invisibility, being somehow more erotic, more concerned with life energy, a sense almost wasted on words, so it becomes mind films." Their sex plays out filmically, activated by what Wojnarowicz calls "the looming sex life energy in imagination." When "greasing up and penetrating," Wojnarowicz wrote of

> feeling humility before all his personal belongings, feeling absent with pale sections of his time and living; his personal past, all these wall and table things all his private dreams revealed only in them and not even from his own eyes—thinking of Jean Genet thinking of the slow motion thump of torsos, thinking about the hole in the stone prison walls, the breathing in of erotic personal smoke, the lifted peephole.[96]

Like the holes that emerged in the decaying warehouses on the Manhattan waterfront, the dilapidated window performs an important voyeuristic purpose. In Genet's film, the prison wall is anthropomorphized as a bodily orifice, activated orally and embedded with traces of its habitation by young men removed from ordinary bodily temporality and familial identity, Halberstam's "paradigmatic markers of lived experience."

Wojnarowicz was turned on, too, by the punitive context of Genet's film, the fact that these men were, most likely, criminals. As in Genet's later novel *The Thief's Journal* (1949), the "toughs" that inhabit Wojnarowicz's erotic waterfront writing are depicted as angelic. Describing an erotic memory of a "tough angel" smoking in the shadows of a Parisian cruising ground, like the Louvre or the Tuilleries, he wrote that "each puff of a cigarette" produced a "dissipating rough halo."[97] For Genet, the criminal act of theft was enhanced by a erotic "nervousness provoked by fear, and sometimes by anxiety, [that] makes for a state akin to religious moods." His boy gangs are "their own heaven," and their quasi-religious erotic appeal is represented as indivisible from their criminality.[98] "I like criminals," Wojnarowicz wrote in lyrics for a song in 1980, returning to the erotic memory of seeing *Un Chant d'Amour* as a younger man in San Francisco, "I like their postures / building small fires behind prison walls."[99]

Later that week, Wojnarowicz returned to the waterfront to cruise and extended his filmic cruising metaphor and comparison with Genet in a journal entry. There at the piers, he wrote,

> bodies bump and [drift] like images out of a hallucinated UN CHANT D'AMOUR free of prison bars and stone rooms but the same sexual drift, the consciousness of it all, the angular body motions through the night evolving with shadows and light and merging with darkness again, just pale shades of arms and shirts or trousers or anything light or white but like a grainy film.[100]

In *City Boy*, Edmund White made similar allusions, recalling how bodies and buildings merged together filmically in the darkness of the piers, where there were "no lights at all beyond the occasional flare of a match seeking a cigarette," and "a sudden phosphorous flash" might reveal that

> what you thought was an embracing couple was actually a thick stump of wood with a rusting chain wrapped around it, or what you saw as a gull's wing was really someone's shirttail. Ramps led up to rooms with missing doors and floorboards, to a seething Laocoön entwined by snakes or by arms as he held fast to his sons or lovers.[101]

The poet Tim Dlugos, whom Wojnarowicz met at the piers in the late 1970s, used similarly filmic and temporally complex language. "It's nice," he writes, "to drift through the history / of film within your own view," thinking about "Laura Mars ensconced in *New York* magazine's idea of luxury / where gay men sunbathe nude along the rotten / pier" and "Al Pacino swaggering in leather and chains, / four blocks to the south" in the movie *Cruising* (1980).[102] Looking at the waterfront from his friend's apartment, "Chez Jane," Dlugos looks out at the

> skyline
> complicated, unfamiliar, from Bedloe's
> (now known as Liberty) Island, past Hoboken
> and the great green docks, up to where the giant cup
> of Maxwell House is yielding its last drop. It's good
> to have this vantage point, to fill in the river's
> graduated silvers with your eyes, and watch the gray
> of sky and street diverge to gold and misty blue,
> like the eyes of a mariner. "I feel like one, too."[103]

For Dlugos, White, and Wojnarowicz, memories of earlier erotic experiences merged with recollected snippets of films and fantasies, just as the bodies in these buildings merged with their dilapidated surroundings and recalled the longshoremen who once occupied these spaces, and as, to use Rechy's term, "sextime" in this dark space confused regular distinctions between day and night, past and present.

Anthropomorphic descriptions of the piers and warehouses abound in Larry Kramer's satirical evocation of the waterfront cruising scene. The Hudson River docks, around "the Erie and Lackawanna dockage area," he writes (most likely referring to the area around Twenty-Third Street, where the Lackawanna railroad barge docked, rather than the Erie Lackawanna warehouse on the New Jersey shore, whose sign was visible from the Lower West Side of Manhattan), was known as "Ellie to her friends." The warehouses there are not only anthropomorphized in Kramer's description, but gendered, feminized. The buildings are rendered as an architectural Miss Haversham, awaiting a lost erotic cargo, "a windswept, storm toss'd, fire-ravaged skeleton of former grandeurs!" She is "a huge black hole of Calcutta,"

> fingers jutting out to the water, pilings sinking, a wrought-iron inspiration with sagging seams, a mammoth cavern now useless to the outside world, a hoary giganticism.

She is, although "sinking," a "home away from home." Kramer is impressed that she is "still standing!" Kramer anthropomorphizes the piers not to eroticize them but to draw humorous, and condemnatory, parallels between the queer persistence of the dilapidated structures and what he saw as the superficial character of gay cruising cultures in the 1970s: egocentric and focused on external, physical features. As the aging character Anthony Montano lies, stoned, "flat on his back in the darkness of the Erie Lackawanna terminal," anxious about his dwindling physical appeal, he muses on the ruination of the warehouse:

> with your three stories gutted yet still here. Holes in you for entrance, holes within your stockings, fetid waters underneath, your bottom twisted and rippling like wooden waves, *You Are a Woman!* Our Ellie, Barbra, Kate, Bette, Diana, Marlene, Tallulah, *Judy!* Survivor, standing from all these ravages upon your face and body, from users and abusers of your finery.

Reflecting on the aesthetic appeal of these collapsing structures motivates Montano to

> go out, go up, go show them that I'm still Alive! Show them that I'm still gorgeous and still gutsy and desirable, and while I may be going down the tubes, I'll go down getting my cock sucked.[104]

## Nostalgia for the mud

Andrew Holleran ruminates on the erotic pull of the piers in similar terms, both poetic and pejorative, in "Nostalgia for the Mud," a short essay for *Christopher Street* magazine, first published in 1983. The title translates a French idiom, *nostalgie de la boue*, that was first used in *Le Mariage d'Olympe* (*The Marriage of Olympia*, 1855), a play by Émile Augier. While the central character Camille, a courtesan, marries a nobleman, she cannot escape the pull of her earlier, lower-class life. "Put a duck on a lake in the middle of swans," one character remarks, "and you'll see that he will miss his pond and end up going back there." "Ah," replies another, "nostalgia for the mud."[105] The phrase had appeared more recently, and in a New York context, in Tom Wolfe's scathing critique of liberal Manhattan society, "Radical Chic: That Party at Lenny's," published in *New York* magazine in June 1970. Wolfe skewered the composer Leonard Bernstein's social circle for associating themselves with the Black Panther Party politically—inviting members to parties, serving up soul food—in order to advance their social and cultural standing. It amounted to, Wolfe argued, a "*nostalgie de la boue*, or romanticizing of primitive souls."[106] Holleran's evocation of this loaded phrase to describe the draw of the piers as a cruising space resonated beyond its historic use as a metaphor for aspirational class politics. Holleran, like Wojnarowicz, Rechy, and White, was drawn by the material character of the harbor's abandoned buildings. He renders the eroticism implicit in Augier and Wolfe's description of the nostalgic pull of the derelict or disenfranchised physical and tactile.

Holleran's essay follows three friends as they visit *Inner City* at the Whitney Museum of American Art, a "room-sized reconstruction" by the artist Michael McMillen "of three entire blocks of a warehouse district in Los Angeles"—a "very evocative doll's house," Holleran noted, "for anyone who has haunted such decaying blocks in reality." Each building in the installation was meticulously recreated in the gallery space, "complete with scaled down neon signs, fire escapes, window shades." As a waterfront cruiser himself, Holleran was struck by the faithful depiction of his favored erotic quarter:

> This is the door, the darkness, the music to which I have been drawn, irresistibly, so many winter nights; this is the ruined neighborhood, the lonely street, the crumbling building (its shades drawn or half drawn); this is the sordid, deserted, poignant place so many of us have wandered in for years.

The three men are led to wonder: "Why do gays love ruins? . . . The Lower West Side, the docks. Why do we love slums so much?"[107] Holleran's use of the term "slums," of course, evokes the long-standing practice of "slumming," which Seth Koven has described as activities, not always explicitly sexual but almost always erotic, "undertaken by people of wealth, social standing or education in urban spaces inhabited by the poor [and] figured as some sort of 'descent' across urban spatial and class, gender and sexual boundaries."[108] Holleran's characters wonder what exactly draws them to these ruined places. "Why," one friend inquires, "do I feel a strange sense of freedom the moment I enter a decaying neighborhood?" "Why," he asks, retracing evenings spent cruising the Lower East Side, when walking by "a tenement with a collapsed wall . . . do I imagine giving a party there—or better yet, conjure up a slender fellow, half hidden by the rusted doorframe, inviting me into the rubble to make love, entirely in ruins?"

McMillen's installation would be an even more accurate depiction of the dilapidated region that this group cruised, Holleran observes, had he modeled a "gang of tiny teenage boys waiting for a solitary man to walk by so they can beat him up." Holleran, initially convinced that "surely, we would never have come to the purlieus of the Lower West Side but for the fact that they are the hunting grounds of other men looking for a certain style of sex," then frames the waterfront more broadly as a space for the city's marginalized citizens. Watching a young boy visiting the installation "peer into a room where, in real life, young Chicanos or Puerto Ricans would surely cluster around the table," he asks, "Who else knows this inner city? The poor, the recently arrived, the Hispanic." Cruising the waterfront, Holleran argues, was a completely different sexual experience, one to which he was "irresistibly" drawn by "the erotic longing you feel walking home late at night in a rundown neighborhood, when physical loneliness corresponds exactly to psychic isolation." "We all wanted to escape," one friend offers, and "you escaped to the city. Would you ever have ended up in the ruins had you not been gay?"[109]

Why, wonders another of the companions, referring to the slumming aesthetic of Man's Country's decor, is there "a truck without a chassis on the eighth floor of the baths so that people may do the curious thing of going to the baths to make love in a truck (or a jail cell or a cheap hotel room)?" Holleran concludes his meditation on this queer nostalgia, this "strange axis between the extremely aesthetic" and "the extremely sleazy," by walking to the Lower West Side piers. "Whatever their attraction, whatever their meaning," he asserts, "these ruins were real."[110] For him and his cruising friends, these warehouses have a queer sort of material authenticity that is cast into relief by their ruination. These are the same visibly rotting buildings that the novelist Henry Miller described in *Sexus* (1959) as "immediate and palpable, not only in their substance but in their essence." It was only at the piers, "in this despised section of the city," Miller wrote,

> that I could meet up with an interesting character. The crumbling architecture itself was an inspiration, to say nothing of the morbid, sordid streets leading to the waterfront. What a world there was here, perhaps still is, despite all the efforts to clean it up![111]

For Holleran, too, the historical suggestiveness and ruinous dereliction of these spaces are markers of the harbor's temporal and spatial disjunction from the rest of the city and from heteronormative sexual cultures and productivity—and so add to its appeal as a cruising space, in terms of both safety and fantasy. One of Holleran's friends, an "alumnus of the Mineshaft," ponders what will happen "if Westway [a proposed development] is ever built" and "the shoreline made pretty by city planners":

> When the city is totally renovated, when gays have restored all the tenements, garden restaurants have sprouted on the Lower East Side, and the meatpacking district is given over entirely to boutiques and cardshops—then we'll build an island in New York Harbor composed entirely of rotting piers, blocks of collapsed walls, and litter-strewn lots.

"Ruins," he concludes, "become decor, nostalgia for the mud."[112] Holleran saw this "nostalgia for the mud" as a temporally complex appeal that hinged upon the warehouse's material ruination. Implicit in his tongue-in-cheek description of the pull of ruins is a willful resistance to urban renewal and normative, or at least progressive, economic production. The queer ruin persists, as Miller had noted a quarter century earlier, "despite all the efforts to clean it up!" The proliferation of gay cruising cultures in ruined buildings on the Manhattan waterfront in the 1970s underlined the failure of municipal authorities to redevelop this once-prosperous industrial space or to properly police the fringes of the city. As New York continued to reel from its industrial and economic decline, its heteronormative fabric also began to fray at the edges.

The ruin, then, for all of these writers, was both the place where the past is reactivated and the material that reactivated it. The queer archival tendencies perceptible in writing on cruising the waterfront in late 1970s New York speak as much to the physical and imaginative potential of the ruin as to the nonlinear, ephemeral practice of urban cruising. As a "process of counter movement" that "necessarily resists totalizing ways" of narrating its queer temporality,[113] of archiving itself, cruising finds its spatial parallel not in the metaphor of the busy street, the modern bathhouse, or the public park, but in the waterfront ruin, dilapidated and decaying, economically functionless and willfully nonproductive, where, in Wojnarowicz's queer narrative, a teleological vision of progress in the city, of "times passage[,] becomes irrelevant."[114]

# 2

# The Whole World and the Cemetery: The Queer Visual Culture of Ruins

In Chantal Akerman's film *News from Home* (1976), New York City appears as a queerly ruined place, perpetually shrouded in dusk or darkness, bright with artificial light. The city teems with activity but has a distinctly lonesome quality. In a series of mostly fixed-camera shots, some lasting over a minute, Akerman directs the viewer through a network of dilapidated streets, ragged subway cars, and fluorescent-lit corner stores. Her city seems at times to be empty or nearing abandonment. When fellow citizens do appear, they glance briefly at the camera before returning to private contemplation or labor, or fail to notice it entirely, absorbed in their own activities. There is no visual narrative beyond this languid excursion around lower Manhattan. Accompanied by rattling subway cars or the squealing of waterfront gulls, Akerman reads intermittently from a series of letters sent to her in New York by her mother in Belgium, the titular "news from home." The letters are read softly, and some of the news—about family and friends, parties missed, relationships neglected—is obscured by urban noise.

While the banal correspondence and dispassionate documentation of downtown Manhattan may initially appear to coexist comfortably, the emotional content of the letters addresses an affective split between mother and daughter and between "there" and "here." Akerman's mother is surprised not to have heard from her daughter. "All we ask," she implores, "is that you don't forget us." As the extent of Akerman's disconnection from "home" becomes clearer, the seemingly detached visual narrative and the city's empty spaces acquire an emotional weight. Akerman creates a powerful sense of place, an indelible image of a now-lost New York, by underscoring her familial placelessness, her dislocation from the "home" of the film's title. Her anonymity in these spaces, her separation from those around her, is key to her liberatory experience of the city. The emptied downtown streets enable Akerman to exist untethered in the postindustrial city, to embrace displacement and move freely through lower Manhattan's broad avenues, side streets, neon-bright bodegas, subway stations, fish markets, and piers. In the film's closing scene, we watch as the camera pulls out of a pier by the South Street Seaport and sails toward Governor's Island or the Upper Bay, with lapping water as the only soundtrack, until Akerman's camera runs out of film.

This disconnection imbues the apparently dispassionate camera direction with a sense of what Giuliana Bruno has called an "erotic nomadism."[1] This "nomadism" is perceptible in the ways in which Akerman occupies the city as both a resident and an outsider with emotional links to another "home." But it also visible in the oblique glances she takes at fellow citizens and in the spaces in which she wanders, largely at dusk and seemingly without purpose. Playing on her sense of separation from those around her by focusing on the city's architecture, rather than its residents, Akerman, according to Timothy Corrigan, inverts "the touristic gaze" that tends to "appropriate spaces and places as imagistic possessions like postcards."[2] These spaces are instilled, in the viewer's mind, with that displaced affect. Focusing on the city's interstitial sites—streets, subway platforms, the waterfront—Akerman instead cruises nocturnal Manhattan for spaces that permit free, anonymous occupation. The reading of the letters, whose subject is longing, nostalgia, and separation, suffuses the shots of recognizably dilapidated places—visibly the domain of the impoverished, the overworked, the lonely and marginalized—with a romantic quality and a sense of latent intimacy, depersonalized but deeply erotic.

Akerman shared with Wojnarowicz a keen interest in the potentially dissonant relation between text and image, between lone introspection and social interaction, and in the "erotic nomadism" that lower Manhattan's half-empty, dusky thoroughfares permitted in the late capitalist moment of the late 1970s. Akerman's desolate streets, imbued with an erotic longing that moves between bodies and buildings, are the same Manhattan spaces that Wojnarowicz, Peter Hujar, Alvin Baltrop, Samuel Delany, Andrew Holleran, John Rechy, Edmund White, and Tim Dlugos wandered in search of sex and aesthetic and literary inspiration. The detached glances she casts upon these ruined sites and the people who occupy them recall the work of photographer Shelley Seccombe, who captured the queer culture of the piers and warehouses near Westbeth Artists Housing at Bethune Street, near West Street, where she lived with her family during the late 1970s (figure 2.1).

Similar erotic allusions punctuate artist Gordon Matta-Clark's writings on his work from the same decade. In "Work with Abandoned Structures,"

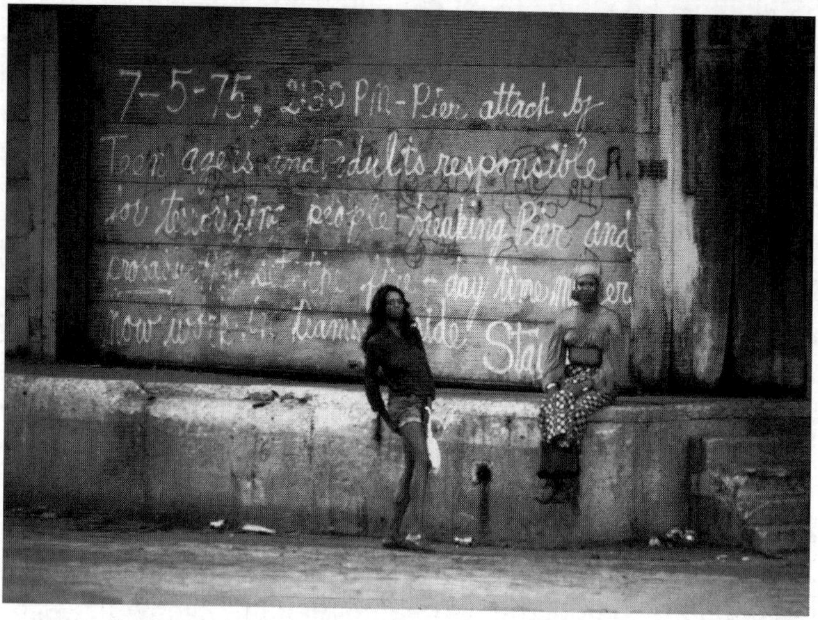


FIGURE 2.1. Shelley Seccombe, *Wall Newspaper—West Street at 11th Street*, 1975. © Shelley Seccombe.

written in 1975, Matta-Clark notes that focusing on ruined urban structures and spaces was part of his broader "concern for the life of a city" on the brink of bankruptcy. Like Akerman, Wojnarowicz, and Holleran, Matta-Clark found liberatory potential in the city's collapse. "The omnipresence of emptiness, of abandoned housing and imminent demolition," he writes, "gave me the freedom to experiment with the multiple alternatives to one's life in a box." As well as offering an affective critique of impending gentrification, Matta-Clark's presence in the city's ruined spaces has a perceptible erotic charge. He writes suggestively of his experiences of "New York's least remembered parts," "driv[ing] around in my pick-up hunting for emptiness, for a quiet abandoned spot on which to concentrate my piercing attention."[3]

Matta-Clark's experience of the city's abandoned spaces as simultaneously erotically loaded and politically charged relates closely to both Akerman's inversion of touristic perspectives on Manhattan and Wojnarowicz's queer sexual occupation of its derelict waterfront. While the previous chapter looked at the erotic charge of the ruin in bodily terms in urban cruising cultures, this chapter considers these overlapping perspectives on late 1970s New York and the complex interrelations between art, sex, space, and the collapse of the postindustrial city in the late 1970s, particularly the convergence of erotic and artistic energies amid the ruins of the waterfront. I explore how Wojnarowicz and other queer New York artists, such as Peter Hujar and Paul Thek, engaged with ruins visually in their artwork; trace the development of a queer visual culture that focused on ruins as both subject matter and medium; and examine that culture's relation to a critical aesthetic interest in urban processes of abandonment, ruination, and renewal that gained traction in the broader downtown Manhattan art scene in this period, visible in the work of Matta-Clark and of fellow New York artists Robert Smithson, Joan Jonas, and Vito Acconci. I explore how this work might appear, achronologically, different from the homoerotic vantage point of cruising, itself a queer way of looking in the city and a visual culture interested in ruins and in the places where the city's heteronormative fabric falls apart. In drawing literal and figurative connections between queer sex, the photography of ruins, urban architecture, and urban renewal, I am concerned with how and why a queer visual culture of ruins developed with such fervor in the late 1970s and early 1980s, and how artists throughout downtown Manhattan manipulated the city's very real dilapidation in this period to their creative, as well as erotic, advantage.

## Watching the piers, picturing America's ruins

In his journals from the late 1970s, Wojnarowicz often offered detailed descriptions of the visual culture of the cruising scene and the waterfront landscape, with its collapsing warehouses and ruined piers, in place of erotic recollections of his own sexual encounters. Vignettes of nights spent in orgiastic abandon in the piers are interwoven with meticulously rendered scenes of evenings passed on the waterfront watching other men cruise from a distance, or observing sex workers wandering in and among the warehouses and nearby parked cars, hustling for business or "primping in the side mirrors." In an entry from July 1979, Wojnarowicz recorded an evening spent in the West Village in the company of his friend John Hall. He wrote of their walking "down Christopher Street in the night," watching "crowds of bar characters, homeless cowboys and street sleepers, the roughneck crowds and the junkies on the stoop next to Boots and Saddles," a leather bar on Seventh Avenue popular with the cruising characters who also frequented the piers.[4] The pair pass by the Silver Dollar Café on Christopher Street between Washington and Greenwich Streets, walking west toward the piers. At the intersection with West Street, they pass Badlands, another leather club, situated on the geographical divide between the West Village and the waterfront. A former seamen's clothing supply store, Badlands sat in the same terrain as Rechy's fictional bar the Rushes, in the "shadows of the tangled iron network" of the elevated rail line, which "divide[d] the street into grey and black patches," the night "dusted orange by the lights from the area of the piers."[5] Wojnarowicz's account of the scene outside Badlands focuses similarly on the play of artificial light on concrete, on the "racing night traffic" along West Street, and on the "glitter of lamps and glass broken on the street." Moving uptown to the intersection of West and West Tenth Streets, Wojnarowicz briefly mentions "the tittering of transvestites" standing outside Peter Rabbit, a bar that looked out onto the piers, but his focus is on the visual and aural experience of this wild landscape, "the ocean roll of traffic and hiss of wheels the shoosh of bypassing autos and the glimmer of the river not too far away."[6]

Hall and Wojnarowicz cross West Street and sit "on the waterfront board walk," where they "watched the characters easing in and outta the shadows of the pier warehouses, along the brick walls like rats and emerging into the phosphorescent shine of bathing streetlamps along the lapping posted walls."[7] Moving cautiously inside one of the warehouses, most likely that on the Christopher Street pier, at the end of West Tenth Street, directly opposite Peter Rabbit, they stand in the doorway, watching the play of light on the water and on "white T-shirts," the "pale gleam of white skin in the darkness," the "gold breathin' light across the surface of the dark rolling river."[8] Aside from a brief encounter with a man keen to share his bottle of amyl nitrate with Wojnarowicz and a memorable recollection of a cruising encounter so "brutal and fast and almost violent" it knocks a participant to the "surface of the pier boards," poetic descriptions of light take precedence over reports on the erotic encounters taking place here.

Hall and Wojnarowicz spoke of their joint visits to the piers in a conversation recorded on New Year's Eve, at the start of 1980. Hall remembered "feeling really uptight, very nervous, very self-conscious" on their first trip. They walked there, Hall recalled, feeling particularly "horny" after a night at Danceteria. He ended up spending three days. Their comments suggest that for both men the erotic appeal of the piers gave way to an aesthetic interest relatively quickly. "You get over the initial excitement of one type," Hall remarks, "but it's just a fascinating place. I like the visualness of it. What goes on there. The actual things that you see. You see this . . . I mean there's so many things about it that are interesting. On different levels. So many different things go on there." The piers have, Wojnarowicz interjects, "some very wild visuals." The visual appeal of the spaces in which this cruising scene operated parallel the visual culture of cruising itself. Cruising is, to return to Mark Turner's definition in *Backward Glances*, a "moment of visual exchange," a culture constructed from, or at least enabled by, glances.[9] At the piers, Hall notes:

> Everything is quiet or silent. And or near silent there. A lot of it, the cruising . . . it's quiet, you know. There's no question as to why people are there. . . . There's none of, having to go to a bar and deal with conversation. It's really very direct. If you don't want to make it with somebody . . . Visual acknowledgement of eye contact; that's usually all that's required.

Yet "even when's nobody's there," Hall remarks:

> aesthetically I find the place fascinating. Just weird and different and interesting. It's the kind of thing that I'd be into. Forgetting the sexual nature or orientation of people meeting there. Not even thinking about that, just the fact that it's this big abandoned place like that. The way it looks, burnt out. The space. The sun coming in. The windows. The halls. The light. All-natural light. Things smashed in. It's just weird. It's a combination of so many different senses and visual aspects and suggestions, memories, things you've seen in movies that are bombed out, burned out.[10]

Hall's description of the piers and his recounting of the specifically visual pleasure he took in ambling there is echoed in comments by Wojnarowicz in a 1990 interview with Barry Blinderman that documenting the "sound quality" and the visual experience of "the slow disintegration" of the waterfront warehouses was as important a creative task as recording the queer sexual cultures active there. He spoke, too, in aesthetic terms of "visions of people that appear out of darkness and disappear into darkness" in the ruined warehouses, an experience he described as "completely hallucinatory and very much like film."[11] Similarly, in February 1980, soon after his recorded conversation with Hall, Wojnarowicz wrote in his journal of cruising in a dark warehouse corridor and imagining the body of a single muscular man multiplying erotically into thousands of desired bodies, "like the bleak lit evolution of a Muybridge series."[12] Relating the visual experience of cruising at the piers to film and Eadweard Muybridge's photographic motion studies suggests both Wojnarowicz's feeling of disconnection from many of the men who cruised there, where he often preferred to remain an outsider or voyeur rather than a participant, and his sense that the warehouses were sites loaded with historical memory, which emerged both erotically, as explored in chapter 1, and visually. In his account of his and Hall's earlier visit to the Christopher Street pier, Wojnarowicz had written of wandering the warehouse, likening the "series of rooms windows bordering the river" to the sequence of frames in a reel of film. He and Hall walk from room to room, each space separated from the next by a "doorframe empty of door" and lit by "diamonds of gold light with shadows crossing window frames." The "visual scenes" this light throws up are, for Wojnarowicz and Hall, "so unexplainable" and have a "wounding nature." Outside the warehouse, the pair continue watching "from a discreet distance," walking by "numerous autos from Jersey" and "trucks lined up silver and motionless," parked beneath "bright lights and lampposts burning continuously beneath the Westside Highway structure," and Wojnarowicz is struck by what he calls "the timeless photographical nature" of these spaces and of the visual experience of cruising there.[13]

In evoking photographic practice and film as temporally complex forms of documentation and of relating to space, Wojnarowicz's descriptions of the ruined piers appear to allude, although often out of time, to Peter Hujar's extensive archive of photographs of the same spaces. Wojnarowicz and Hujar spent time at the piers, together and with others, as photographs in both artist's archives make clear. Hujar's photographs of the Christopher Street pier in the mid-1970s show a lively community of cruising men sunbathing, chatting, and flirting on the open pier (figure 2.2). Stanley Stellar photographed Hujar "get[ting] his dick sucked" in Pier 46 in the summer of 1981. In a contact sheet among Wojnarowicz's papers, Hujar is captured in the act of photographing the architectural degradation of the piers, focusing on points of intersection between abandoned rooms, on peeling wallpaper and broken windows, as he had in his photograph *Pier—Four Doors* (1981; figure 1.1). Later, in the same set of images, Hujar can be seen, with his camera hanging around his neck, posing in front of a drawing of a faceless Saint Sebastian, graffitoed on another warehouse wall by Wojnarowicz.[14] Hujar also took photographs of site-specific artwork by Wojnarowicz, Mike Bidlo, Luis Frangella, and others at the Ward Line pier in the spring of 1983. Although he and Wojnarowicz spent time at the piers together and clearly took photographs there on these visits, ruined architecture, discarded objects, and abandoned or disused postindustrial landscapes had been recurrent themes in Hujar's work since the mid-1970s, predating his relationship with Wojnarowicz, whom he first met in January 1981.

Along with the warehouses of New York's derelict waterfront, Hujar photographed New Jersey junkyards, Manhattan car parks at night, and bankrupt, shuttered shops. Not just personal investigations of ruined places, his images are studies of the formal properties of crushed automobiles, of steel shavings, of torn paper, of discarded shoes and items of clothing, of weeds growing through fences and in the hallways of emptied buildings. They fixate upon the waste products of American industry and draw our attention toward the debris that accompanies hurried exits or evictions, the visual culture of late capitalism's ruins. Like Wojnarowicz's, Hujar's ruins are formally fascinating and approached with aesthetic as well as erotic interest. While both artists

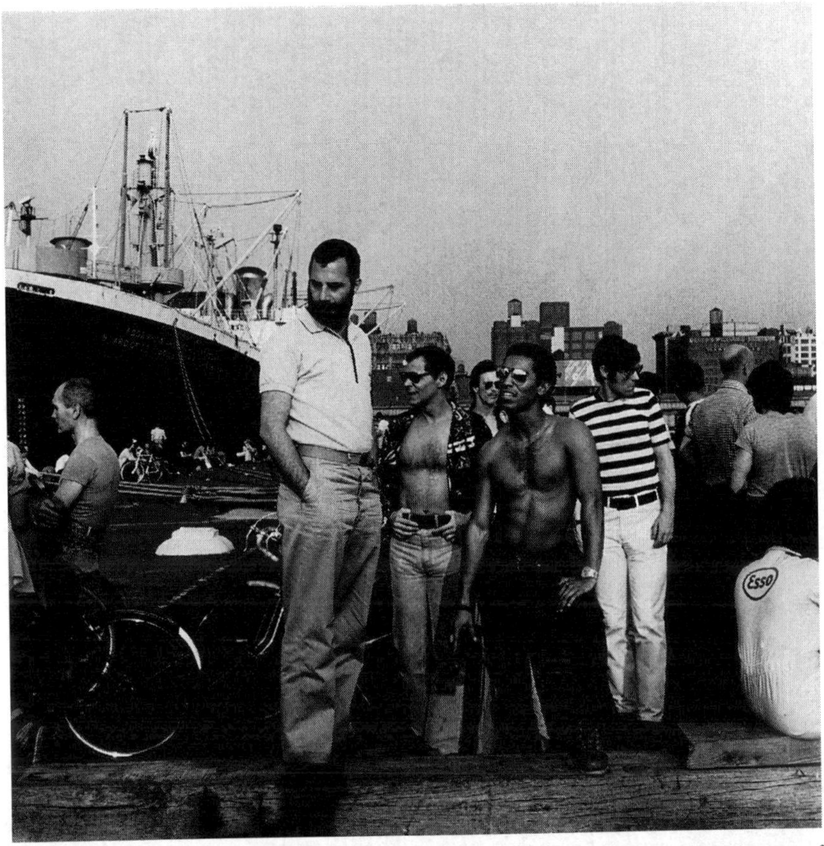


FIGURE 2.2. Peter Hujar, *Christopher Street Pier #4*, 1976. © 1987 The Peter Hujar Archive. Courtesy of Pace/MacGill Gallery, New York; Fraenkel Gallery, San Francisco.

play with the image of the ruin as willfully functionless, a symbolic parallel to the nonproductivity of queer sex, Hujar's photographs are less explicitly concerned with a critique of heteronormative teleology than was Wojnarowicz's waterfront work. They offer, however, a richly rendered place from which to reflect further on the imbrication of queer sex, urban decay, and American industrial collapse in the forgotten fringes of late 1970s New York.

In 1978 Hujar shot a series of photographs in metal junkyards in Newark, New Jersey. A crushed automobile, presumably once curved and smooth, now reduced to a ragged cube, sits at the center of *Steel Ruins #13* (1978; figure 2.3).[15] Hujar's black-and-white image gives the viewer little sense of the character of the surrounding dump, reducing, even crushing, the sense of space between the viewer and this lumpen form. While the compression of space and compositional focus on a simple form suggest abstraction, this

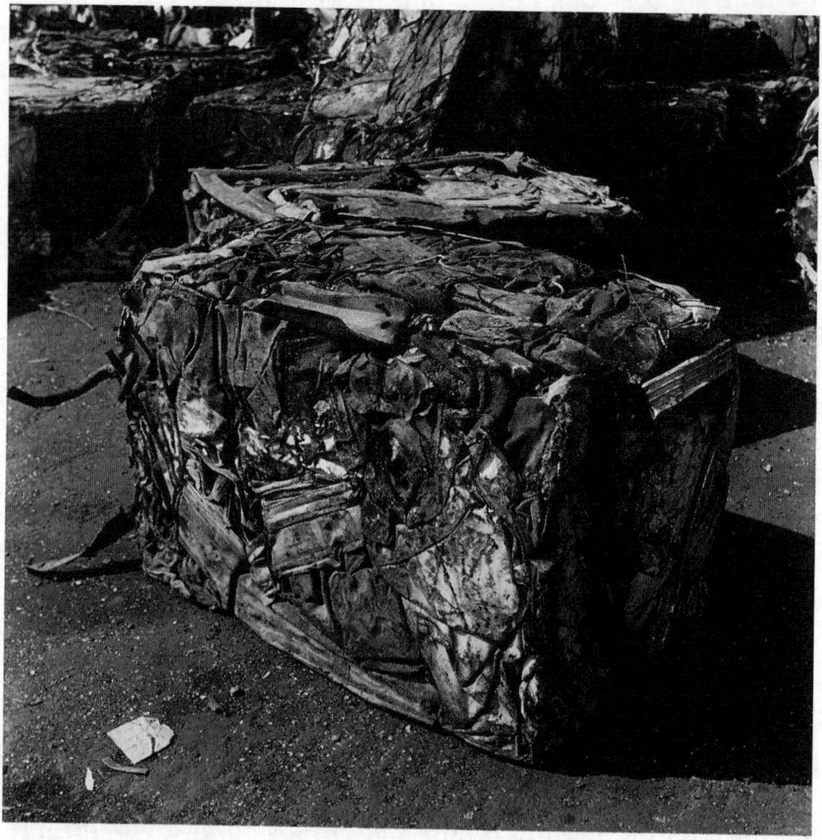

FIGURE 2.3. Peter Hujar, *Steel Ruins #13*, from the series *New Jersey: Metal Dumps*, 1978. © 1987 The Peter Hujar Archive. Courtesy of Pace/MacGill Gallery, New York; Fraenkel Gallery, San Francisco.

photograph is resolutely not abstract. The punctum is the moment of recognition of the form as a car, the realization that what sits here is an item once invested with value, now wrecked beyond repair, transmuted into this new shape in preparation for a new economic function, the resale of the ruined remainders of American industry. In *Steel Ruins #7* (1978; figure 2.4), most likely taken in the same junkyard, Hujar turns his gaze to another, further reduced output of this deconstructive industry, steel shavings stored in heaps, oddly gleaming. Small, tubular automobile parts are visible at points across the image, reminding the viewer of the provenance of these strange mounds. Decontexualized beyond easy recognition, this accumulation of curled shavings loosely resembles a mountain range or a grassy cliffside. The metal junkyard is presented here as a new genre of American landscape, offering the photographer a subject that in its entropic ruination sits between abstraction and figuration, just as it straddles past and present.

Hujar's interest in the landscape of the metal dump as a photographic subject echoes Walker Evans's exploration of the same theme in the early 1960s. The "nadir of all landscape scenery," Evans wrote in an essay accompanying the publication of some of his (color) photographs in *Fortune* magazine in April 1962, "is the great American auto-junk scrap pile." "Pictorially speaking," he writes, the visual impact of these spaces and these objects is one of "chaos abstracted." This has "considerable curious interest in itself." Yet his interest is not wholly formal. Focusing on cars in partial ruination, with doors or windows or tires missing, rusting beyond repair, he finds an anthropomorphic power in them. "Agonized travesties of what was once grandeur, they

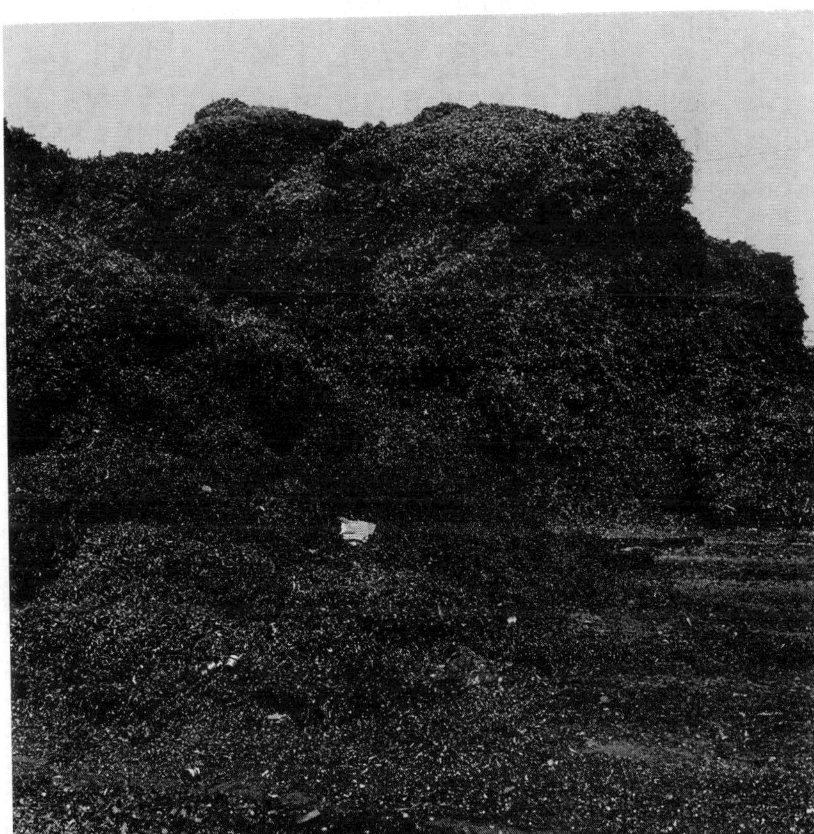

FIGURE 2.4. Peter Hujar, *Steel Ruins #7*, from the series *New Jersey: Metal Dumps*, 1978. © 1987 The Peter Hujar Archive. Courtesy of Pace/MacGill Gallery, New York; Fraenkel Gallery, San Francisco.

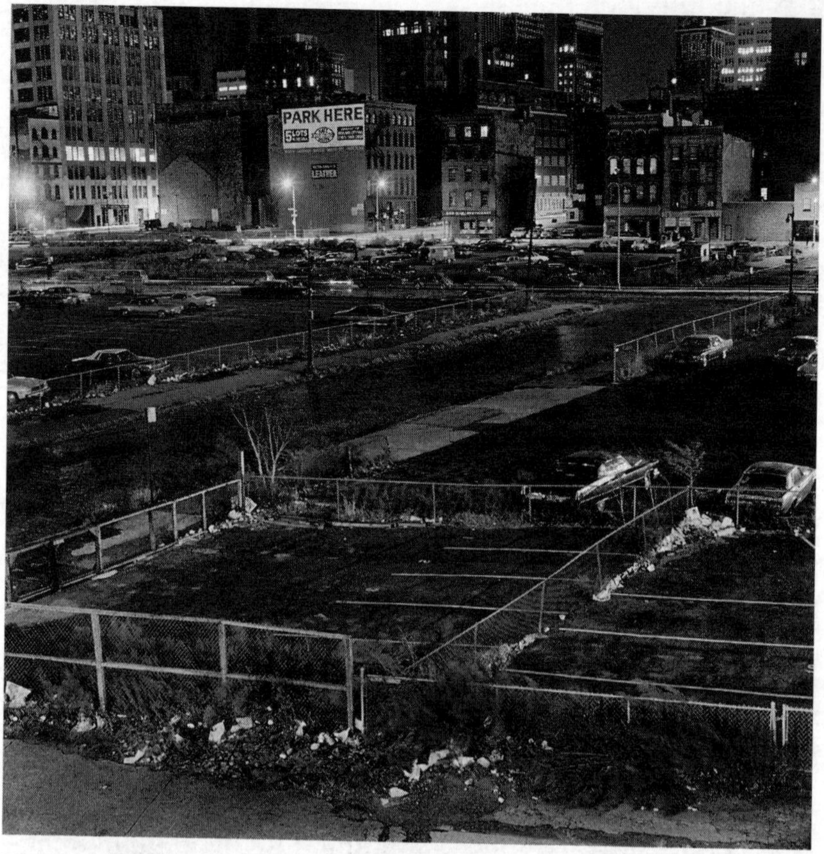


FIGURE 2.5. Peter Hujar, *West Side Parking Lots*, 1976. © 1987 The Peter Hujar Archive. Courtesy of Pace/MacGill Gallery, New York; Fraenkel Gallery, San Francisco.

gasp on their sides, or stack crazily on high, looking like the aftereffect of some timeless carnage."[16] Evans's insistent references to the anthropomorphic qualities of these abandoned cars present an interesting lens through which to view Hujar's photographs of half-empty parking lots on Manhattan's West Side at night. In *West Side Parking Lots* from 1976 (figure 2.5), the same year as *Christopher Street Pier #4* (figure 2.2), Hujar gazes down from above, perhaps from an adjacent warehouse or apartment building, on a large lot partially lit by streetlamps. A billboard at the top of the image bids passersby to "PARK HERE." While the area below is occupied by cars, large portions of the lot, including that at the front of the composition, are empty. Trash has gathered and weeds grown along its fences. While at first glance this might appear to be an image of a functionless place, considered in the context of Hujar's photographs of the Christopher Street pier, it becomes clear that is also an image of a cruising space. As with Baltrop's photographs of the ruined waterfront, we have to cruise this image for clues as to content or context. As we do, this solemn image of a desolate part of the city acquires a playful edge, a dark humor. Hujar plays with the viewer in visual and linguistic terms: "PARK HERE" the billboard proposes, above a sign advertising "LEATHER" goods. Hujar does not need to anthropomorphize the cars that punctuate the image to establish a queer erotic mood.

"Scenes like this," of junkyards and decaying cars, Evans posits, "are rich in tragicomic suggestions of the fall of man from his high ride." The gaudy tone of his color photographs adds to the sense of tragic comedy, in contrast to Hujar's ostensibly somber, black-and-white exploration of the same landscape. While, for Evans, making use of a now-abandoned term for the gently comic, "nothing could be gayer than the complete collapse of our fanciest contrivances," for Hujar, nothing could be queerer. His decontextualized images of ruined automobiles point to a keen interest in the queer visual culture of nonproductivity and decay that also characterizes Wojnarowicz and Holleran's literary engagements with the abandoned warehouses on the New York waterfront. Beyond recognizing in ruination an opportunity for experimentation and freedom from sociocultural regulation, all three find a darkly humorous parallel to their own alienation and queer nonproductivity. Importantly, Hujar draws these connections, or rather, makes these visual allusions, without anthropomorphizing ruins. He appropriates the visual culture of ruin without drawing causal connections between queer sex and bodily decay or sociocultural ruination, unlike Evans, who finds "suggestions of the fall of man." Hujar's visual culture of ruins is emphatically not an aesthetic expression of a social or cultural fall, of what Gayle Rubin has called the "domino theory of sexual peril," of the line that "appears to stand between sexual order and chaos," that "expresses the fear that if anything is permitted to cross this erotic DMZ [demilitarized zone], the barrier against scary sex will crumble and something unspeakable will skitter across."[17] Rather, Hujar points, through a sidelong appropriation of the visual language of American landscape photography, to sex in ruins as a creative reuse of his own exclusion and a refiguring of the tragic gaiety of the deteriorating automobile, symbols of decay or death, and, often as Evans's photographs suggest, ciphers of heterocultural fears of social and economic change.

Hujar's visits to metal junkyards in New Jersey in the late 1970s also recall Robert Smithson's excursions in his home state in the late 1960s. In "A Tour of the Monuments of Passaic, New Jersey," published in *Artforum* in 1967, Smithson recounts a trip by bus to the banks of the Passaic River, near the Passaic Concrete Plant, where wooden and steel bridges and beams and industrial machinery sat quietly, unguarded and, as Smithson visited on a Saturday, inactive. Such a landscape, Smithson observes, makes it difficult to distinguish old from new, past from present; it is an exemplary entropic landscape, offering as well a vision of a future in which Passaic's steel industry is outmoded and no longer economically productive. A highway being built along the river, he notes, appears, labor being suspended over the weekend, "part bulldozed and part intact," "confounded into a unitary chaos," and becomes, in his monumental vision, an antiromantic ruin.[18] Interestingly, Smithson's description of Passaic's provisionally obsolescent machinery, its soon-to-be ruins, develops into a homoerotic reading of the imminent nonproductivity of mechanized industry in late capitalist America. A large pipe, connected to the river bank by a set of pontoons, looks to Smithson as though it "was secretly sodomizing some hidden technological orifice." "A psychoanalyst," he notes, "might say that the landscape displayed 'homosexual tendencies,' but I will not draw such a crass anthropomorphic conclusion, I will merely say, 'It was there.'" However, as he expands upon the entropic pull of these temporary ruins, Smithson seems to mock industrial construction efforts at Passaic that, like all construction, will not fall "but rather *rise* into ruin," drawing connections between industrial and economic obsolescence and the non-reproductivity of gay sex, its "failed" sexual economy—what Smithson calls, with reference to the imagined impending uselessness of Passaic's mechanical landscape, the "memory-traces" of its "abandoned sets of futures."[19]

Later in the essay, Smithson rejects any further inclinations to anthropomorphize this queerly ruined landscape. Much as Hujar focused his photographic gaze upon abandoned architecture, rusting steel, and crushed cars, Smithson observes that in interstitial places like suburbs, factories, or riverbanks, "time turns metaphors into *things*" and that this objecthood problematizes efforts to establish a linear relation between past and present, much as the ruins on the Manhattan waterfront muddied clear distinctions between then and now, land and sea. Smithson was "convinced that the future is lost somewhere in the dumps of the historical past; it is in yesterday's newspapers," just as, for Wojnarowicz, the ruination of the piers and their partial separation from the main body of Manhattan made thoughts of time's passage irrelevant.[20] For Wojnarowicz, and for Hujar, this lack of temporal direction echoed the spontaneity of the cruising excursion. Hujar appears to play with this idea of impulsive passage and undirected movement in his photographs of the Canal Street pier, taken on visits with Wojnarowicz in the early 1980s. Like *Pier—Four Doors* (1981), *Hallway, Canal Street Pier* (1983; figure 2.6) takes a corridor as its subject, a space of heightened in-betweenness in this already interstitial place of casual wandering and spontaneous queer sex. As

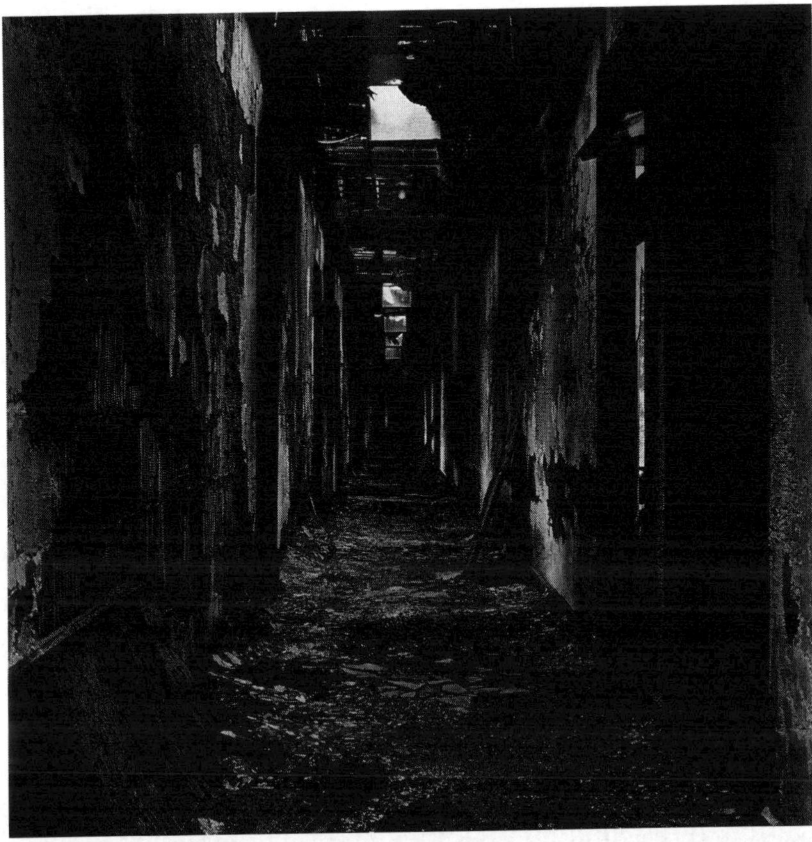

FIGURE 2.6. Peter Hujar, *Hallway, Canal Street Pier*, 1983. © 1987 The Peter Hujar Archive. Courtesy of Pace/MacGill Gallery, New York; Fraenkel Gallery, San Francisco.

light streams in from an opening in the ceiling, the viewer's eye is drawn to the dilapidated condition of the walls and the fragments of metal and glass that have collected along the edges of the walkway. What is striking, however, is not only the extensive ruination of the Canal Street pier, but the signs of its frequent usage. A flattened pathway through the debris is clearly visible on the floor, with larger obstacles leaned against the walls, allowing easy passage. Hujar's interest in the queer visual culture of the ruin was a playful one that recognized the ruin as an appropriative emblem of queer liberation, as well as a symbol of industrial collapse. Rumors of the pier's total abandonment were, Hujar points out, greatly exaggerated.

As the title of Smithson's essay suggests, the industrial architecture of Passaic has, for him at least, a monumental quality. Without contemporary indicators of time and place like street signs, billboards, license plates, or even lamps, Hujar's photographs of strange accumulations of waste objects in junkyards, like his images of hauntingly empty parking lots, also acquire a monumental sense through their dislocation from the heteronormative time-space and functional economy of the city. Hujar's visual interest in the monumentality of the ruin, its memorial potential, and its queer objecthood, can be traced back to a much earlier series of photographs he took on a trip to the catacombs at Palermo, Sicily, in 1963 with his friend and lover, the artist Paul Thek. In these monastic burial grounds, the dehydrated and often embalmed bodies of Capuchin monks were installed along the corridors. Later, local residents were interred in small niches in glass coffins that were visible to grieving relatives who visited the catacombs to pray with the deceased or give offerings. Indeed, the crypts were maintained through donations from relatives of the interred, leading to the development of the catacombs as a tourist destination in the nineteenth century.

While photography in the space is prohibited, Hujar took a series of black-and-white photographs of bodies positioned against the corridor walls, in ornate clothing and decorated glass caskets. As Hujar furtively photographed the encased corpses, Thek opened a coffin, stopping to pick up what he thought to be a piece of paper. It crumbled into dust in his hand, and he realized that it was in fact "a piece of dried thigh." "I felt strangely relieved and free," he recalled in an interview with Gene Swenson in 1966. While "we accept our thing-ness intellectually," he observed, the "emotional acceptance of it can be a joy."[21] In response to this experience at the catacombs, Thek produced a small sculpture, *La Corazza di Michelangelo* (1963; figure 2.7), a cheap souvenir reproduction of an armored breastplate that he encrusted with fleshy lumps of red and pink wax. Thek appears to animate the lifeless torso, but he does so by adding ruptured flesh, by creating an image of a body in pain. It is a powerfully visceral work that offers the viewer an impression of a body suspended between life and death, past and present. Might we, Thek appeared to wonder here, be able to experience the intellectual and emotional impact of loss simultaneously, as he had when he picked up that little piece of thigh and watched it disintegrate? Can we view life and death together, as Hujar and Thek felt they had at the Palermo catacombs? In his remaking of a monumental object, itself already ruined, headless, with limbs lost, Thek presents an image of the ruin that is colorful, emotive and, most importantly, multitemporal, both past and present. Thek's later *Technological Reliquaries*, such as *Warrior's Arm* (1967; figure 2.8), examine the emotional complexities of bodily thingness in more depth and acquire a powerful objecthood in their own right in the much same way as the small *Corazza di Michelangelo*. In becoming things, Thek's work after Palermo preempts Michael Fried's

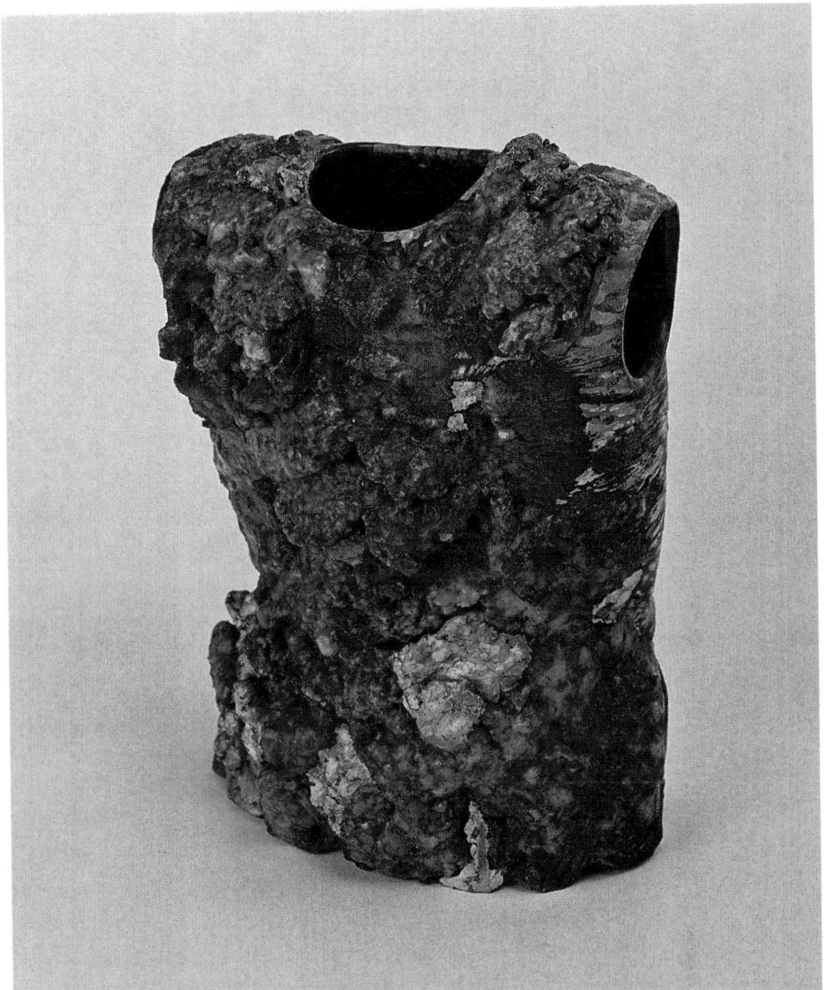

FIGURE 2.7. Paul Thek, *La Corazza di Michelangelo*, 1963. Wax, acrylic on plaster. 40 × 30 × 15 cm. Courtesy of Deichtorhallen Hamburg/Fallen Collection. Photo: Egbert Haneke.

critique of "the blatant anthropomorphism" and theatricality of Minimalism; the literalist work has been waiting for him.[22] In Thek's vision of sculptural objecthood, Fried's anxieties are literalized and challenged, just as Thek felt his ontological superiority as a living thing distorted, rendered pointless, if not ruined, on his visit to Palermo.

Thek and Hujar's interest in the catacombs as a kind of ruin, perceptible in Hujar's focus, as much on the forms of the caskets and the contrasts between rotting cloth and the peeling walls of the crypts as on the bodies interred

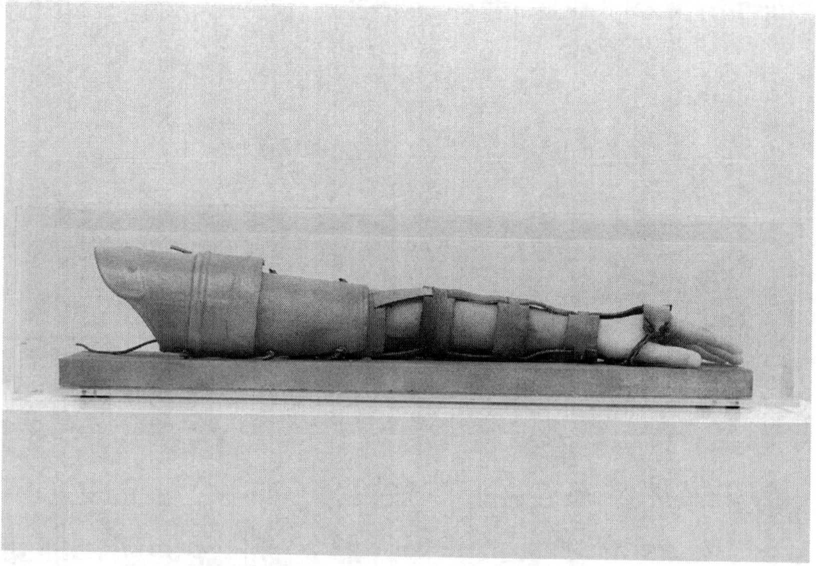

FIGURE 2.8. Paul Thek, *Warrior's Arm*, 1966–1967. Wax, paint, leather, metal, wood, and resin in a Plexiglas case. 8½ × 35½ × 9½ inches. Carnegie Museum of Art, Pittsburgh. Henry L. Hillman Fund, Mr. and Mrs. James H. Rich Fund, Carnegie Mellon Art Gallery Fund, and A. W. Mellon Acquisition Endowment Fund, 2010.3.

within them, can be seen as an echo of an even earlier series of photographs by Hujar, taken on a trip to Villa Vizcaya, the industrialist James Deering's estate in Dade County, Florida, in the summer of 1956. Deering died in 1925, and the grand property was acquired by the county in 1952, to be restored and opened to the public as a tourist attraction. While visiting the property with their friend Joe Raffael, Thek and Hujar came across the boathouse, which had been left unreconstructed, a ruin, and wandered inside. Hujar's photographs of the site, shown in the exhibition *Paul Thek and His Circle in the 1950s*, cocurated by Jonathan David Katz and Thek's friend Peter Harvey at the Leslie-Lohman Museum of Gay and Lesbian Art in New York in 2013, bear striking formal similarities to his photographs of the Manhattan piers taken twenty-five years later. In untitled images of Thek (figure 2.9) and Raffael and Thek (figure 2.10), as in *Pier—Four Doors* (1981) and *Hallway, Canal Street Pier* (1983), Hujar focuses on the intersections between doorways, windows, and hallways, on places of connection and passage. Both of these Deering boathouse photographs feature figures framed by doorways looking directly at the viewer, and indeed, the photographer, adding an erotic urgency to the images and to this ruined place, a distinct sense of cruising or being cruised.

As in his photographs of the Canal Street pier and the Newark junkyard, Hujar pays close attention to the material degeneration of the building itself, focusing on cavities in interior walls and on places where the walls' component layers—wood, plaster, wallpaper, paint—become individually visible, offering a cross-sectional view of the building's structure. In a third photograph (figure 2.11), Thek and Raffael are seen walking up a flight of stairs inside the ruined building. Raffael looks out at Hujar, the photographer, while Thek, blurred through motion, advances up the stairs. Wooden interior beams are visible, offset by peeling paint and a crumbling trefoil stone arch. In his introduction to the 2013 exhibition Katz suggests, paraphrasing Harvey, that the pleasure Hujar, Thek, and Raffael found in exploring the boathouse ruins stemmed in part from their sense that this was "historically gay ground," since James Deering, a confirmed bachelor, had designed Villa Vizcaya with the artist and

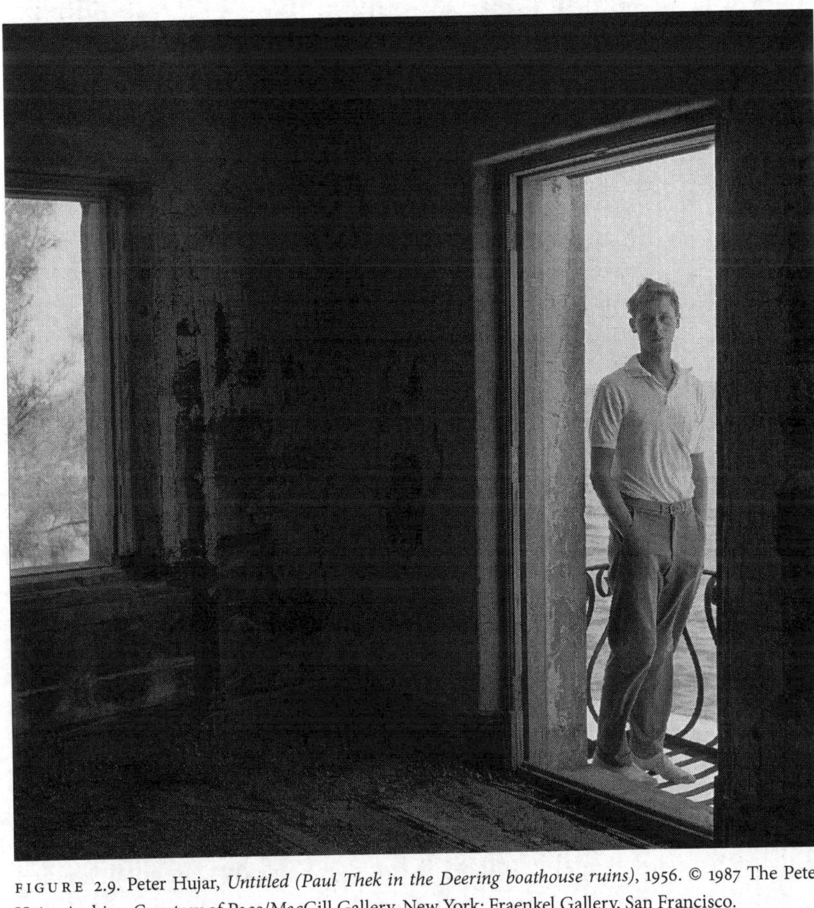

FIGURE 2.9. Peter Hujar, *Untitled (Paul Thek in the Deering boathouse ruins)*, 1956. © 1987 The Peter Hujar Archive. Courtesy of Pace/MacGill Gallery, New York; Fraenkel Gallery, San Francisco.

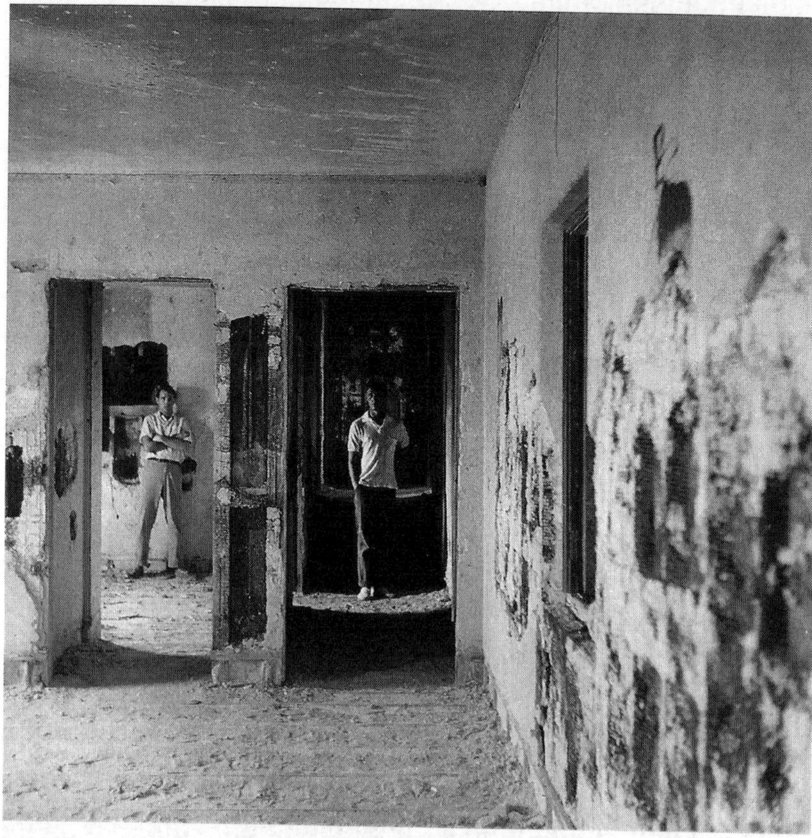

FIGURE 2.10. Peter Hujar, *Untitled (Joe Raffael and Paul Thek in the Deering boathouse ruins)*, 1956. © 1987 The Peter Hujar Archive. Courtesy of Pace/MacGill Gallery, New York; Fraenkel Gallery, San Francisco.

interior designer Paul Chalfin, rumored to be his lover, and had entertained other artists thought to be queer there, including the American painter John Singer Sargent.[23] The dilapidated boathouse seemed to offer Hujar, Thek, and Raffael a queer point of connection with Deering, Chalfin, and their circle, outside of time and away from municipal redevelopment initiatives.

Like Hujar, Thek appears to have embraced ruins, in part, as a creative reuse of his enforced social exile. In an essay for the short catalog that accompanied *Paul Thek and His Circle*, Peter Harvey quotes from a series of letters Thek sent him in the mid-1950s. They are anxious and romantic and often address Thek's experiences of rejection from heteronormative society in terms of space. "It is not that the world has suddenly found itself without room for us," Thek wrote. "It is that the world has quickly gone about making no room for us. You know we are dangerous."[24] We might conclude, then, that attending to the ruined boathouse on the fringes of Deering's estate, forgotten as the house and much of the grounds underwent restoration for a wider tourist public, was both an act of claiming a liminal space in a place "without room for us" and an opportunity to pay respects to a hallowed "gay ground" as it was in the process of being restored, its elusive queer history under threat of erasure. Fittingly, Harvey concludes his reflections on his friendship with Thek in the 1950s with a quotation from T. S. Eliot's long poem *The Wasteland* (1922), in which the poet reflects on the restoration of Europe after the trauma of World War I: "These fragments I have shored against my ruins."[25]

While the impact of the Palermo trip on Thek's sculptural practice is relatively well known, owing in part to the widespread publication of Hujar's photographs of Thek posing before a group of preserved monks in the catacombs (figure 2.12), the relation between Hujar's photographs of dried

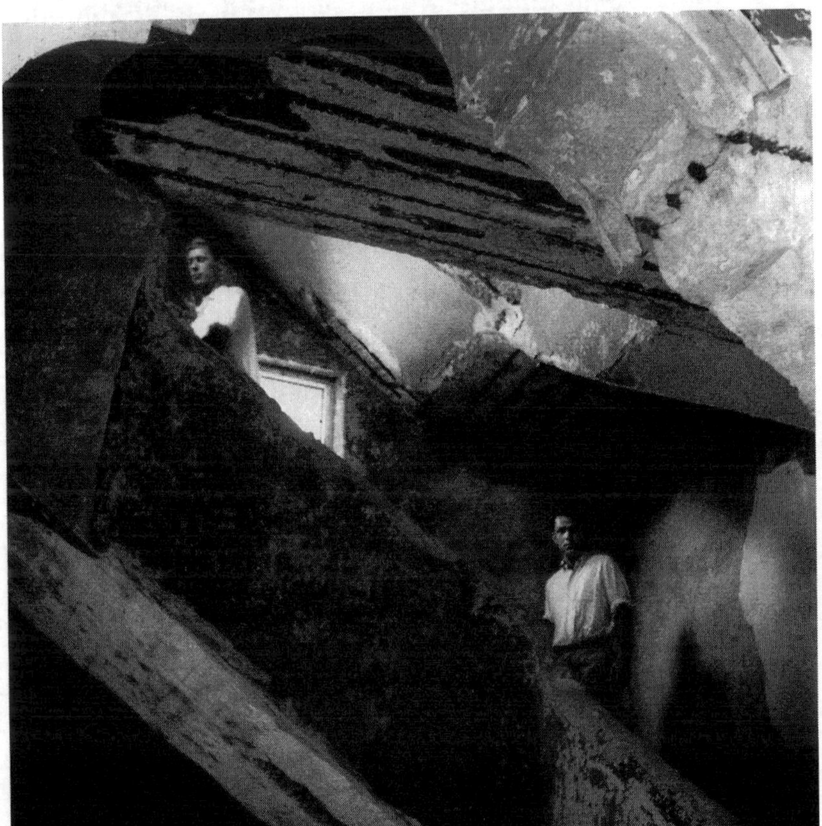

FIGURE 2.11. Peter Hujar, *Untitled (Paul Thek and Joe Raffael in the Deering boathouse ruins)*, 1956. © 1987 The Peter Hujar Archive. Courtesy of Pace/MacGill Gallery, New York; Fraenkel Gallery, San Francisco.

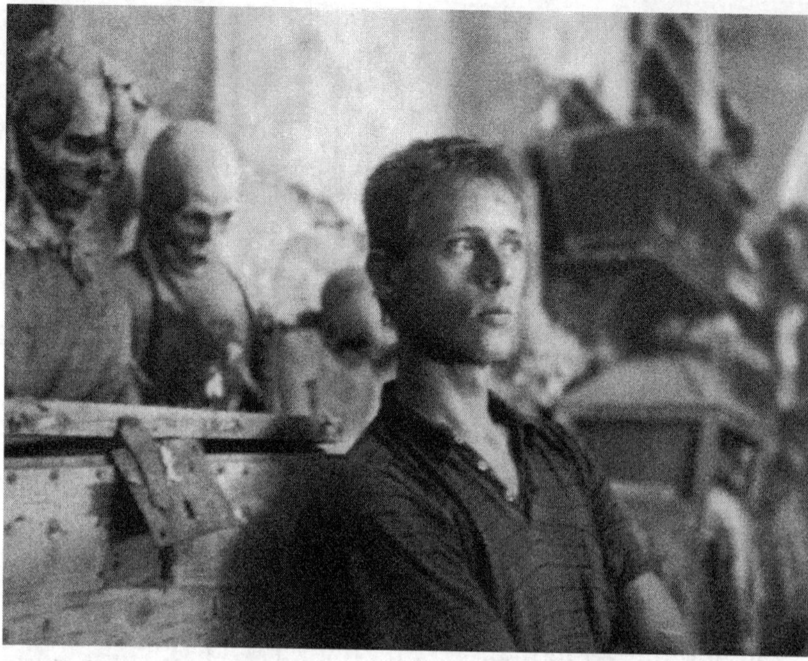

FIGURE 2.12. Peter Hujar, *Thek in the Palermo Catacombs*, 1963. © 1987 The Peter Hujar Archive. Courtesy of Pace/MacGill Gallery, New York; Fraenkel Gallery, San Francisco.

corpses at Palermo and his later work with ruined buildings and industrial decay has not been explored in depth. Thek's work after Palermo was famously concerned with corporeality, relaying the impression of bodies suspended between past and present. Meanwhile, Hujar gave the name *Portraits in Life and Death* to a 1976 book that featured portraits of living friends intermixed with his photographs of corpses from the Capuchin catacombs. The juxtaposition is as jarring and explicit as the book's title suggests. It does not make the Capuchin corpses appear as if living, or turn his living friends into mummified visions of future death; rather, it suggests queer parallels among the figures and suspends both sets between life and death. Hujar's key interest seems to be the impact of photography on the perception of the figure and the ability of the medium to facilitate this suspension between temporal frames. In her introduction to the book, Susan Sontag argues that photography "turns the whole world into a cemetery."[26] For Hujar, photography appears to turn everything into a kind of object and to hasten the "emotional acceptance" of our "thing-ness," but with pleasure rather than dread.[27] The photograph, as it makes the photographed subject material, takes on a material life of its own. A photograph, Hujar stated in a recorded interview with Wojnarowicz from the mid-1980s, is not a frozen moment, but "an echo" of one; it takes on its own life and exists according to its own temporality:

> It doesn't seem like a freezing of life, but of—it's like taking the shape of that moment, of what's happening, and making something else out of it. It's not frozen. Sometimes people freeze moments of life and they become memories. That's one kind of way of doing it. I keep hoping that when I do a picture that it has its own life, it really has nothing to do with that moment. It's not something frozen. It's the echo of that time. And what's on that piece of paper has its own life. Which is very different from the life that was in that moment in which the picture was taken. . . . In the end it has nothing to do with it.[28]

The photograph, as it has its own material life, cannot suspend the ruination it depicts. Hujar's photographs are not an attempt to suspend or stall the dereliction of the piers; they will also degenerate. Instead, like his photographs of the Deering boathouse ruins, they offer a trace of Hujar's presence and an image (that will, in turn, disappear) of "gay ground" in the process of disappearing.

One of the most productive points of connection between this interest in the temporal complexity of the ruin and the queer materiality of the photograph, Thek's work after Palermo, Hujar's photographs of the catacombs, and his later images of New Jersey junkyards and the Manhattan waterfront is Robert Smithson's essay "Entropy and the New Monuments," published in *Artforum* in 1966, the year prior to his "tour of the monuments" on the banks of the Passaic River. Surveying recent work by Thek (such as the meat piece *Hippopotamus*, 1965), Dan Flavin, and Larry Bell, Smithson detects a new kind of sculptural monumentality that is, he argues, "a visible analog" for entropy, the second law of thermodynamics, a celebration of what Flavin had called "inactive history." Like the dormant machines at Passaic, "instead of causing us to remember the past like the old monuments, the new monuments seem to cause us to forget the future":

> They are not built for the ages, but rather against the ages. . . . Both past and future are placed into an objective present. This kind of time has little or no space; it is stationary and without movement, it is going nowhere, it is anti-Newtonian, as well as being instant, and is against the wheels of the time-clock.[29]

As Smithson explores this notion of time as spatial, antiprogressive, and nonteleological, informed by "grand and empty" new forms of architectural construction such as Mies van der Rohe and Philip Johnson's midtown Union Carbide building, he describes time itself as a kind of place. This displacement of normative understandings of time as linear facilitates a material experience of time; it "allows the eye to see time as an infinity of surfaces or structures, or both." "Time becomes," Smithson writes, "a place minus motion. If time is a place, then innumerable places are possible. . . . Time breaks down into many times. Rather than saying, 'What time is it?' we should say, 'Where is the time?'" Breaking down, going nowhere, "not built for the ages"—Smithson's new monumental space-time appears to be a kind of ruin.[30]

Writing about the "putrid finesse" of Thek's *Technological Reliquaries*, Smithson cites a passage from William S. Burroughs's novel *Nova Express* (1964) in which Burroughs describes the ruined place where the "Addicts of the Orgasm Drug" reside, among "Flesh juice in festering spines of terminal sewage—Run down of Spain and 42nd St. to the fish city of marble flesh grafts." The references to animal waste locate this scene vaguely within one of the city's waterfront districts, where "the green mist had formed a carpet of lichen over the bunks and floor of what looked like a vast warehouse."[31] Beyond this, as Smithson borrows tropes from avant-garde science fiction writing and modernist architecture, as well as the scientific language of thermodynamics, he inadvertently constructs a convincing theory for figuring the queer occupation of the ruins of the piers and the temporality of cruising in relation to Thek's and Hujar's own artistic practice and understanding of time. Time there, as Hujar's photographs make clear, had broken down "into many times." Wandering for hours, if not days, at the piers, as Wojnarowicz and Hall did, walking from room to room along decrepit hallways and looking through holes that appeared in decaying walls, "rather than saying, 'What time is it?' we should say, 'Where is the time?'"[32]

### The ruin and the "crummy space": Public space, private time

Peter Hujar's photographs of ruined and abandoned sites in New York and New Jersey also speak to a growing interest in dereliction in the city's downtown art scene in this period, perceptible in the work of Smithson, Gordon Matta-Clark, Vito Acconci, and Joan Jonas, among others. As industrial lower Manhattan was systemically emptied out in the late capitalist moment of the mid- to late 1970s, as traditional shipping and light manufacturing industries declined, numerous artists made creative use of the surplus of empty buildings, either as cheap studios or as collective arts spaces, and made work that reflected critically on the sociocultural impact of urban abandonment and economic decline. As the critic Nancy Foote noted in an essay on PS1 in Queens, published in *Artforum* in October 1976, many of the early alternative spaces were in "crummy" buildings that encouraged radical artistic experimentation as much they fostered radical politics. The work shown in these spaces was often ephemeral and frequently unsalable. One of the PS1's earliest successes was, Foote wrote, the *Rooms* show in June 1976, a "remarkable spur-of-the-moment exhibition" in which around eighty artists participated. Artists such as Robert Ryman, Joseph Kosuth, and Acconci "hacked, gouged, stripped, dug, poured and picked away" at the building's "rotting hulk."[33] Matta-Clark produced a cutting work that extended through all three floors of the once-derelict building. The spaces themselves seemed to demand this kind of revolutionary approach. A "crummy" space, Foote wrote, "can be brutalized, destroyed, completely restructured; it can be 'amended' subtly by small additions that comment on its nature and adapt their posture to its own; it can serve as medium, directly or indirectly, also as subject." A place "ravaged by time and use," she argued, "offers a far richer lode from which to mine ideas than any clean, well-lighted place."[34]

PS1's elevation of the "crummy" spaces appearing across New York City in the 1970s and its embrace of the visual culture of the ruin occurred contemporaneously with the development of the downtown alternative arts space 112 Greene Street (also know as 112 Workshop), run by the artist Jeffrey Lew. A year later, Matta-Clark and Caroline Goodden opened Food, a space for inexpensive food and informal discussion in SoHo, designed to redirect cheap and empty buildings in lower Manhattan to function as "a tangible support system that fulfilled basic everyday needs for a community of artists."[35] Like PS1, 112 Workshop and Food came out of the antagonism of 1960s protest groups, such as the Art Workers' Coalition, toward institutionally sanctioned arts spaces like the Museum of Modern Art. Exhibitions and events at 112 Greene Street were largely spontaneous events, and the building was not renovated. The space displayed proudly the marks of "decades of industrial usage," having been the home of a rag-salvage business prior to Lew's purchase of the property in 1970.[36]

As well as providing studio space, 112 Greene Street was the setting for Anarchitecture, a small group of artists "dedicated to the voids, gaps, interruptions, and movements in the physical environment." Over the course of a year, members including Matta-Clark, Laurie Anderson, Tina Girouard, Richard Landry, and Richard Nonas, met weekly to discuss " 'anarchitectural' facts." Resisting urban or artistic utopianism by foregrounding collaboration and thematic ambivalence, Anarchitecture was, according to Jackie Apple and Mary Delahoyde, "the epitome of the 112 Greene Street mission."[37] Its anarchic approach paralleled the rough material character of the Workshop space: no group leader was designated, and subcultural, populist, and industrial subjects were presented equally, promoting dialogue between these diverse practices.

However, the building's dilapidation was not always viewed in such utopian terms. In an article for *Studio International* in 1980, Rudolf Baranik criticized the unrefined appearance of 112 Greene Street, disputing whether the so-called alternative space could ever represent a genuine alternative to the institutionalized gallery. Lew spoke abstractly of his hesitation to "fix" 112 Greene Street as stemming from his reluctance "to disturb the raw power of the space," Baranik branded its unrenovated quality a "focus on surface trappings instead of content . . . a carefully regulated dinginess, a kind of studied poverty, where the enemy became not philistine levelling but white walls and a contemplative space."[38] The structural character and "dinginess" of 112 Greene Street emerged from a post-Minimalist artistic attitude to its downtown location—highlighting its place within the former Cast Iron District, a working neighborhood, yet ensuring that the art produced there was unsalable. As Martin Beck has argued, this attention to surface quality and inclination to maintain a "material 'rawness' " within the exhibition space was an impassioned representation of the contempt of Lew and his peers for the growing hegemony of the white cube gallery space. The building's decay was highlighted because it functioned, in part, as "a metaphor for freedom from restrictive definitions of art making."[39]

Lew was not the first artist to explore the creative and curatorial possibilities of outmoded industrial buildings in the city. In December 1968, the artist Robert Morris organized an exhibition, *9 at Leo Castelli*, at the dealer's uptown storage warehouse on West 108th Street. The nine artists featured—Giovanni Anselmo, William Bollinger, Eva Hesse, Stephen Kaltenbach, Bruce Nauman, Alan Saret, Richard Serra, Keith Sonnier, and Gilberto Zorio—were invited to create works that specifically engaged the vast space and would be exhibited there for only fifteen days. Morris said little about the choice of venue, except that "things were simply 'possible' there."[40] Writing in 1986, Douglas Crimp characterized the warehouse show as an "assault" on aesthetic presumption, where "strewn upon the cement floor, affixed to or leaning against the brick walls, were objects that defied our every expectation regarding the form of art and the manner of its exhibition."[41] Serra contributed two works to the show, *Splashing* and *Prop*. To create *Splashing*, Serra threw molten lead against a concrete wall in the warehouse where "it adhered to the interior of the angle of the architecture and hardened into an uneven line,"[42] producing a work with "no definable shape or mass , , , no legible image." "There it was," Crimp writes, "attached to the structure of that old warehouse on the Upper West Side, condemned to be abandoned there forever or to be scraped off and destroyed."[43] As Martha Buskirk has argued, *Splashing* was, like Serra's film *Hand Catching Lead* (1968), a physical manifestation of an intellectual turn toward reevaluating the "specific relationship between action, site, and material."[44]

*Staircase–3 Landing–Leaves* by Rafael Ferrer, who was not named on the show's invitation, further questioned the parameters of Morris's curatorial project. "Without a doubt," Ferrer lamented, "consistency is an important factor for the art market."[45] Installed in one of the warehouse's most interstitial spaces, a stairwell, his work addressed the often ephemeral processes of site-specific sculpture, as did that of others in the show, drawing attention to a kind of aesthetic temporality that resisted sale, and, in using nontraditional media—industrial materials like lead and rubber, or, in Ferrer's case, organic matter like leaves—acknowledged the alternative functions and other "lives" of the materials employed. "Without fanfare," Ferrer observed, the Castelli warehouse "became the first 'alternative' art space."[46] Even in these earliest creative interventions in postindustrial spaces, artists viewed these interstitial spaces as permissive sites for artistic and social experimentation.

In the winter of 1970, curator and critic Willoughby Sharp organized an installation of the work of twenty-seven artists at the abandoned Pier 18 on Manhattan's Lower West Side, documented in around 350 images by photographers Harry Shunk and Janos Kender ("Shunk-Kender") and exhibited at the Museum of Modern Art in the summer of 1971. As Lynne Cooke notes in her introduction to the exhibition *Mixed Use, Manhattan* at the Museo Nacional Centro de Arte Reina Sofia in Madrid in 2010, "the project was something of a guerilla action, given that Sharp, predicting official refusal due to the wharf's derelict condition, had not sought permission to work there."[47] "Assuming that the wharf could not safely accommodate an audience," she writes, Sharp "conceived the project from its inception as a museum presentation" to be shown elsewhere, unlike *9 at Leo Castelli* which was a temporary and, most importantly, ephemeral sculptural engagement with the space and its prior uses.[48]

While a number of the works that made up *Projects: Pier 18* address the social and spatial marginalization of this space despite its proximity to the occupied core of Manhattan, for many involved, including the curator, the pier was seen as a backdrop, a stage. The most striking collaboration was arguably between Shunk-Kender and the twenty-seven artists. Photographs of John Baldessari's piece *Hands Framing New York Harbor* show the artist "framing" the World Telegram pier with his hands, an image that is in turn framed by Shunk-Kender's secondary image. Dan Graham revisited his collaborative photographic performance piece *Body Press—Hands Off* for the waterfront site, and Shunk-Kender's documentation of the performance was exhibited at MoMA alongside the images from Graham's camera, playing the role of the second participant.

For Sharp, Cooke argues, "the location (the pier) was valuable primarily for its convenience (its openness and extensive space) and its lack of associations with artmaking." The project thus brought up questions of who might claim ownership of the pier, and what sites or spaces might be permitted to host "public" art. The harbor's failed redevelopment in the 1970s rendered the waterfront a stagnant public space that highlighted wider legislative failings in the city. The presence of artists was itself an indicator of its municipal and industrial dereliction, if not its social abandonment. It is for this reason that Cooke posits *Projects: Pier 18* at the outset of the trajectory of downtown artworks addressing urban renewal traced in *Mixed Use, Manhattan*, and Sharp's work with Shunk-Kender at Pier 18 as the founding moment in a narrative of creative engagement with the decaying downtown landscape of 1970s and early 1980s Manhattan. "Clearly the role played by photography in *Projects: Pier 18* was not simply one of documentation," she argues, "even if that may have been the initial presumption on the parts of Sharp and Shunk-Kender." Each artist involved, Cooke notes, "had reflexively 'detourned' the assignment to address, among other things, the ways in which pictorial knowledge is produced, the relation of this marginal venue to the city beyond, and the terms in which site could be defined visually and materially."[49]

Vito Acconci's contribution to Sharp's exhibition, a durational performance work titled *Security Zone*, consisted of the artist standing blindfolded and with his ears plugged at the edge of the pier, making a quite literal reference to the subject of isolation in the derelict and potentially dangerous space of the abandoned waterfront, but also alluding, through loose insinuations to bondage and penetration, to its appropriation as a gay cruising space. In an untitled work from earlier the same year, the artist invited friends to another abandoned warehouse at 1:00 a.m. over a series of twenty-nine nights, where he proceeded to "reveal to that person something that hasn't been revealed about me before, something that I would normally keep concealed."[50] Both works spoke to Acconci's broader rejection of "the gallery as the space where art itself occurred while someone else watched," the boundaries between voyeur and viewer becoming blurred, as they were in the cruising that took place in the same waterfront landscape. The unregulated, abandoned site of the warehouse allowed Acconci "to work *in* a public rather than *in front of* a public," relatively unmediated.[51] Distinct from Sharp's earlier project, which was focused on documentation for a museum audience and, indeed, could be recorded photographically at all, Acconci's second pier piece was performative to the point of being visually inconceivable, contingent upon and enhancing the waterfront's interstitial qualities and its dereliction.

Writing on the subject of "private time" and public space in 1990, Acconci reflected on the false openness and impenetrability of much civic space. His argument appears to extend from this early performance work on the abandoned waterfront and to address attitudes to public space and public sexuality. The article reflects the various politically charged contests over the use of postindustrial sites in late 1970s New York, exemplified by the appropriation of the derelict waterfront as a cruising zone and as a location for body-oriented performance art. He demonstrates the central role of municipal policy in the city's artistic culture, in regard to regulating housing and studios, stabilizing rents, and legislating treatment of queer association in the city. "The establishment of certain space in the city as 'public,'" he argues, "is a reminder, a warning that the rest of the city isn't public. New York doesn't belong to us." Acconci suggests, however, that space may rendered public in two ways: either designated by "right," that is, permitted by city authorities, or "made public, a place where the public gathers precisely because it doesn't have the right—a place made public by force." Like the derelict waterfront, this latter kind of space is "a place in the middle of the city but isolated from the city."[52] The idea of public space is not in itself exclusionary, he argues, since both legislated and appropriated spaces can be conceived of as public. All public space, whether cruised or not, is inherently sexual, Acconci proposes, because "the public space of the city is the presence of other bodies":

> public space is an analogue for sex—either it's a composite of objects of the desire for sex, or it's a composite of images that substitute for sex. . . . You liberate yourself into public space when sex at home closes you up inside a relationship and "sex" becomes reduced to a subcategory of "relationship." Public space is the refusal of monogamous relationships and the acceptance of sex that has no bonds and knows no bounds.

"New York doesn't belong to us," but, Acconci suggests, it might be made ours, if only temporarily, through the "refusal of monogamy," a kind of sexual interaction fostered by (though not limited to) the cruising encounter as it rejects heteronormative sexual privacy in favor of a form of unbounded erotic engagement that takes place in similarly boundless urban spaces.[53]

Acconci's erotic vision of the liberatory occupied city clearly draws on his own performance work in the semipublic urban space of the abandoned waterfront in the early 1970s. It also evokes the quasi-erotic language of Joan Jonas's performance work in the same spaces in the same period. In a short essay for the *Drama Review* in 1975, Jonas remarked that her "thinking and

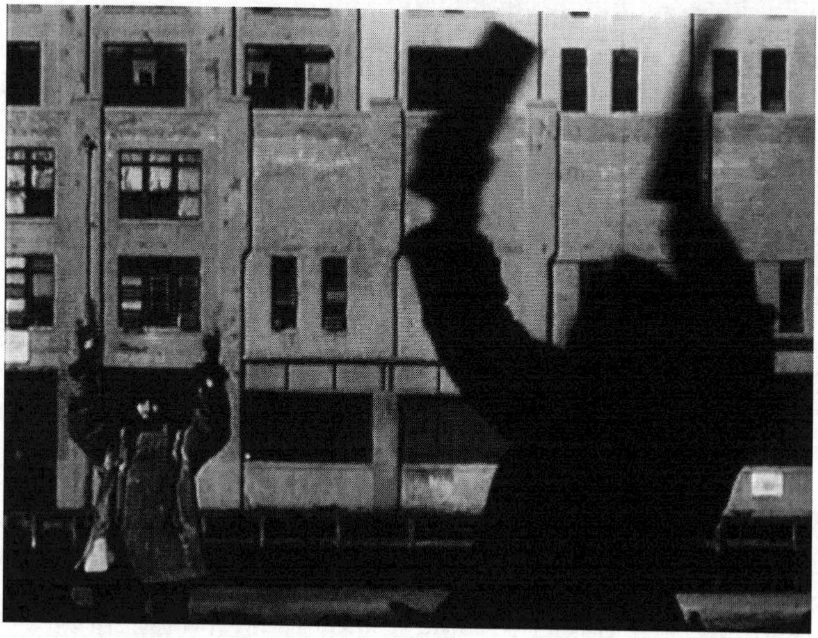

FIGURE 2.13. Joan Jonas, *Songdelay*, 1973. Courtesy of Electronic Arts Intermix (EAI), New York.

production" in the early 1970s "focused on issues of space—ways of dislocating it, attenuating it, flattening it, turning it inside out, always attempting to explore it without ever giving to myself or to others the permission to penetrate it."[54] In 1972 Jonas made the spaces on and around the Lower West Side waterfront the focus of her "thinking and production" with the performance work *Delay Delay*, "translated" into film as *Songdelay* in 1973 (figure 2.13).[55] Against a backdrop of downtown apartment blocks, piers and warehouses along the Hudson River, and factories on the New Jersey harborside, performers including Carol Goodden, Robin Winters, Gordon Matta-Clark, and Jonas herself play with the viewer's sense of space and scale, performing a series of visual set pieces with a variety of props: a large hoop, a broom used as a paintbrush, wooden blocks used to clap with. Jonas toys with the "delay" between visual and aural comprehension and the viewer's sense of what these sorts of places are for. As the performers stand in apparently abandoned stretches of the waterfront, the audio track evokes the sounds of crowds and the blasting horns of passing ocean liners. Using a telephoto lens, Jonas's exploratory eye spans a range of city spaces that were, in this period, as Douglas Crimp has observed, often empty but available for creative reuse.[56] Our perspective on the waterfront is fragmented both aurally and visually by Jonas's play with filmic scale. The landscape of lower Manhattan—its apartment buildings, rubble-filled demolition sites, abandoned warehouses with defunct corporate signage, and rooftops—appear as if layered upon a flat backdrop, a collaged picture plane rather than a bustling, multidimensional city.

By presenting the city's fringes in this abstracted, flattened way, Jonas points explicitly to their value as spaces for aesthetic and social exploration, dislocated, attenuated, flattened, and penetrated without permission.[57] Jonas uses "these techniques," Crimp has argued, "to thwart our desire to know or possess the city beyond our immediate experience of it in the moment of use." Her fragmented view leaves the city open for further reclamation, underscoring Acconci's belief that while "New York doesn't belong to us," to artists, it might be made ours, at least temporarily, through creative practice. After all, Crimp concludes, we only ever "see the city in fragments . . . in our peripheral vision—and in recollection."[58] Jonas, like Acconci and Hujar, places this sense of dislocation at the center of her work about the experience of place, so that it becomes an investigation of what is possible rather than what is prohibited in the ruined city.

## "Hunting for emptiness": Matta-Clark's ruins

Themes of fragmentation, dislocation, reclamation, and ownership also sit at the heart of Gordon Matta-Clark's work on the waterfront in this period. Matta-Clark had been involved in Willoughby Sharp's show at Pier 18, producing "an untitled performance in which he hung from the ceiling by a rope above a pile of debris." In 1973 he exhibited *Pier In/Pier Out*, a work made up of fragments taken illegally the previous year from the windows and corrugated iron door of the abandoned Pier 14 and displayed as a totemic freestanding sculpture.[59] In the summer of 1975, Matta-Clark spent two months working on *Day's End* (figure 2.14), a large-scale cutting work in Pier 52, located opposite Gansevoort Street in the Meatpacking District, in the waterfront area known as the Gansevoort Peninsula. "During the months of July and August," he wrote in a letter to a friend,

> I totally devoted myself to a working vacation by the water on the Hudson. My "studio retreat" consisted of appropriating a nearly perfectly intact turn-of-the-century wharf building of steel truss construction having virtually basilical light and proportions. A beautiful shape for such an industrial "hangar."

He spent the two months "cutting and working out sections of dock 10–18" thick, roof, walls and heavy steel trusswork," creating a vast almond-shaped orifice in the side of the warehouse, opening its empty interior up and allowing light to stream into the dark space.[60]

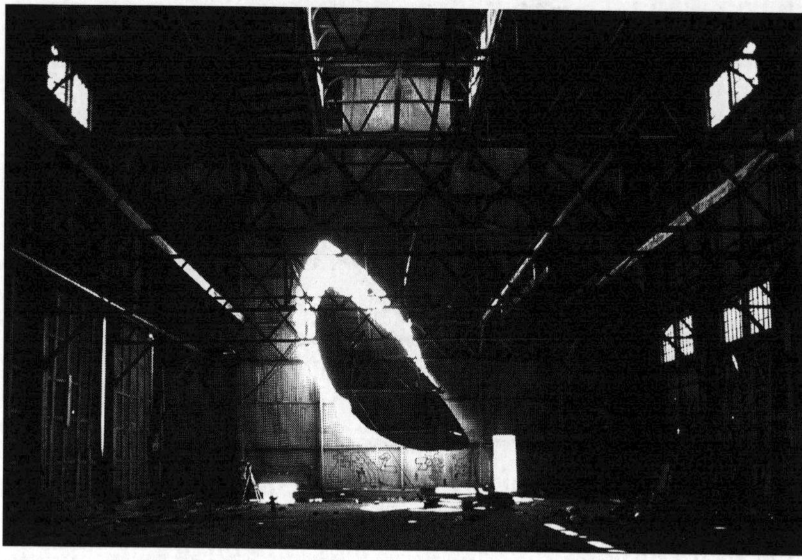

FIGURE 2.14. Gordon Matta-Clark, *Day's End*, 1975. Building cut at Pier 52, New York. © The Estate of Gordon Matta-Clark. Courtesy of the Estate of Gordon Matta-Clark; David Zwirner, New York/London/Hong Kong.

As Pamela Lee notes in her study of Matta-Clark's practice, *Object to Be Destroyed*, the work's title—*Day's End*—alludes to the temporal progression of light through the riven space: major cuts across the warehouse "charted the course of the sun throughout the day, beginning with a thin arc of light around noon that gradually swelled into full radiance by dusk."[61] This effect relied upon the physical presence of the viewer at various junctures throughout the day. Like Acconci's and Jonas's earlier work on the waterfront, Matta-Clark's piece interrogated the contingencies of a site-specific artwork's production and display, and offered the derelict waterfront as an in-between space where the ephemerality of such site-invested artistic interventions was cast in relief. As Thomas Crow has argued, the "actual duration of [*Day's End*] is limited because its presence is in terminal contradiction to the nature of the space it occupies"—the work is a reflection on an emptiness that it negates through its presence. Rather than taking something away, Matta-Clark's cutting added aesthetic and social interest to the warehouse, making an apparent ruin functional again, even temporarily, as an art object. "Contradiction," Crow writes, "is the source of [the work's] articulateness, so brief duration is a condition of meaning and is presupposed in its founding stipulations. If the piece could persist indefinitely, the contradiction is illusory."[62]

Similarly, Lee argues that Matta-Clark's choice of location was not simply an aesthetic or practical one; it was directly connected to the commercial decline of the waterfront, documenting and intervening in what Matta-Clark called "the metabolization of old buildings."[63] He shaped the warehouse to function as what Lee calls "a kind of late capitalist pantheon." As the poetic dualism of the work's title suggests, "the falling of light in the space was allegorically charged as well. . . . Its passage within *Day's End* was structurally coincidental with the building's historical passage into outmodedness, illuminating the twilight of the pier itself."[64] These explicitly political readings of the work are compounded by the controversy in which Matta-Clark became embroiled shortly after the work's completion. Pier 52 was one of the only piers on the largely abandoned Lower West Side waterfront that was still in some use in the mid-1970s. Although in poor structural condition, it was a garbage shipping dock—known as a marine transfer station—for the New York City Department of Sanitation. *Day's End* was discovered a few days prior to its completion by a department employee, and the New York City Economic Development Administration shut down an opening held at the pier on August 27. An investigation was launched into Matta-Clark's trespassing. At trial, the artist argued that the work was "a part of the 'public domain'" and should be considered legally permissible because it "represented an artistic contribution to a 'decaying city.'" Although, in one sense, the court case destroyed Matta-Clark's work, in another it enabled the work to function properly as a critical commentary on the use value of and access to ruined spaces.[65] Its subject, after all, was the "terminal contradiction" of the ruin, the tension between municipal decline, industrial abandonment, and urban poverty that coalesced in a strikingly visual way at the city's edge. Unlike Wojnarowicz and Hujar, however, Matta-Clark's interest in dereliction was not solely connected to the creative opportunities ruined buildings might present for artists. Speaking about the relation of his slightly earlier work *Splitting* (1974), a cutting in a derelict domestic building in Englewood, New Jersey, to the aesthetic and political interests of Anarchitecture, Matta-Clark recalled that as a group their "thinking about anarchitecture was more elusive than doing pieces that would demonstrate an alternate attitude to buildings." Instead, "we were thinking more about metaphoric voids, gaps, leftover spaces, places that were not developed"—that is, spaces that were "metaphoric in the sense that their interest or value wasn't in their possible use" but, with *Day's End* at least, in their abandonment.[66]

This interest in "leftover spaces" and "gaps" also shapes the experience of viewing *Day's End* after its destruction. Like Acconci's and Jonas's waterfront work earlier in the decade, *Day's End* exists now only in photographic documentation and on film, heightening the sense of impending "metabolization" inherent in the original work and underscoring Matta-Clark's interest in "illuminating the twilight of the pier itself."[67] The film footage of the work, recorded by Betsy Sussler on Super 8 color film, focuses on its construction. It shows Matta-Clark on a makeshift suspended wooden platform, blowtorch in hand, making incisions in the warehouse's west wall. The sliced metal is then pulled out of the building using a series of ropes, leaving a cat's eye-shaped cut in the warehouses and allowing light to stream in from the harbor. Sussler plays with this act of exposure in the film itself. As she moves from documenting the interior space of the warehouse to capturing its exterior from the vantage point of the peninsular pier, she leaves the aperture wide open. The film is saturated with light to near-abstraction as sunshine reflected off the steel surface of the warehouse's exterior fills the frame. The later portions of the film show Matta-Clark cutting into the floor and foundations of the pier itself, extending the cat's-eye incision into the Hudson River below. The dislocating darkness of the warehouse, captured in the film, is ruptured by its cutting, and Sussler records both the pier's proximity to the water, that is, its status as not-land, a manmade construction, and the proximity of other piers and warehouses. We look, with her and Matta-Clark, through the cat's-eye to the other dilapidated spaces along the waterfront, a vantage point on this ruined place that, in watching the film, we understand to be temporary.

Writing about Sussler and Matta-Clark's film, Juan Suárez suggests that both the work itself and its filmic documentation "partake of the indexical character that Rosalind Krauss attributed to much 1970s art." According to Krauss, Suárez writes, indexicality is a quality "not so much encoded in the work as captured and impressed on its surface."[68] "Spatial occupation," he argues, was indexical because "it was a way of framing and capturing sites that were contiguous with art-making at the time: former location of production and profit now available for play." That many of these waterfront buildings were indexical markers of an industrial portion of Manhattan shifting into outmodedness is underscored by Sussler's focus on the movement of sunlight and the relentless rippling of the river underneath the pier, very briefly "captured and impressed on its surface." However, rather than emphasizing the piers' use value as spaces now available for play, as Suárez argues, the filmic record of the making of *Day's End*, a work with its own powerful indexicality, also focuses on the warehouse's decay, on its material decline, as it appears to be absorbed by the river on which it sits. Although Matta-Clark was interested in opening the pier out, in "[making] it possible for people to see it . . . in an unmenacing kind of way,"[69] the film, like the original work, does

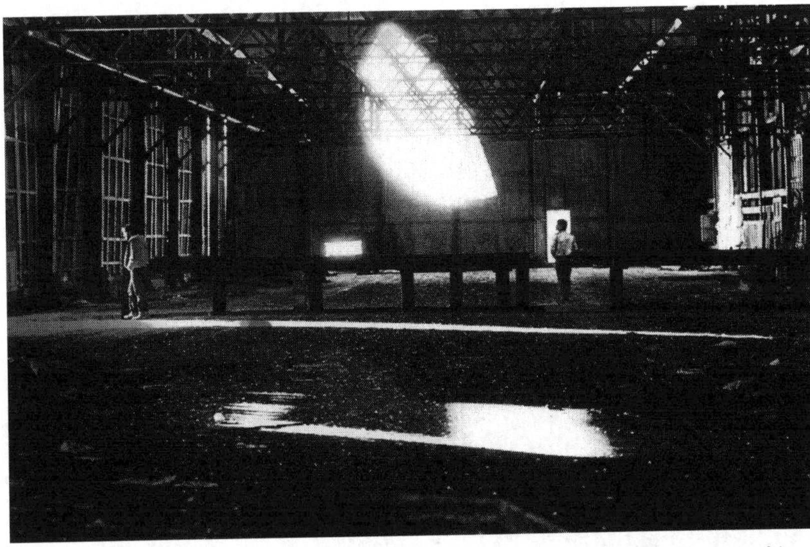

FIGURE 2.15. Alvin Baltrop, *Pier 52 (Gordon Matta-Clark's "Day's End" building cuts with two people)*, n.d. (1975–1986). Photograph courtesy of the Alvin Baltrop Trust. © 2010 Third Streaming, NY; Galerie Buchholz, Berlin/Cologne/New York. All rights reserved.

not function simply as a celebration of the empty spaces that the "base mismanagement of the dying harbor" made available; it also offers a solemn but nuanced critique of the appearance of these gaps in the first place.[70]

The playful side of Pier 52's "twilight" years was captured in Alvin Baltrop's photographs of the pier cruising scene (figure 2.15). His work provides invaluable documentation of *Day's End* and of the impact of the work on the unsanctioned use of the space as a cruising ground. Matta-Clark was not unaware of the other creative uses these ruined waterfront buildings had been put to, though he often addressed them in a disparaging tone. Speaking to Liza Bear in March 1976 about the development of *Day's End*, he recalled that "the [piers] that I found originally were all completely overrun by the gays."[71] In the letter in which he describes the experience of creating *Day's End*, Matta-Clark writes of having to "secure the space from other intruders, mainly S & M cruisers."[72] He was startled by the proliferation of muggings and physical violence at the unpoliced piers. However, Douglas Crimp notes that Matta-Clark "not only disavowed any bond with the gay men who were using the piers as cruising ground but went so far as to lock them out," an act that, to Crimp at least, conflicted with the artist's engagement in his earlier work with the city's homeless, exemplified by *Garbage Wall* (1970), a shelter built out of trash, and with disenfranchised young people from the South Bronx through his *Graffiti Truck* (1973).[73] In Baltrop's photographs of Pier 52, we see the "S & M cruisers" Matta-Clark maligned in the work itself, responding to the new patterns of light and shadow that the cutting generated, transforming its erotic potential as once-hidden, shadowy spaces were exposed. As a work that related to Matta-Clark's broader interest in exploring "New York's least remembered parts," the spaces "between the walls of views inside out," Baltrop's photographs of *Day's End*, making use of the playful binaries of light and shade, occupation and abandonment, suggest that the siting of the work on the waterfront and the work's aesthetic and political impact drew, in part, on Matta-Clark's appropriation of the visual culture of pier cruising as he himself wandered the ruined city, "hunting for emptiness, for a quiet abandoned spot on which to concentrate [his] piercing attention."[74]

## The Ward Line pier project

Just as Matta-Clark's oblique interest in the visual culture of cruising in New York's ruins is echoed in Baltrop's photographs of his work, his interest in the spaces "between the walls of views inside out" and in sites threatened with "metabolization" reverberates in David Wojnarowicz's artistic appropriation of an abandoned warehouse at the end of Canal Street in 1983. In February of that year, Wojnarowicz and the artist Mike Bidlo, a painter and performance artist active in New York's East Village arts scene and known for his meticulous recreations of paintings by Jackson Pollock and Picasso, invited friends and fellow artists to join them in staging an illegal "take-over" of the dilapidated Pier 34.[75] Wojnarowicz and Bidlo met when they both exhibited at the Gracie Mansion Gallery's *Famous* show in 1982. In an interview with Sylvere Lotringer in 2006, Bidlo recalled that, for around six months in 1983, he and Wojnarowicz were "co-curators, supposedly," of what the artists named, informally, the Ward Line pier project, after the shipping line that operated in the warehouse until the early 1950s. But, Bidlo asserted, "it wasn't a curated show":

> It was just something we told people about and got people excited about: the ultimate alternative space, where anybody could come and do almost anything they wanted, if they had the time, the energy, and the effort.[76]

Indeed, Bidlo and Wojnarowicz set out "to start off a show that would allow anyone the chance to explore [an] image in any material on any surface they chose," freeing them to do "something no gallery [would] tolerate, nor be large enough to accommodate." There is, they wrote, "no rent, no electricity, no running water, no dealers, no sales, no curatorial interferences. There is 24 hour access, enthusiasm, deep sudden impulse and some sense of possibility for dreaming." The warehouse's ruination was key. "This is something possible wherever there are abandoned structures," Bidlo and Wojnarowicz wrote. "This is something possible everywhere."[77]

Hundreds of artists responded to Wojnarowicz and Bidlo's word-of-mouth call. Established downtown artists like Ruth Kligman worked alongside younger East Village painters like Judy Glantzman and Luis Frangella. Artworks were largely produced in situ and displayed in almost every available space in the vast warehouse, its three floors filled with murals, graffiti, and sculpture. Many of the works' maritime subjects addressed the port's naval past and its contemporary cruising culture, inspired by earlier waterfront murals by the artist Tava, whom Wojnarowicz met in the late 1970s.[78] Other works at the Ward Line pier interacted with its labyrinthine layout and rundown quality. The decaying building was interpreted not as a canvas but as a participatory element in the work's execution.[79] The aesthetic potential of ruins was central to the work produced there. Wojnarowicz found pleasure in the waterfront's ruination and in imagined visions of its prehistory, encouraging participants to engage with the warehouse as a dangerous and primal space, to "make gestures on the walls, treating abandoned structures as caves."[80] In a statement circulated by Wojnarowicz and Bidlo a few weeks into the Ward Line project, the artists observed that, in the space of the warehouse,

> people are affected by light, by wind from the river, by the subtle deterioration of the surroundings, by the movement of strangers through broken doorways, by the shift of sky and water from blues to greys in the evenings, by elements of risk and danger, by suddenly discovered work where hours before there was none.[81]

Wojnarowicz spread grass seeds through empty rooms (figure 2.16), the "disintegrated plaster that had fallen out of the ceiling" providing sustenance for them to grow, transforming the rooms into what he called fields in an "industrial meadow" and an ephemeral "multi-authored artwork" fostered by architectural circumstance and municipal neglect.[82] "Those are some of the gestures that I loved the most and got the least attention," he told Barry Blinderman, "because they were the most anonymous—you couldn't sign a blade of grass that says Wojnarowicz."[83] Although Cynthia Carr argues that Wojnarowicz selected the Ward Line pier because "it wasn't a cruising ground. At least not during the day," and first made work at the Ward Line pier so that "he could be alone," viewing the site as a colossal studio, the project quickly acquired a collective ethos.[84] Its emergent collaborative spirit became key

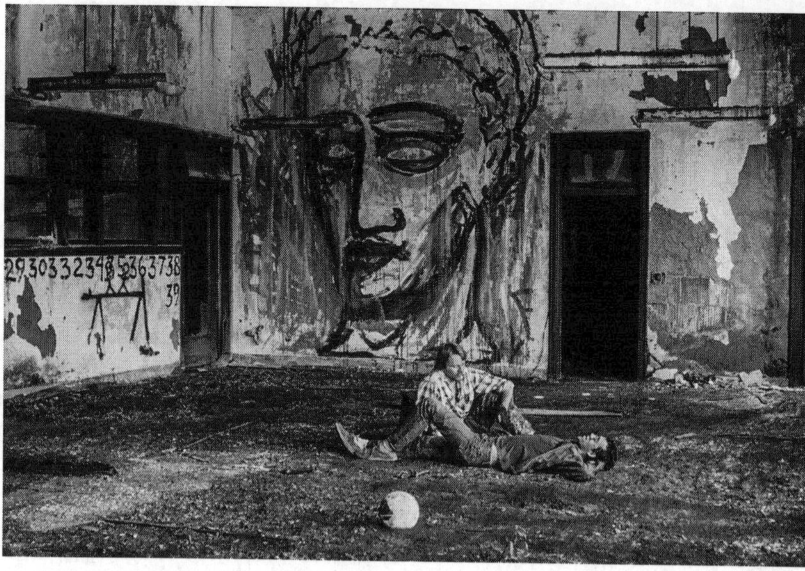

FIGURE 2.16. Mike Bidlo and David Wojnarowicz at Pier 34, New York, 1983. Photo © Andreas Sterzing.

to its success and the ruination of the warehouse itself helped support this. "People who lived in this city for years," Bidlo and Wojnarowicz wrote in an unpublished statement,

> said it was the first time they experienced fulfilment in terms of contact with the art scene and strangers. People shared supplies, energy, thoughts, even the surfaces to work with—crumbling walls of plaster, earth floor, metal walkways and hundreds of windowpanes—the work came out in rampages of raw energy.[85]

However, as "generations of word of mouth spread the scene became more crowded. Some people reacted territorially," the collaborative spirit was compromised, and "work got painted over." Everyone "had to in some way learn to give up the desire for possession. Possession of territory, possession of walls, of materials, of approach to creative impulse, of personal taste or directions for the place. It [has] become a simultaneous process of building up and tearing down."[86]

The project was documented unofficially by the young photographer Andreas Sterzing, who had arrived in New York from Germany in 1982, initially living in Brooklyn. By 1983 he was immersed in the arts scene of Manhattan's East Village and regularly photographing in its clubs and galleries. That February, after hearing murmurings about a guerilla art project on the city's waterfront, Sterzing made his way through lower Manhattan to Pier 34 to photograph it. A small selection of his images, nine from a collection of well over a hundred, were featured in the German magazine *Stern* in 1984.[87] While Sterzing had initially envisioned the documentation of the pier project as a launch pad for his own career as a photographer, he considered many of the images of his artist friends and their ephemeral works, destroyed by city authorities a year earlier, to be too personal for international publication and withdrew consent.[88] Although some were included in Lotringer's *Five or Six Years on the Lower East Side* in 2006 and in the exhibition *The Piers: Art and Sex along the New York Waterfront* at the Leslie-Lohman Museum of Gay and Lesbian Art in New York in 2012, the majority of the images discussed here remain untitled and unpublished, part of Sterzing's personal archive.

Sterzing's photographs capture the extent of the pier's dereliction and convey the romantic appeal of its ruinous state: the vast expanse of the warehouse space, the discarded bureaucratic papers of its abandoned offices, its crumbling walls and cracked windows (figure 2.17). Artists are depicted walking through hallways and vast rooms littered with plaster and defunct metal fixtures, and among the homeless people who appropriated the space for shelter in the winter months. In the ground-level storage area of the warehouse, the Italian sculptor Paolo Buggiani produced a performance based on the story of Icarus, as part of his *Urban Mythology* series, performing in a handmade glider adorned with painted flames. On the concrete pier outside the

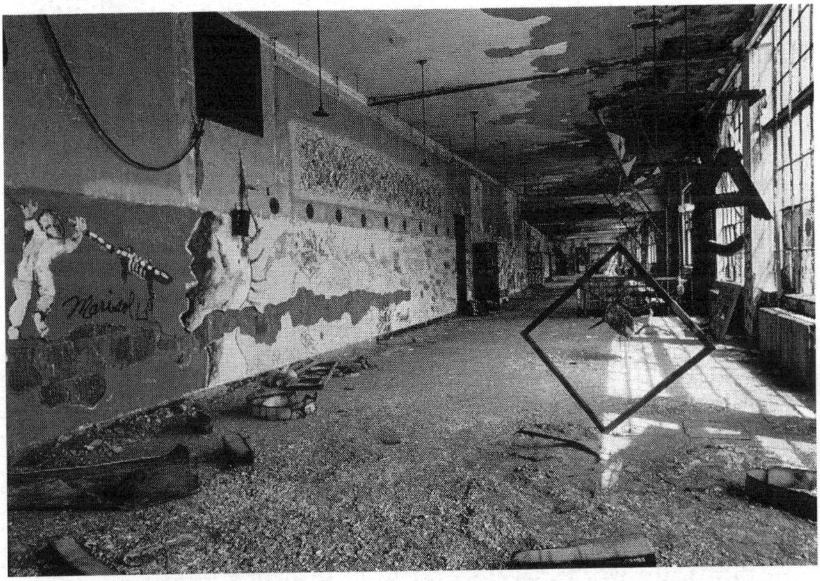

FIGURE 2.17. Pier 34, New York. 1983. Room facing Canal and Spring Streets. Photo © Andreas Sterzing.

warehouse, he installed a "Trojan Horse" sculpture, an armored bicycle that spat fire through customized pipes. Ruth Kligman, well known in New York as an Abstract Expressionist painter and for her relationship with Jackson Pollock, produced a line drawing in pencil and chalk of a nude woman. Mike Bidlo had befriended Kligman as he immersed himself in Pollock's past prior to his performance as Pollock at PS1 in 1982, a performance Kligman participated in. Situated on a peeling, crumbling wall, her work at the Ward Line pier addressed the vulnerability of the site and of those who wandered its hallways and corridors, drawing attention to its broadly masculine history and queer sexual appropriation (figure 2.18). Nearby, Michael Otterson employed aquatic symbolism that referenced the proximity of the Hudson River and the maritime life that suffered during the waterfront's industrial prime. In a large wall drawing, Otterson drafted a red-scaled fish, its insides filled with a horizontal nude female figure, a regendered transposition of the biblical tale of Jonah and the whale (figure 2.19). Torn cubicle walls in the warehouse toilets were appropriated as panels or "canvases" by the theatrical set designer Huck Snyder, who painted babies emerging, upside down, from phantom wombs, and labeled with dates and times of "birth"—"4.54 p.m. 5.22.83," "5.22.83 5.14 p.m"—emphasizing the immediacy, specificity, and ephemerality of the works and the space itself. His paintings extended to the surrounding walls, and the small bathroom space, painted in reds and pinks, appeared as a womb, the fleshy origin of this painted progeny.

Throughout the pier, the proliferation of ephemeral artworks accentuated the aesthetic quality and sculptural dynamism of the decaying structure. Judy Glantzman painted expressionistic figures directly onto disintegrating wallpaper, ensuring the painting's impermanence. In a photograph by Sterzing, she stands facing the camera, in front of her work, playfully blowing bubble gum and holding her paint-soaked brush like a torch, emphasizing the casual, convivial atmosphere of the pier project (figure 2.20). Glantzman's paintings bear much visual and painterly likeness to Luis Frangella's grand nudes. At the Ward Line pier, he painted gargantuan male and female torsos in the upper levels of the warehouse that recalled classical sculpture and erotic wall paintings at the House of the Vettii in Pompeii (figure 2.21). Frangella was also involved in the spontaneous social life of the pier project. "Luis used to always have parties," Mike Bidlo recalled. "He would have food on the stove, cook potatoes, and people would come over."[89] Frangella's wall paintings surrounded the room that Wojnarowicz appropriated, anonymously, as his "industrial meadow."[90]

Rag and newspaper figures by the sculptor David Finn punctuated the grand storage spaces of the warehouse's lower levels (figure 2.22). Finn was

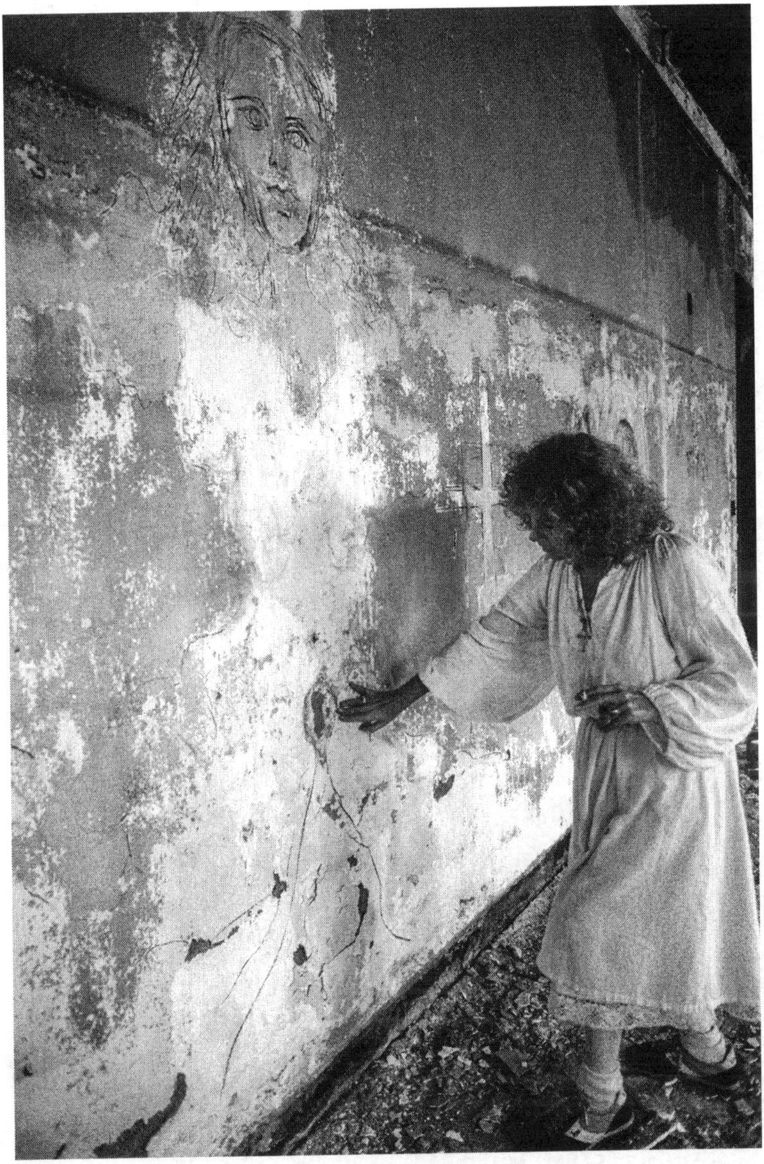

FIGURE 2.18. Ruth Kligman at Pier 34, New York, 1983. Photo © Andreas Sterzing.

well known on the Lower East Side and in the South Bronx, where his life-size bodily work had appeared on corners and sidewalks since 1982. In his earliest series, *Newspaper Children*, he wrought small figures from discarded urban paraphernalia, and in *Masked Figures*, a lengthy project begun in 1982, added colorful painted masks to the sculptures. The figures in both series

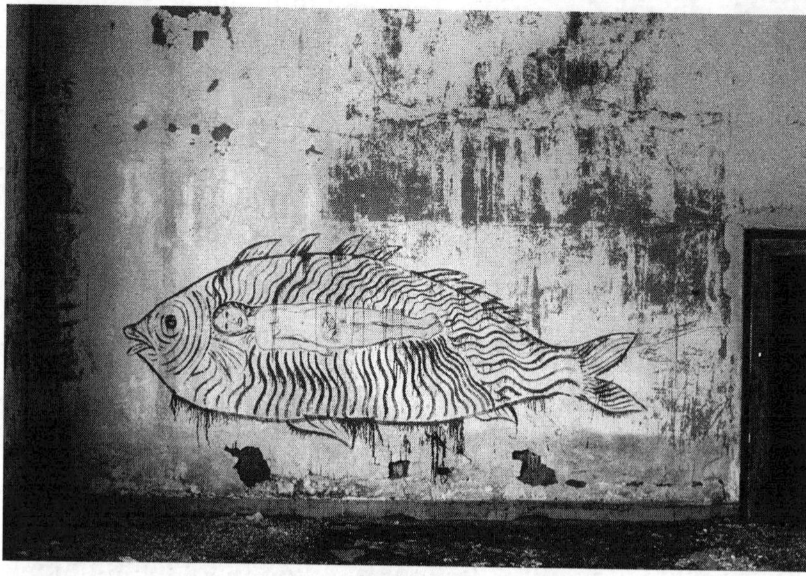

FIGURE 2.19. Pier 34, New York, 1983. Work by Michael Ottersen. Photo © Andreas Sterzing.

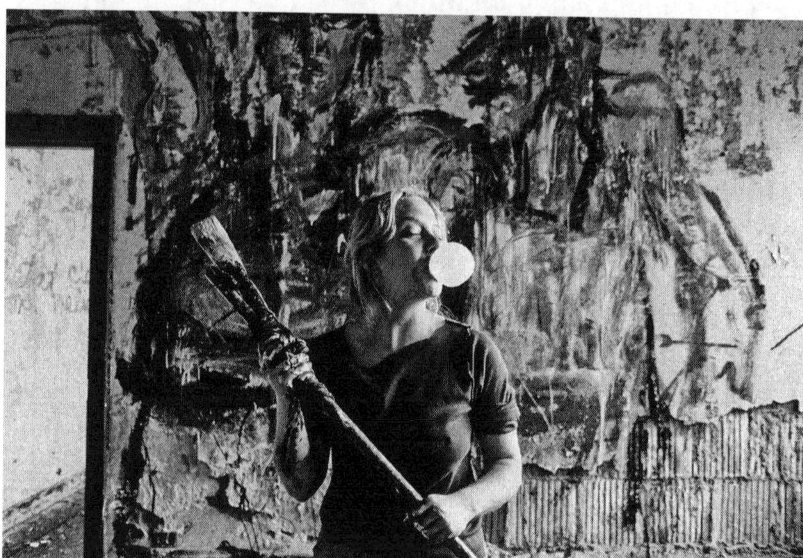

FIGURE 2.20. Judy Glantzman at Pier 34, New York, 1983. Photo © Andreas Sterzing.

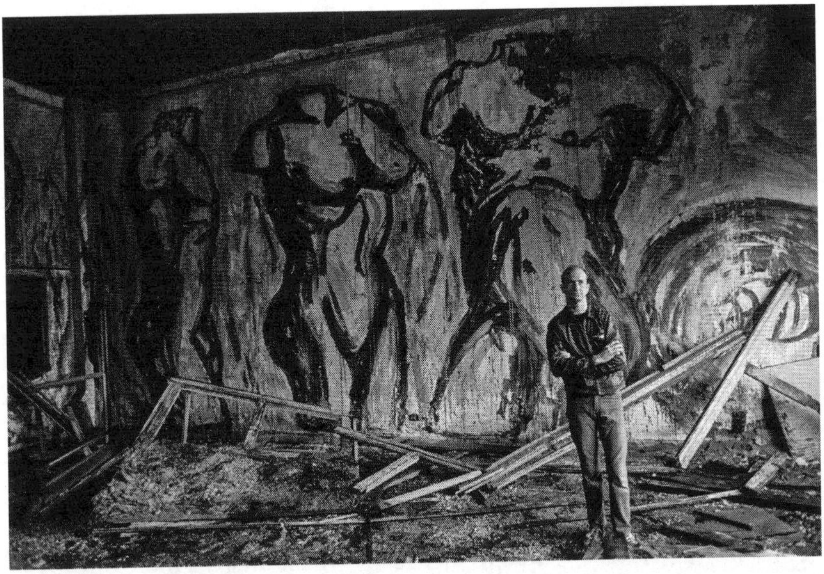

FIGURE 2.21. Luis Frangella at Pier 34, New York, 1983. Photo © Andreas Sterzing.

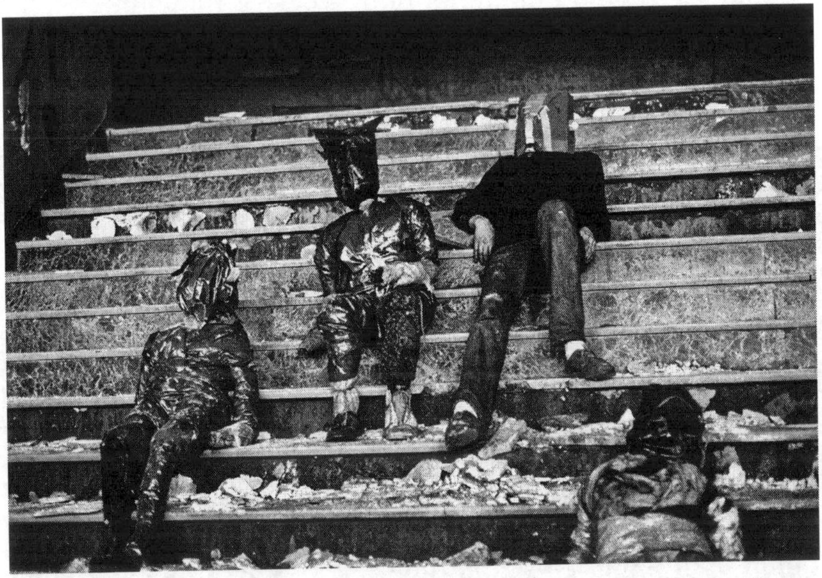

FIGURE 2.22. David Finn with some of his figures at Pier 34, New York, 1983. Photo © Andreas Sterzing.

were simultaneously ghostly and solidly material, constructed from the city's by-products. Placed in deprived pockets of Manhattan and the South Bronx, they offered a bitter commentary on the city's human "waste," on who might be considered expendable in a gentrifying or neglected neighborhood. In the Ward Line warehouse, Finn's figures were strewn across the interstitial space of the stairwell, some casually reclining, others contorted as if dead or dying, like the building itself. James Wines placed these figures among the most important works of public sculpture in 1980s New York. "The ultimate power of Finn's images," he argued, "comes from his use of figuration to describe the relationship between viewer and environment," drawing heavily "on the audience's expectations about an urban setting, using this as the basis for an integration of content with context."[91] The abandoned waterfront was, then, an apposite location for these refuse sculptures, drawing attention, as Matta-Clark had done in the mid-1970s, to the pier's historical neglect and the displacing effects of urban regeneration.

Matta-Clark's intervention in Pier 52 was memorialized more directly at the Ward Line pier by the artist John Fekner. Fekner had met Matta-Clark while working as a teacher's assistant in SoHo in the mid-1970s and would regularly visit 112 Greene Street and Food.[92] Along an exterior wall at the Ward Line pier, Fekner stenciled the phrase "4 Gordon 2 U" (figure 2.23). Another artist made a tiny cutting in an upstairs window, in homage to *Day's End*. Like

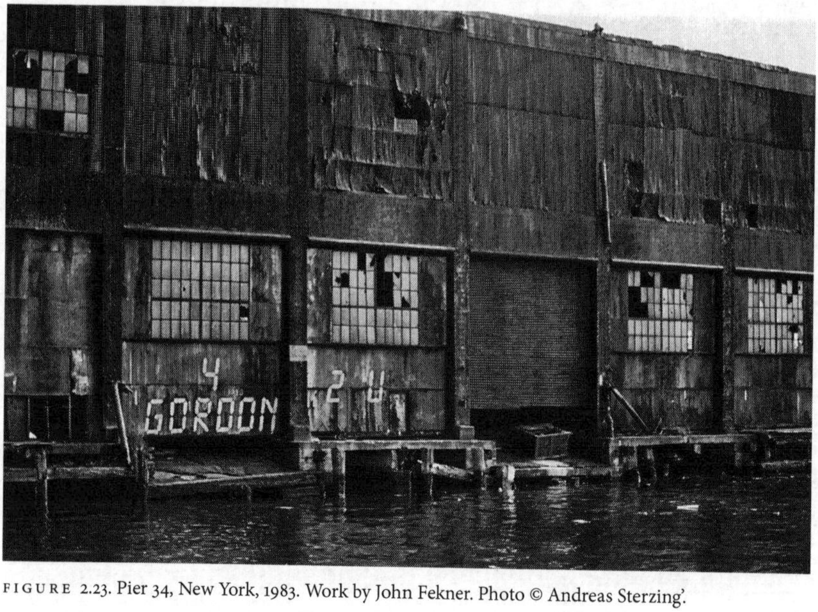


FIGURE 2.23. Pier 34, New York, 1983. Work by John Fekner. Photo © Andreas Sterzing.

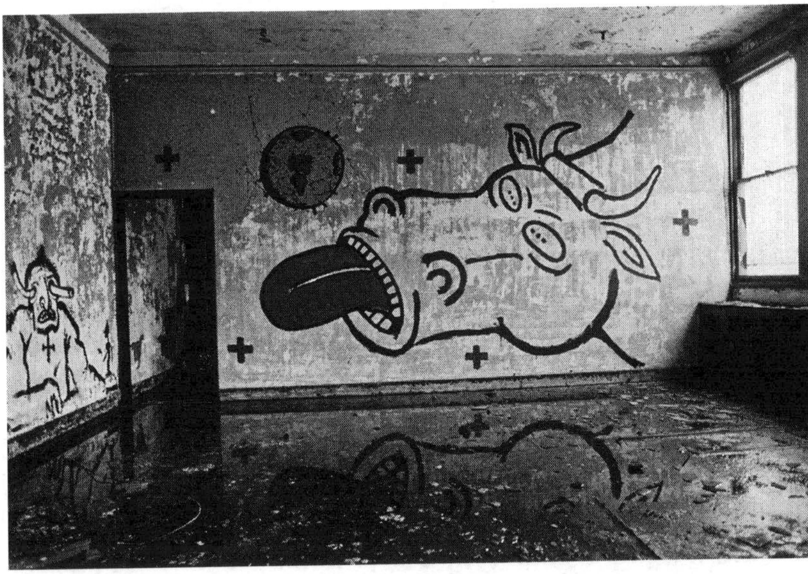

FIGURE 2.24. Pier 34, New York, 1983. Work by David Wojnarowicz. Photo © Andreas Sterzing.

Matta-Clark's original cutting, Fekner's homage was complexly nostalgic, a memorial to Matta-Clark, who had died from pancreatic cancer in 1978 at the age of thirty-five but continued to speak to the waterfront's decline and decay in the early 1980s, as the piers were again threatened with demolition.[93]

At the Ward Line pier, Wojnarowicz painted two large murals of animals in pain: a screaming pterodactyl, an extinct, prehistoric creature, and a gagging cow, suggestive of the abattoirs in the nearby Meatpacking District and inspired by recent trips to New Jersey farms with Hujar, where they photographed animals, trees, and empty sheds (figure 2.24).[94] The "scale and clarity" of these works, Mysoon Rizk notes, "not only call[s] attention to the impossibility and strangeness of coming upon either animal in this abandoned urban structure, but also makes their actual arrival seem magically imminent (as wild animals depicted on cave walls in prehistoric times might have seemed to Palaeolithic people)," further complicating the line between the urban and rural, the contained and the wild, the past and the present in a ruined city space that was itself approaching extinction.[95] In *Soon All This Will Be Picturesque Ruins*, a painting produced in 1984, the year after the Ward Line pier project, Wojnarowicz overlaid a collage of postcard images of the Parthenon with painted depictions of two skulls, mouths ajar, atop rubble and in front of a burned-out building. This group of bodily and architectural ruins is framed by an eroded grid pattern, suggestive of Manhattan's orderly street network, and a photograph of a dead dog. An imagined classical past

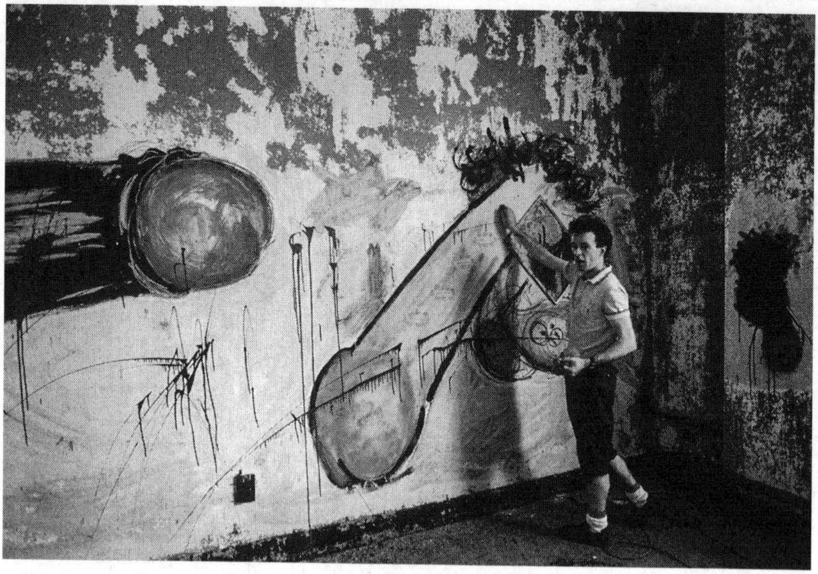

FIGURE 2.25. Keith Davis at Pier 34, New York, 1983. Photo © Andreas Sterzing.

is united with an American late-capitalist present through the image of the ruin, a fetishized symbol of glory as much as a marker of decay and failure. Ruination is imminent, and, as the buildings of downtown New York decay in the disappearing present, they are, Wojnarowicz suggests, both pitiful and picturesque, crass and classical.

While, as Cynthia Carr noted, Wojnarowicz first started making work at the Ward Line pier because "it wasn't a cruising ground," much of the work produced there did reflect on the queer erotic appropriations of the piers. On a discarded door there, Wojnarowicz sketched a composite homoerotic vision of Saint Sebastian and a sailor in Breton stripes. Richard Hambleton covered some of the steel walls of the warehouse's lower levels with orgiastically contorted shadow figures, arranged in a linear band that recalls classical frieze sculpture. In a smaller room, one of Hambleton's figures was paired with a disembodied head that fellated its erect penis. Keith Davis's exuberant paintings of giant phalluses are perhaps the most explicitly homoerotic works at Pier 34 and draw clearly on the visual culture of pier cruising. In Sterzing's photographs, Davis, a designer for *Artforum*, is seen, smiling, in the act of painting a monumental cock on a peeling wall (figure 2.25). Davis added a mirror to the base of the penis, alluding to the erotic voyeurism of cruising, its reliance on seeing and being seen, and the long-standing status of the piers as a cruising ground. The filmmaker Ivan Galietti echoed Wojnarowicz's perception of the piers as closer to "the faraway past than the recent past" in his film *Pompeii New York*, a meditation on the erotic "catacombs" of Pier 46 and what Galietti saw as the expulsion of its queer inhabitants from mainland Manhattan.[96] The film documented the queer life of the pier as it faced demolition later in 1983. Galietti described the film, which features a cameo from Wojnarowicz, as an effort "to recreate that atmosphere of men moving in the half-light, in this distant night world on the Manhattan shore . . . to suffuse it with the sexuality of the frescoes and taboos," to record the demise of "a surreal monument, half-destroyed, bathed in strange light, a poetical, 'post-Vesuvian' ruin," to document "the ravaged beauty of this landmark of alternative lifestyles" at the moment of its disappearance.[97]

Sterzing's photographs of the Ward Line pier end with the project's own conclusion: its repossession and demolition by city authorities. The participating artists, including Wojnarowicz, were reprimanded or arrested for trespassing. As the surrounding walls were torn down, Wojnarowicz's cow's head mural was exposed to passers-by. A figurative sculpture by Bill Downer was mistaken for a trespassing artist, and police attempted an arrest.[98] The placement of a municipal "No Trespassing" stencil over Ward Line graffiti urging New Yorkers to vote captures the complex and contradictory understanding of civic engagement that was integral to city authorities' struggle to "reclaim" the waterfront and underscores the exclusive conception of public access that was central to the harbor's neglect and the case for its renewal. With the majority of the remaining waterfront warehouses demolished later in the year, the Ward Line project was the endpoint of Wojnarowicz's visual waterfront work. The demolition erased, for a time, signs of the creative habitation of the harbor space, as well as the small graffito memorials that had been appearing there since the earliest reported cases of what would become known as AIDS in 1981.[99]

The repossession and demolition of the pier underscored Acconci's assertion that "New York doesn't belong to us." However, as the Ward Line project made clear, it might be made ours, temporarily, through artistic occupation that refuses commercial and "curatorial interferences," an appropriation Wojnarowicz and Bidlo felt could only take place in a neglected space like the piers.[100] As Gordon Matta-Clark's, Peter Hujar's, and Paul Thek's work with ruins in the 1950s, 1960s, and 1970s also suggests, the visual culture of ruins is a distinctively queer one. The ruined spaces of lower Manhattan look different from the homoerotic vantage point of cruising, a queer way of looking in the city and looking at the places where the city's heteronormative fabric falls apart. In approaching the "memory-traces" of the piers' "abandoned sets of futures," Wojnarowicz, Hujar, and others approached these ruins as a site that through their industrial nonproductivity could facilitate and sustain queer creative and cultural presence.[101] This, as Wojnarowicz suggested, is a liberatory perspective on socioeconomic decline in the late-capitalist city that draws on both the culture of cruising and the visual culture of ruins, the whole world and the cemetery: "This is something possible wherever there are abandoned structures. This is something possible everywhere."[102]

## "I miss you dearly"

John Fekner's memorial gesture for Gordon Matta-Clark at the Ward Line pier was echoed in 2014 in a work for Pier 54 by the artist Jill Magid, titled *Postcards from the Pier*. In a handwritten postcard addressed to Matta-Clark at Pier 18, Magid writes longingly, "I am on the pier but there is nothing left here to remind me of you" (figure 2.26). The work formed part of an exhibition at the derelict but extant stone Pier 54 that responded to Willoughby Sharp's *Projects: Pier 18*, recalling its experimental engagement with an industrial landscape but resisting its gendered elisions; where Sharp had invited twenty-seven men to participate, *Pier 54* featured only female-identified artists, including Magid, Emily Roysdon, and Xaviera Simmons. The exhibition recast the masculinist pioneer aesthetic of Sharp's project by inviting these artists to respond both to the space itself and to histories of its artistic

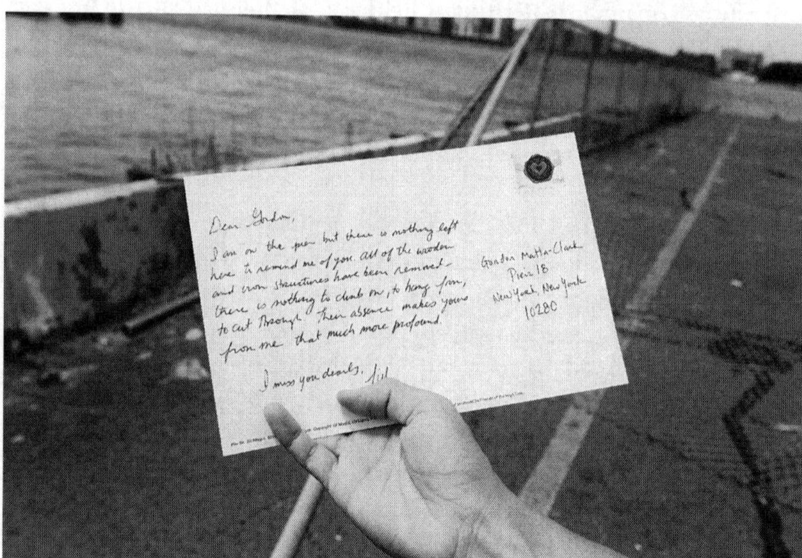


FIGURE 2.26. Jill Magid, *Postcards from the Pier*, 2014. Photo by Liz Ligon for the exhibition *Pier 54*. © 2014 Jill Magid, Liz Ligon, and Friends of the High Line. Commissioned and produced by Friends of the High Line.

appropriation, specifically Sharp's project and Shunk-Kender's photographic documentation of it. Photographs by Liz Ligon documenting the new exhibition were displayed nearby in a pop-up space on Eleventh Avenue.

While the funding of the latter project by the High Line, a powerful gentrifying agent in the landscape of contemporary downtown Manhattan, complicates the critical charge of this work and its relation to the continuing redevelopment and privatization of the waterfront, *Pier 54* and the Ward Line pier project share a concern with the disappearance of unregulated public spaces that foster artistic experimentation and community. In November 2014, shortly after the opening of *Pier 54*, the Hudson River Park Trust announced that Pier 54 would be demolished and replaced with a landscaped garden funded by the businessman Barry Diller. Many of the individual works that make up *Pier 54* reflect critically on the imbrication of personal loss, the erosion of free public space, and the impact of gentrification on the lived experience of people who live, work, and play near the piers in the present. A press release for the show describes it as "an exhibition conceived as a tribute to and a reaction against *Pier 18* . . . both a re-enactment and an exercise in historical revisionism."[103]

In keeping with this dual curatorial and artistic approach and the sense of loss at impending redevelopment, Magid's postcard to Matta-Clark relates one artist's personal sense of loss and her creative tribute to a predecessor who died nearly forty years earlier to the broader context of ongoing gentrification. "All of the wooden and iron structures have been removed," she writes. Like Akerman's *Letters*, Magid's postcards resist the possessive relationality of "the touristic gaze" and draw connections with a lost past through the disarming dynamic of friendship. "There is nothing," she continues, "to climb on, to hang from, to cut through. Their absence makes yours from me that much more profound. I miss you dearly." In a similar mode, Xaviera Simmons's *Number 18/Number 19* took photographs of the cruising cultures at the piers in the late 1970s as the point of departure for a set of performances on Pier 54 by female-identified dancers, which were in turn photographed by Ligon (figure 2.27). Simmons's performances present "a conversation between image and movement," drawing upon photographs by Baltrop and others of men together in this space to construct "a pier-based dictionary of gesture and movement" stemming from archival materials. The dancers kiss, touch, laugh together. For Simmons, as for Hujar and Wojnarowicz, cruising cultures at the piers in the 1970s and the architectural ruins that remain and recall them drew upon a unique visual vocabulary that is specific to cruising but could be meaningfully deployed as a means of memorializing this queer

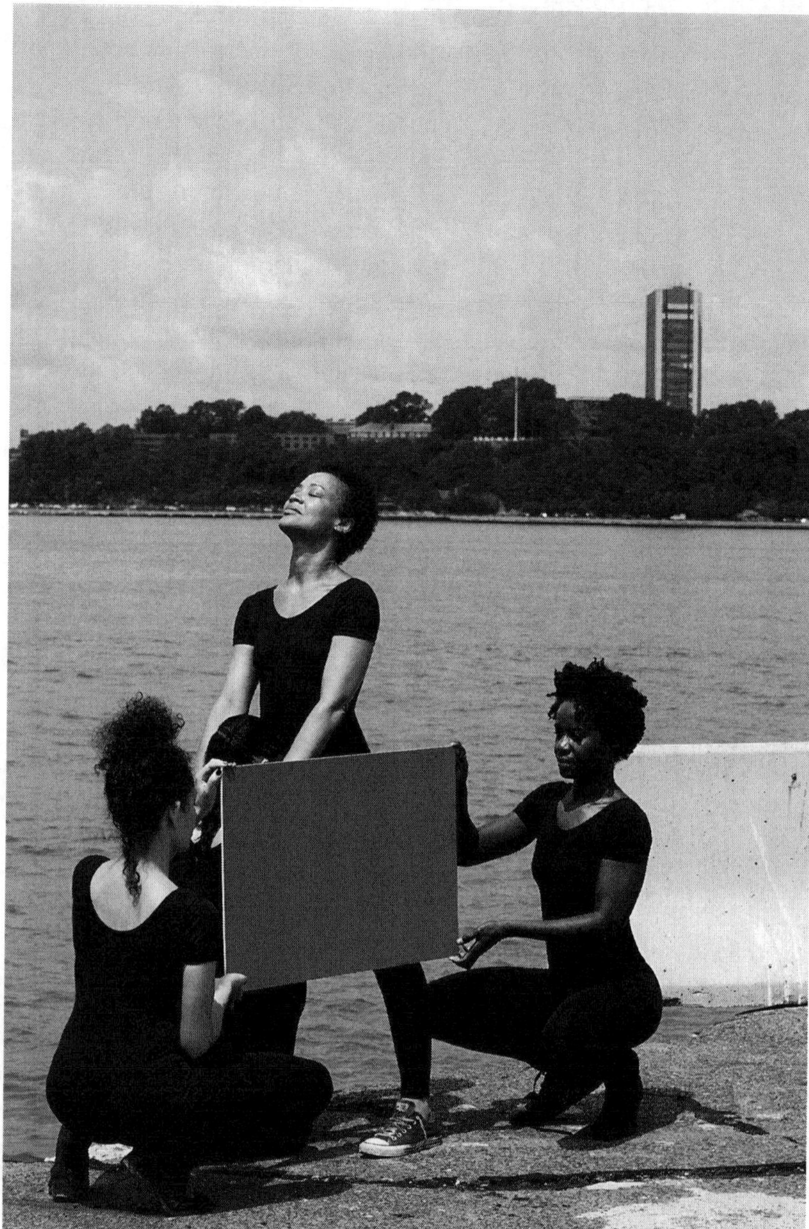

FIGURE 2.27. Xaviera Simmons, *Number 18/Number 19*, 2014. Photo by Liz Ligon, for the exhibition *Pier 54*, 2014. © 2014 Xaviera Simmons, Liz Ligon, and Friends of the High Line. Commissioned and produced by Friends of the High Line.

visual culture of ruins without ossifying it. Rather than "something possible everywhere," for Simmons, it is something made possible through the historical suggestiveness of the ruins of the piers and through the methodological practice of tentative, individual research in artistic archives, a kind of cruising in ruins that Simmons and Magid, like Hujar and Wojnarowicz, engaged in as a means of conjuring pleasure in the present and marking the personal and political value of Manhattan's lost and disappearing public spaces.

# 3

# Cruising Ghosts: David Wojnarowicz's Queer Antecedents

"He wanted me to move as if I was made up of moments in history."[1]

Time on the waterfront was in ruins. For Wojnarowicz, the material decay of the piers and their queer erotic appropriations also suggested the possibility of temporal overlap. Past and present, his writings suggest, coalesced in these ruinous buildings, and as his waterfront writing developed in the late 1970s, the transparent figure of the ghost became the ideal symbol with which to articulate this temporal coexistence, this encounter with time in ruins. An ontologically slippery character, the ghost was, for Wojnarowicz, a "pale wordless," even shapeless, figure, "containing whole histories and geographies and adventures."[2] In the metaphor of the ghost, like that of the ruin, the temporal distinctions between "ancient" monks and heretics, and propositioned young men, became irrevocably blurred. In the "blue night halls" of the waterfront's empty warehouses, where "figures could appear and disappear, become vacant or nonexistent," both were "strangers, . . . discs of black silhouette outlined briefly as each car passes, one after the other, pale interior faces turned against the windows, then fading into distance."[3]

In *Spectres of Marx* (1994), Jacques Derrida introduces his theory of hauntology, a pun on ontology that elucidates what he calls "the spectral moment." This moment, he argues, "no longer belongs to time," is "beyond the living present in general—and beyond its simple negative reversal." Thinking of time as haunted, Derrida wrote, offered "a linking of modalised presents (past present, actual present: "now," future present)." For Derrida, haunting is "historical to be sure, but it is not dated, never docilely given a date in the chain of presents, day after day, according to the instituted order of a calendar."[4] Rather, "a spectral asymmetry interrupts . . . all specularity," all spectral temporality, and as with the multiple, coexistent temporalities of Wojnarowicz's waterfront writing, it does not simply fragment, rather, "it desynchronizes, it recalls us to anachrony," just as, by the spring of 1980, Wojnarowicz's journals were populated by "toughs" imagined as spectral versions of his favorite writers, living and dead.[5] One man, for example, is described as having "a tough face, square-jawed and barely shaven, tight-cropped hair, wiry and black, intensely handsome like some face seen in old boxer photos of Rocky Marciano, a cross between him and [the Russian Futurist poet Vladimir] Mayakovsky, a nose that might've been broken in some dark avenue barroom in the waterfront district of a distant city." Another recalls Jean Genet: "grizzled and dirt lines in the creases of his neck skin, vaguely handsome, red print worker's hankie around his throat, shorn hair, white and stubble."[6] Wojnarowicz's erotic waterfront hauntology refigures time and temporal relations according to the logic of cruising, resisting the normative, essentialist teleology of heterosexual familial genealogy, Jack Halberstam's "paradigmatic markers of lived experience."[7]

In this chapter, extending the notions of cumulative erotic architectural and material histories explored in the first chapter, I lend the conceptions of hauntological time, spectral presence, and inspiration to the temporally problematic cruising spaces of the abandoned New York waterfront, and to artists like Emily Roysdon who have been influenced by Wojnarowicz's cross-temporal cruising and have tread the same temporally slippery poetic spaces. I explore the development of Wojnarowicz's ghostly idiolect in the late 1970s and early 1980s, from his cruising of anonymous "toughs" reimagined as Genet, Mayakovsky, and Rimbaud, to his reimagining of the late works of William S. Burroughs in the queer space of the piers, examining the erotic possibilities that this temporal intermingling presented in the context of the cruising encounter. Going beyond the single, anonymous intimate encounter and the new personal temporalities Wojnarowicz generated through this cross-temporal poetic practice, I examine the political dimensions of this queer literary multiplicity, thinking through the possibilities for imagining alternate ways of being together, as queer, across and through time that it offered him.

Like Elizabeth Freeman's theory of "erotohistoriography," Wojnarowicz's spectral cruising practice was "distinct from the desire for a fully present past, a restoration of bygone times."[8] Described by the playwright and performance artist Penny Arcade in a review of Wojnarowicz's published journals, as "multigenerationalism,"[9] it was a form of what Roland Barthes, in "The Death of the Author," termed "multiple writing," in which

> everything is to be distinguished, but nothing deciphered; structure can be followed . . . in all its recurrences and all its stages, but there is no underlying

> ground; the space of the writing is to be traversed, not penetrated: writing ceaselessly posits meaning but always in order to evaporate it: it proceeds to a systematic exemption of meaning.[10]

For Wojnarowicz, this hybrid present does not distinguish between itself and that which is past. Linearity inhibits the temporal interaction that he generated through his reading of Rimbaud, Genet, and Mayakovsky, which he found necessary to his existence as a queer man in late 1970s New York. "Being homosexual is, to me," he remarked in an interview with his friend Keith Davis, recorded in 1983,

> it's like you're not working with the support of society, not living with the support of society at large. And that's something political in itself. Here's masses of people who have been taught that something is not right, not correct, as a way of living, as a life, as a life form. And so in your being queer, you're living without support, without the total support of society. You're living on your own strength.

The writers he read and admired, he told Davis, figured in his mind not as superiors, erotic or literary precedents, but as "peers":

> What attracted me to them when I started reading [Genet and Burroughs] was basically their feelings of no guilt. Their sense of no guilt for anything they did or lived. And it gave me, it became, if there were peers those became peers, and were the people I felt the closest to.

Wojnarowicz's description of intergenerational influence as a relationship between peers speaks, in part, to the powerful confidence he performs throughout this conversation with Davis and to his belief in the value of nonlinear time:

> Future time is as vivid for me as past time. All it takes is being in the right state for it. And the right state is usually set off by things about light and, you know, solitude. Usually walking by myself somewhere and usually close to a river.[11]

Figuring his connections with these writers as erotic, mapping them onto the bodies of cruised anonymous toughs, onto men with whom he shared sex, conversation, a cheap coffee in the Silver Dollar Café, Wojnarowicz asserts a peer-to-peer dynamic of sharing and receiving influence that recalls Michel Foucault's theory of "friendship as a way of life," which "can be shared among individuals of different age, status, and social activity" and "can yield intense relations not resembling those that are institutionalized." For Foucault, cross-generational relationships between men hold the potential for a rethinking of social and sexual relations:

> Two men of noticeably different ages—what code would allow them to communicate? They face each other without terms or convenient words, with nothing to assure them about the meaning of the movement that carries them toward each other. They have to invent, from A to Z, a relationship that is still formless, which is friendship: that is to say, the sum of everything through which they can give each other pleasure.[12]

Wojnarowicz's passionate connection to writers like Rimbaud and Genet, figured through cruising and sexual connection, was also one of admiration and veneration. This relationship evokes Catherine Grant's theory of the value of the fan in thinking through the relation between radical second-wave feminism in the 1970s and radical, often queer, feminist artmaking in the 2000s, including Emily Roysdon's *Untitled (David Wojnarowicz Project)*: "The passionate attachment to the object of interest is one that is not passive, but instead alters the object to suit the fan's needs, taking a fascination for something as a starting point, which can then also start a process of negotiation and transformation of the object." The connection is not necessarily sexual but, like all fandom, can be erotically charged, even if never consummated. Fandom, Grant argues, is a dynamic "that does not simply revere or reject, combining the past and the present in an active dialogue, one that does not seek to simply reinstate the past, but to rework it differently, passionately, and perhaps even politically in the present." Grant draws upon Elizabeth Freeman's notion of "temporal drag" since, she argues, it "explores the revisions needed when thinking about generational models of relationships."[13] As Freeman argues,

> "Generation," a word for both biological and technological forms of replication, cannot be tossed out with the bathwater of reproductive thinking. Instead, it may be crucial to complicate the idea of horizontal political generations succeeding one another, with a notion of "temporal drag," thought less in the psychic time of the individual than in the movement time of collective political life.[14]

An encounter with the past in the present was, for Wojnarowicz, always a multiplicitious encounter, a friendship, a collaborative erotic experience, and a bodily one. As Freeman puts it, an erotohistoriographic encounter with the past in the present "uses the body as a tool to effect, figure or perform that encounter." It "sees the body as a method, and historical consciousness as something intimately involved with corporeal sensations." It "does not write the lost object into the present so much as encounter it already in the present, by treating the present itself as hybrid."[15] The erotohistoriographic narrative that Wojnarowicz created in his waterfront writing was, then, a queer one. As

Judith Butler asserts in the closing chapter of *Bodies That Matter*, if the term "queer," and the collection of meanings and identities it both incorporates and generates, "is to be a site of collective contestation, the point of departure for a set of historical reflections and future imaginings, it will have to remain"—like the derelict waterfront—"that which is never fully owned, but always redeployed, twisted, queered from a prior usage."[16] Like queer time and ruined space, the specter "remains difficult to name," for it is also "neither soul nor body, and both one and the other. . . . It is flesh and phenomenality that give the spirit its spectral apparition, but which disappear right away. . . . One does not know whether it is living or if it is dead."[17]

## The return of the dead: Wojnarowicz's Rimbaud

In 1980 the Manhattan paper *Soho News* published a black-and-white photographic series by Wojnarowicz with the title *Arthur Rimbaud in New York*. It was one of his first forays in the practice of cross-temporal collaboration, produced between 1978 and 1979. In it, Wojnarowicz appears, along with three or four friends, wearing a life-size mask of the nineteenth-century French writer Arthur Rimbaud, appropriated from Ray Johnson's cover for the New Directions edition of Rimbaud's *Illuminations* (itself a reworking of Etienne Carjat's 1871 photograph of the poet), first published in the United States in 1966. The photographs were staged in various locations around New York City, sites that Wojnarowicz himself frequented (figures 3.1, 3.2). The masked "Rimbaud" stands next to porn movie theaters in Times Square, among butchers in the Meatpacking District, in empty warehouses on the abandoned waterfront, on the subway, and in dive coffee shops. An unpublished note for a *Rimbaud in New York* film details Wojnarowicz's plans for shots of "rimbaud along lower west side . . . inside piers and in dusk in hallways with milling groups of cruisers."[18] The series was "playing with," Wojnarowicz wrote, "ideas of compression of 'historical time and activity' and fusing the French poet's identity with modern new york urban activities mostly illegal in nature."[19] In a journal entry from 1980, Wojnarowicz recorded a meeting with the *Soho News* prior to the paper's publication of the work. "I explained that it was a vision of Rimbaud with what was known of his sensibilities," he wrote, "only here in New York at this time and place in history. What he'd get into, what areas he'd be drawn to."[20]

While Henry Miller described his personal study of Rimbaud, *The Time of the Assassins* (1946), as "the outcome of a failure to translate, in the fashion intended, *A Season in Hell*" and an effort to render this "text in a language more

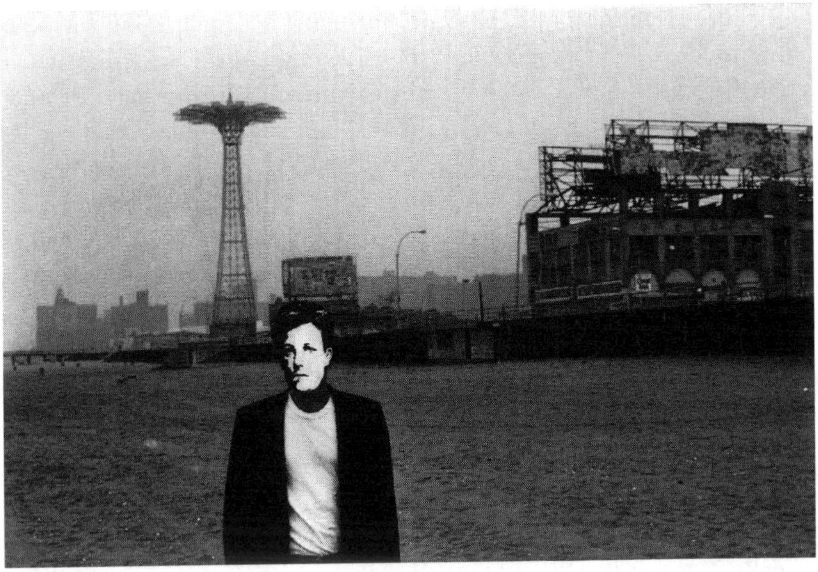

FIGURE 3.1. David Wojnarowicz, *Arthur Rimbaud in New York (kissing)*, 1978–1979. Courtesy of the Estate of David Wojnarowicz; P•P•O•W, New York. © David Wojnarowicz.

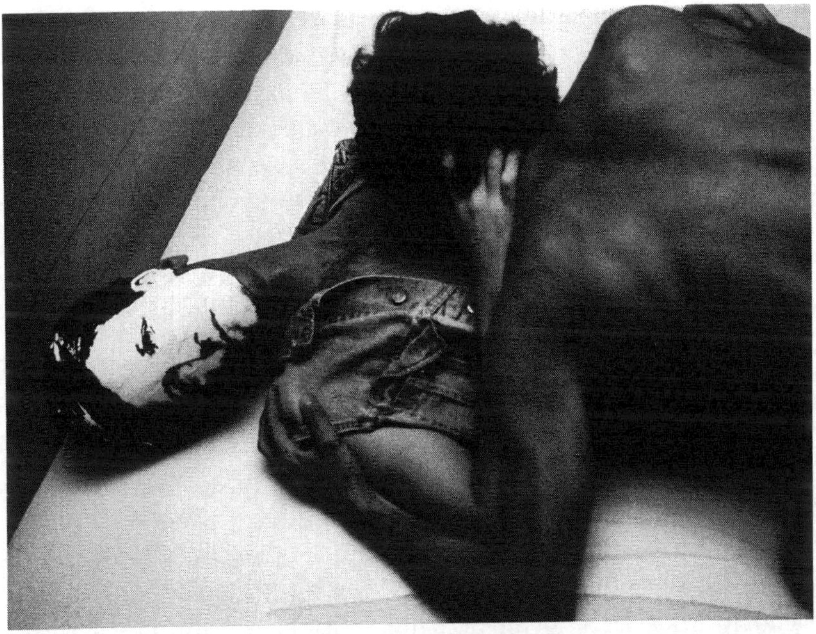

FIGURE 3.2. David Wojnarowicz, *Arthur Rimbaud in New York (coney island)*, 1978–1979. Courtesy of the Estate of David Wojnarowicz; P•P•O•W, New York. © David Wojnarowicz.

proximate to Rimbaud's own," Wojnarowicz's series attempted a distinct, visual transposition, inviting Rimbaud into the present, representing a proximate relation that was already active and making it material.[21] In a journal entry from 1978, Wojnarowicz attached a postcard of Henri Fantin-Latour's painting *Un Coin de Table* (1872), which depicts Rimbaud and his mentor and lover, the poet Paul Verlaine, among the so-called *villains cathars* of the Parisian literary scene. In the photo series, the poets of 1870s Paris are replaced by ordinary citizens of 1970s New York, riding the graffiti-covered subway, hustling in Times Square, and cruising the waterfront. For Wojnarowicz, Rimbaud's poetry permitted a reconfiguration, a mythologizing of autobiography that appealed to the young writer, who continually rewrote and reinvented the events of his own past. As Rimbaud wrote in *A Season in Hell* of his "bad blood," lamenting his "Gallic" ancestry as providing "no antecedent," Wojnarowicz opened *Close to the Knives* by exclaiming, "my heritage is a calculated fuck on some faraway sun-filled bed . . . conception's just a shot in the dark."[22] Rimbaud "gluttonously" waits for a time when he "will come back with limbs of iron and dark skin and a furious look. . . . By my mask they will think I am from a strong race."[23]

While Miller's revisitation was deeply literary, Wojnarowicz's was largely visual and certainly more erotic. Miller found in his invocation of Rimbaud's poetry and persona a "medium"—both a literary subject and a ghostly channel—in which "one sees backward and forward with equal clarity." Communication, he wrote, "becomes the art of establishing at any moment in time a logical and harmonious rapport between the past and the future." While Miller asked, "had [Rimbaud] come back in this life, what sort of poetry he would have written, what his message would have been," Wojnarowicz wondered where a contemporary Rimbaud might live and cruise.[24] As in his early waterfront poem, "Circulating drunk to midnight music," Rimbaud's desire for a total "derangement of all the senses," endorsed in his letter to Paul Demeny in 1871, was articulated poetically by Wojnarowicz through a derangement of both time and place.[25] Bringing Rimbaud to 1970s New York epitomized his interest in temporal and spatial rearrangement and reflected Rimbaud's own passion for a reconfiguration of time and space.

This confluence was emphatically political; it was a survival tactic for existing queerly in the present. "I wanted," Wojnarowicz noted in 1990, "to consider what [Rimbaud's] life would be like if he lived in New York City in the present." Similarly, his 1979 collage work *Untitled (Genet)*, which places the haloed figure of Genet, appropriated from a well-known 1947 portrait photograph by Brassaï, within a World War II image of soldiers in a ravaged church interior, flanked by armed angels, was a response to a "sense of alienation" that overwhelmed him in the mid-1970s:

> I felt the weight of my experiences and that there was very little chance I could transcend them, or turn them into something useful with the social structure I was living in or outlive those experiences.[26]

To achieve this queer transcendence, Wojnarowicz wrote, he needed "to make a symbol that would show that he would take on the suffering of the vast amounts of addiction that I saw on the streets."[27] To borrow from Elizabeth Freeman, to facilitate survival in the present, Wojnarowicz's *Rimbaud* series, like his Genet collage, "does not write" these queer figures from the past "into the present so much as encounter [them] already in the present, by treating the present itself as hybrid."[28]

*Jean Genet Masturbating in Mettray Prison* (1983) follows the form of a number of Wojnarowicz's collage works from the period: stenciled images superimposed on mass-produced poster advertisements, often connected with the sale of meat or fish from downtown wholesalers. Its production coincides with the peak of Wojnarowicz's activity at the Hudson River warehouses and the Ward Line pier project. The stenciled image depicts two naked male figures masturbating, the prison setting indicated by the barred window in the top right corner of the image, boldly executed in block shading that highlights the languid pose of the foremost figure and delineates his erect penis (figure 3.3). One figure's face is obscured, an absence that plays, perhaps, to Leo Bersani's sense of "the self-shattering and solipsistic jouissance that is sexuality itself."[29] More importantly, this absence suggests the figure of Genet in prison as a referential body for any number of sexual desires and longings, permitting Wojnarowicz to fantasize a collaborative idiom of erotic pleasure and physical oppression that links his own experiences to those of the imprisoned Genet, conflating the two locations by way of the contemporary American commercial poster. Both Wojnarowicz and the viewer are implicated in the position of the masturbating figure. The absence of the face places Wojnarowicz's Genet in a slippery space of anonymity and familiarity that recalls the affective and material distance of the fan, and emphasizes the historical and cultural currency of anonymous cruising sex for Wojnarowicz as a means of documenting and preserving multiple queer pasts, as well as its place in his everyday life.

In his journals, Wojnarowicz wrote of pinning up a poster of Rimbaud upon his arrival in Paris in 1977, an ironic reminder of home, and reading a battered copy of *Illuminations* on the piers in the late 1970s while cruising.[30] The myth of Rimbaud was exalted by a range of writers in New York in the 1960s and 1970s. Marjorie Perloff placed Rimbaud at the head of a canon of what she terms "the poetics of indeterminacy," the author of a poetic "landscape . . . characterized by constant explosive movement and shifting

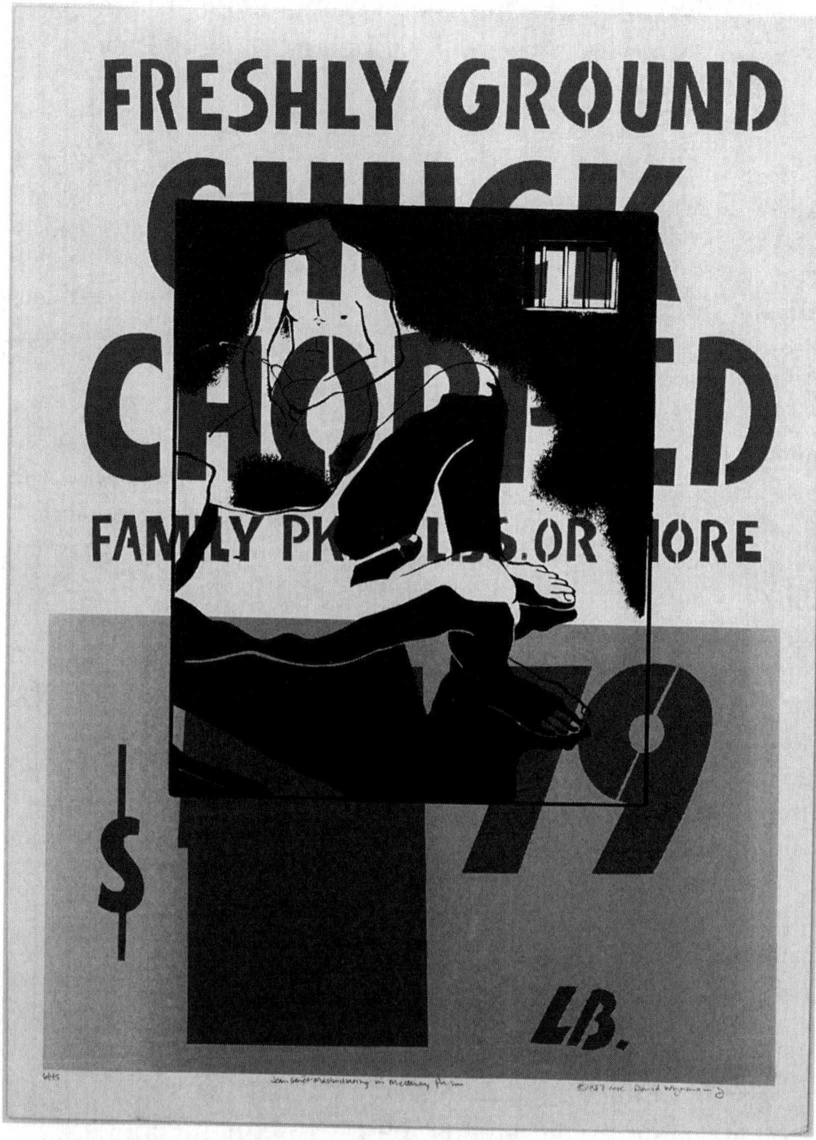


FIGURE 3.3. David Wojnarowicz, *Jean Genet Masturbating at Mettray Prison*, 1983. Courtesy of the Estate of David Wojnarowicz; P•P•O•W, New York. © David Wojnarowicz.

perspective." She opens *The Poetics of Indeterminacy* with a quotation from Roland Barthes, who argued that modern poetry

> stems not from Baudelaire but from Rimbaud [whose poetry] destroyed relationships in language and reduced discourse to words as static things. . . . In it, Nature becomes a fragmented space, made of objects solitary and terrifying because the links between them are only potential.[31]

This indeterminacy, a queer counterpart to a modernist practice of fragmentation, found followers in the New York poets Frank O'Hara, William Carlos Williams, and John Ashbery. Their depictions of urban spaces were, like Rimbaud's literary cities, evoked in *A Season in Hell* and *Illuminations*, and Wojnarowicz's representations of the abandoned Lower West Side waterfront, "dream landscapes at once present and absent, concrete and abstract."[32] Normative linear biography is disrupted in O'Hara's poetry, Perloff argues, as it is "subordinated to a series of hallucinatory visions and memories" and to "absorption in history."[33] Engaging with poets from the past is one way of escaping "the empirical self" of heteronormative narrative and temporality:

> Beneath the lives
> the ardent lover of history hides.[34]

Bob Dylan, Patti Smith, and Jim Morrison were avid readers of Rimbaud's work in the 1960s and 1970s, a connection detailed in Wallace Fowlie's *Rimbaud and Jim Morrison: The Rebel as Poet* (1993), a book inspired by Morrison's letter of thanks to Fowlie for his 1966 English translation of Rimbaud's collected poetry, and Daniel Kane's *Do You Have a Band? Poetry and Punk Rock in New York City* (2017). Smith hung the cover photo of Rimbaud from the New Directions edition of the *Illuminations* above her desk in the apartment she shared with Robert Mapplethorpe in the late 1960s, and in 1973 joined guitarist Lenny Kaye for a concert in celebration of the poet, titled "Rockin' Rimbaud." Her song lyrics feature frequent allusions to the poet's life and work, effecting what Carrie Noland has termed "a *self-legitimating* ritual" of "cultural cross-fertilization" and cross-temporal connection.[35]

Musician and poet Richard Hell, a founding member of the band Television, and later frontman of the early New York punk band the Voidoids, coauthored two translations of "The Drunken Boat" in the 1970s, both concerned less with a rearticulation of the language or content of Rimbaud's poetry than with its enthusiastic desire to "hold many opposed ideas in one's mind at the same time and function fully."[36] The first was written with his Television bandmate Tom Verlaine, with whom Hell also created the fictional poet-prostitute Theresa Stern, a female alter-ego created by overlapping photographs of the two men. As Fowlie wrote of Rimbaud's poem "Memory," in *Rimbaud: The Myth of Childhood*, "in cinematographic procession and juxtaposition all the characters of his life are merged into one—into one eidolon of changing proportions but always of permanent and recognizable traits."[37]

Hell's personal notebooks are filled with references to the writings of the Comte de Lautréamont and Gérard de Nerval, and ideas for "a passionate mimeoed fanzine of (French) Symbolist Poetry," in which "the art of plagiarism" was to be exalted: "Simpering wimps alone use quotation marks."[38] The litany of nineteenth- and early twentieth-century French writers quoted, yet unquoted, in Hell's notebooks works like contemporary montage, which, as Benjamin Buchloh writes in "Allegorical Procedures" (1982) "negates and constitutes itself simultaneously in the act of quotation," as the viewer and reader "encounters a *decentralized* text that completes itself through his or her reading and comparison of the original and subsequent layers of meaning that the text/image has acquired."[39] Hell's "ragged cigar box of fetishistic souvenirs" demands the involvement of the viewer in a collaborative interaction that is, ultimately, an act of what he termed "unrequited narcissism."[40]

Tennessee Williams presents a similarly plagiaristic autobiographical invocation of Rimbaud in his late novel *Moise and the World of Reason* (1975), set in a derelict warehouse by the Greenwich Village waterfront. In its second chapter, the narrator, an aspiring writer, links himself to the poet by way of facial resemblance. "Is this you, baby?" asks his lover of a small photograph: "See, it could be, but it's the poet Rimbaud. . . . I tore it out of . . . a library book about him." The similarities in appearance are extended as the narrator combines phrases from Rimbaud's poetry with his own writing, culminating, as Williams's novel draws to a close, in the inclusion of direct quotations used without citation. A haunting last image, somewhat paraphrased in the lifting from Rimbaud's "The Drunken Boat," is invoked to represent the peculiar experience of living on the Manhattan waterfront. As the narrator "moved east on Eleventh and crossed to Bleecker," walking out to the piers, thinking "of the earth's frozen waters[, he] wanted now only the ditch where a child crouched at dusk to release from his fingers a paper boat, as frail as a May butterfly."[41]

Wojnarowicz's decision to locate his "Rimbaud" in New York, a city the French poet never visited, lay partly in his disappointment with the real late twentieth-century Paris, where he lived intermittently between 1977 and 1979. In a journal entry written shortly before his final departure from France, the gap between his literary expectations and his experience is clear. He recalls arriving in France in "a cloud of old genet novels, cocteauian drawings writings, old photobooks of paris and the whole gloomy waterfront misty wanderings of existentialist [clochards]."[42] Once in Paris, cruising the waterfront along the Seine, he did not find the utopia about which he had fantasized, the literary home of Arthur Rimbaud:

> The bare animal need to experience and react within environments that have contact or construction within the past—the areas that one searches for personal history and understanding—these places are not found in Paris—so far as I've seen. . . . Brassai, Genet, Cocteau. They wrote of the Paris that I subtly carried in my heart. . . . The A.R. [Arthur Rimbaud] vision of side streets and crazed men with the spark of guns beneath their coats.[43]

In his poem "Paris," the American poet Gregory Corso—whom Wojnarowicz described, while traveling to France, as one of his favorite living poets[44]—similarly longs for an imagined Paris:

> Spirits of angels crouched in doorways,
> Poets, worms in hair, beautiful Baudelaire,
> Artaud, Rimbaud, Apollinaire.[45]

Corso laments the state of the contemporary French capital, where the "Seine generates ominous mud, / Eiffel looks down—sees the Apocalyptical ant crawl, / New Yorkless city."[46] Similarly, in a short piece entitled "Paris Please Stay the Same," William Burroughs wrote of the "deep pang of loss" he felt on realizing that the Paris of his youth no longer existed, and mourned its disappearance through paraphrased citations from Rimbaud's early poem "Novel"—"we are aren't serious when we're seventeen"—and William Shakespeare's *Romeo and Juliet*: "well, 'tis gone, 'tis gone."[47] It was, rather, Manhattan that Wojnarowicz's spectral "Rimbaud" would haunt, a place deeply familiar to its author and unknown to its subject. This Rimbaud was a photocopy, queerly anachronistic, ripe for appropriation. Transposing the poet in time had, for Wojnarowicz, made late 1970s Paris, a changed city that appeared to foreclose the "personal history and understanding" he had sought in traveling there, into a place that permitted pleasure and fantasy, slipping "in and out of fictions while movin' through these surroundings, in the midst of lovemaking with some Parisian tough by the dark whirling waters of [the] midnight seine I felt like I was making a man of fiction mine."[48] Displacing him as well in space, to late 1970s New York, made life as a queer man seem possible and emotionally sustainable.

The writer Dennis Cooper dedicated the April 1978 issue of his zine *Little Caesar* to Rimbaud, filling it with "poems for him, about him, comments, live-alikes, a trip to his hometown, etc." It included new writing and new translations of Rimbaud's poetry by Tim Dlugos, Rene Ricard, and Gerard Malanga, Rimbaud comic strip adventures, a Rimbaud-themed crossword, a picture of James Dean with the caption "Rimbaud '55," and one of Johnny Rotten from the Sex Pistols with the caption "Rimbaud '77." The poet Delmore Schwartz, the musician Syd Barrett, and the artist Chris Burden appear elsewhere in the issue as Rimbauds out of time. (None of Cooper's Rimbauds are women, despite Patti Smith's noted fandom.) For Cooper, as his choice of modern-day Rimbauds suggests, the poet was "an ultimate punk": "who needed Jagger, Lou Reed, Hendrix, bla, bla" when you had Rimbaud?[49] While not deployed so explicitly as a queer survival strategy, Cooper's Rimbaud is close to Wojnarowicz's vision of the poet as "peer," embraced for his similarities to one's friends and contemporaries. As Daniel Kane observes, "In Cooper's world, [Rimbaud] was no longer the idealized other about whom one dreamed, for whom one cheered GO RIMBAUD, and idealized."[50]

While Kane argues that Cooper's Rimbaud was "just another suburban 'intellectual teenager' out in the streets, in the clubs, playing in a band," his zine issue's singular focus on Rimbaud and its connections to the development of a broader Rimbaudian-punk culture in New York suggests a degree of veneration beyond celebrating Rimbaud as "just another" downtown punk poet. After all, Cooper wrote, "He'd hate everything my friends and I do now." The floating signifier of Arthur Rimbaud—poet, queer, arms dealer—was both entirely relatable and unique enough to be worthy of respect, of being rescued from the stultifying forces of traditional literary posterity through the act of cross-temporal translation and the cutting and reworking inherent to the practice of zine making. Cooper relates to Rimbaud not as an act of reverence in itself but in order to resist the dull solidification of his poetic practice and his queer legacy in the present, creating space for an earnest and emotional response to his work. This zine was Cooper's "pale tribute" to "the greatest poet I know about, and the most exciting person."[51]

In 1979 Wojnarowicz was visited in Paris by Brian Butterick, a close friend from New York who had participated in the *Arthur Rimbaud in New York* series the year before. Together, they explored Père-Lachaise Cemetery, the final resting place of artists, writers, and musicians such as Frédéric Chopin, Marcel Proust, and Jim Morrison, and a popular destination for American tourists. Wojnarowicz and Butterick performed reenactments of the deaths of the cemetery's spectral residents alongside their tombstones. A photograph, taken by Butterick of Wojnarowicz at the grave of the early twentieth-century French poet Guillaume Apollinaire was included in the published edition of Wojnarowicz's journals (figure 3.4). The unpublished journal features plans for a more extensive series of graveside portraits. They "found ol' guillaume,"

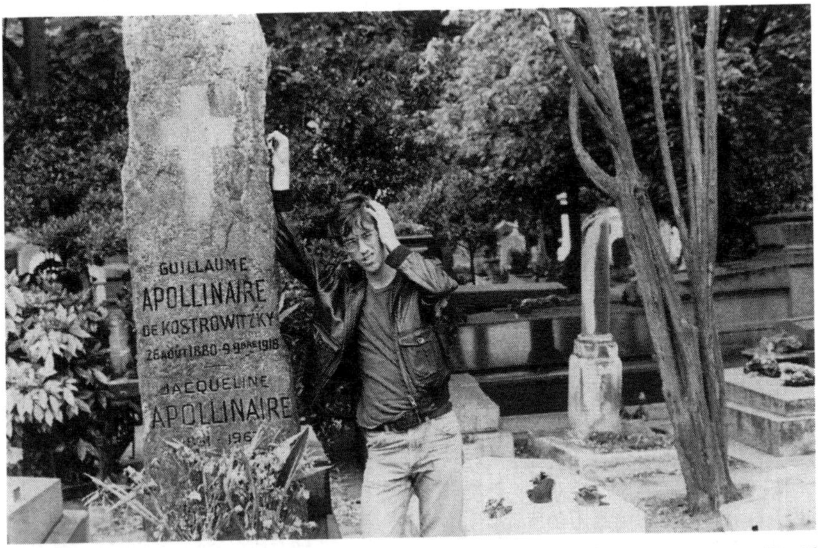


FIGURE 3.4. David Wojnarowicz at Père-Lachaise Cemetery, Paris, 1979. Courtesy of the Estate of David Wojnarowicz; P•P•O•W, New York. © David Wojnarowicz.

and Brian "took a shot of me next to grave holdin' my head, i.e., headwound he died of,"

> then we got an idea for a photo shot series for the *Zone* crime issue entitled: Mimicing the Dead, with inspiration rattlin in our heads we rushed off in search of sarah bernhardt, couldn't find her after much walking and circling among the tombs, finally asked one of the caretakers, semi-elderly with thick glasses and a great rosey face where she might be, he took us on a long winding journey among the tombs and trees and finally brought us upon the grave; brian was gonna pose in an operatic actress manner with his one leg doubled up so as to appear one legged, . . . then on to ol oscar [Wilde] . . . where the grave was a huge crypt with a stone nude man with . . . egyptian angel wings and brian took a shot of me next to it [groping] the ass of the statue, Oscars grave was great, all these nameless characters had etched messages to him like: a tear for you Oscar . . . I be there soon . . . I love you . . . etc. there was a green paper flower stuck into the crypt which I took with me . . . then onto gertrude steins grave where brian rummaged thru the garbage for a loose bunch of [semi-]wilted purple flowers which he laid on her grave, tender gesture . . . then he stuffed his huge leather coat under his shirt for a "fat" effect and posed next to her grave, afterwards we sat and smoked cigarettes and found alice b. toklas name to be etched on the same gravesite and brian put a flower on hers too.[52]

*Zone*, where Wojnarowicz imagined sending the series for publication, was a New York–based zine, but is also the title of a poem by Apollinaire, in which he depicted Paris as a contested space both "absolutely modern," to use Rimbaud's phrase, and haunted, achronologically, by centuries past:

> In the Jewish ghetto the clock runs backwards
> And you go backwards also through a slow life.[53]

The influence of Apollinaire's ahistorical poetics is seen, too, in an unpublished poem by Wojnarowicz, titled "Reading a little Rimbaud in a Second Avenue coffee shop." As Apollinaire wrote in "Zone" of "standing at the metal counter of some dive / Drinking wretched coffee where the wretched live," Wojnarowicz wrote of sitting in a coffee shop where "newspapers draped over the counter tell of the fall of the city."[54]

Wojnarowicz's interest in rearticulated obituaries or alternative memorials, seen in both the imagined photographic series for *Zone* and the *Arthur Rimbaud in New York* series, appears indebted to a French tradition of tombeau poetry, of which the poet Stéphane Mallarmé was a notable proponent. Mallarmé wrote a series of literary homages to writers such as Victor Hugo and the poet Paul Verlaine, Rimbaud's lover, that focused on the material site of the grave, on the tombstone as a tangible marker of bodily absence. In "The Tomb of Edgar Poe," Mallarmé urges the reader to acknowledge the tombstone itself as a marker of the importance of Poe's misinterpreted work: "If our imagination does not carve a bas-relief / With which to adorn the shining tomb of Poe / . . . Let this granite at least forever be a boundary / To the foul flight of straggling Blasphemy in the future."[55] Like Wojnarowicz's *Arthur Rimbaud in New York* series, Mallarmé's tombeaux poems are revivalist works that also shape the reader's interpretation of the "quoted" dead writer.

Mallarmé's poems, in contrast to Wojnarowicz's photographs and waterfront writing, suggest a monumental division between the dead, represented by solid granite tombstones, and the living reader. Marian Sugano's reading of Mallarmé's tombeau poetry, however, suggests a possible parallel between the stone form of the tomb and the ruined nature of the building on the abandoned waterfront. Mallarmé's "framing" of Verlaine and Poe's mortal legacies, Sugano argues,

> perpetrates a certain kind of violence by wrenching the text from its circuit of communication and by placing it in an alien context. The text is preserved, monumentalized, but transfigured in the process.

For Wojnarowicz, the temporal disruption engendered by placing Rimbaud in the "alien context" of the harbor was precisely the intention of the series. "The immobilization involved in building or writing a monument," Sugano concludes, “necessarily contorts the object of one’s attention.” The “deformation” of legacy that Sugano sees in Mallarmé’s tombeaux poems, “does not imbue [the monument] with the qualities we associate with the monumental,” the interpretational framework and mode of teleological historicization that Wojnarowicz sought to disrupt in *Arthur Rimbaud in New York*.[56]

In “Tradition and the Individual Talent” (1917), his essay on authorial lineage, T. S. Eliot argued that “no poet, no artist of any art, has his complete meaning alone. His significance, his appreciation is the appreciation of his relation to the dead poets and writers.” Not only is the writer “inevitably [to] be judged by the standards of the past,” he must also write with an awareness of what Eliot terms “the historical sense,” that is,

> a perception, not only of the pastness of the past, but of its presence; the historical sense compels a man to write not merely with his own generation in his bones, but with a feeling that the whole of literature . . . has a simultaneous existence and composes a simultaneous order.

What Eliot implores the critic to insist upon “is that the poet must develop or procure this consciousness of the past and . . . continue to develop this consciousness throughout his career,” effecting “a continual surrender of himself as he is at the moment to something which is more valuable.” For Eliot, what fundamentally renders a poet traditional is “a sense of the timeless as well as of the temporal and of the timeless together.”[57]

This conjoining of past and present is extended, but its tendency toward binarism undermined, by Roland Barthes as he articulates the literary impact of the “absence of the author.” Time, he argues, “is no longer the same,” and

> The Author, when we believe in him, is always conceived of as the past of his own book: the book and the author take their places of their own accord on the same line, cast as a before and an after: the Author is supposed to feed the book—that is, he pre-exists it, thinks, suffers, lives for it; he maintains with his work the same relations of antecedence a father maintains with his child. Quite the contrary, the modern writer (scripter) is born simultaneously with his text; he is in no way supplied with a being which precedes or transcends his writing, he is in no way the subject of which his book is the predicate; there is no other time than that of the utterance, and every text is eternally written here and now.[58]

In “Burnt Norton,” the first of Eliot’s *Four Quartets*, first published in his *Collected Poems 1909–1935*, the poet opens with a proposition that develops his earlier argument in “Tradition and the Individual Talent” in a manner similar to Barthes:

Time present and time past
Are both perhaps present in time future,
And time future contained in time past.
If all time is eternally present
All time is unredeemable. . . .
What might have been and what has been
Point to one end, which is always present.

Present time is, he wrote, "both a new world / and the old made explicit," a pseudospectral state that is "neither flesh nor fleshless; / Neither from nor towards."[59] As such, it extends the deadly metaphors of "Tradition and the Individual Talent": "you cannot value [the poet] alone; you must set him, for contrast and comparison, among the dead."[60]

Borrowing from Eliot, we might set Wojnarowicz "among the dead" as a means of exploring the nature and extent of his engagement with themes of inheritance, influence, and authorship in his waterfront work through a "hauntological" mode that reflects Wojnarowicz's own spectral symbolism. The figure of the specter provides a useful extension to Barthes's idea of the death of the homogenous author, one that makes this condition of multitemporality, or "multigenerationalism," material.[61] It renders it more literal but highlights, too, its inevitable and necessary indeterminacy and disjunction. For Derrida, the "here and now" that Barthes writes of in "The Death of the Author" "does not fold back into immediacy, or into the reappropriable identity of the present, even less that of self-presence"; its relation to both past and present points out an "irreducible heterogeneity" in the two and in their union.[62] It is this multiplicity that appears in Wojnarowicz's work on and of the abandoned waterfront. A cheap Xerox copy of an appropriated, reworked book cover, his "Rimbaud" could not fit seamlessly into the present or the past. He is a spectral presence in each time-space.

In *The Anxiety of Influence* (1973), Harold Bloom argues for a more aggressive revision of notions of poetic lineage, or "intra-poetic relationships," than Eliot put forward in his literary criticism—one that he terms "poetic misprision," and that employs spectral symbolism in a different manner and to almost contradictory effect. "Weaker talents idealize," Bloom contends, "figures of capable imagination appropriate for themselves."[63] Discussing the poetry of W. B. Yeats and Wallace Stevens, he argues that through appropriation from writers of the past, they "achieve a style that captures and oddly retains priority over their precursors." In so doing, Bloom argues, "the tyranny of time almost is overturned, and once can believe, for startled moments that they are being imitated by their ancestors." In refusing imitation in favor of imaginative recreation, "the mighty dead return but they return in our colors, and speaking in our voices, at least in part, at least in moments, moments that testify to our persistence, and not to their own." They create their own precursors and refigure their meaning and relevance, as "the Kafka of Borges creates the Browning of Borges."[64]

Bloom's notion of *apophrades*—taken from the name for "Athenian dismal or unlucky days upon which the dead returned to inhabit the houses in which they had lived"—was, he argued, "not so much a return of the dead, as a celebration of the early self-exaltation that first made poetry possible," its "central problem" an "anxiety of style," not of the literary representation of lineage or, indeed, the passage and experience of time. Temporality is explored in Bloom's text only insofar as the process of *apophrades* is considered to "hold" a new poem "open to the precursor, where once it was open and . . . the new poem's achievement makes it seem to us, not as though the precursor were writing it, but as though the later poet himself had written the precursor's characteristic work." Past and present have been combined to the point where the later writer's voice disappears, a rejection of Eliot's notion of the simultaneous "historical sense."[65]

Wojnarowicz's *Arthur Rimbaud in New York* series does not engage with Bloom's notion of the role of poetic *apophrades* as that of an "apprenticeship." Instead, Wojnarowicz wrote, in "playing with ideas of compression of 'historical time and activity' and fusing the French poet's identity with modern new york urban activities mostly illegal in nature," Rimbaud returns in both "our colors" and his own.[66] Bloom criticized the work of the French playwright Antonin Artaud for precisely this temporal confusion, for carrying "the anxiety of influence into a region where influence and its counter-movement, misprision, could not be distinguished."[67] Willfully disruptive and antilinear, this was one of Wojnarowicz's aims. In the poem "Reading a little Rimbaud in a Second Avenue coffee shop," for example, Wojnarowicz described the spectral past encountered in the material present as active and perceptibly current:

> going on outside the shop just rushing by in waves of sound & I can't do anything about it it could be nineteen twenty or eighteen sixty or now & it wouldn't make a difference except maybe I wouldn't be reading what I'm reading where I am.[68]

The three times of which Wojnarowicz writes—all "rushing by" simultaneously—have, like Maurice Blanchot's conception of Marx's "voices, three," summarized by Derrida, a "non-contemporaneity with themselves," beyond the "revisionary ratios" of modernist influence Bloom found in the poetry of Yeats and Stevens.[69] Wojnarowicz's poetic time is closer, then, to Eliot's "sense of the timeless," which, he argued, "at the same time . . . makes a writer most acutely conscious of his place in time, of his contemporaneity."[70] The presentness of the current moment is not simply a fragmented, chronological amalgam of various pasts; it is irrevocably disjointed, characterized by "an irreducible heterogeneity, an internal untranslatability."[71] It is comparable to that "disorder" which Roland Barthes considered extant in every photograph, "all practices and all subjects mixed up together," each "a certificate of presence," yet a reminder of the contingent nature of that presentness.[72] Rimbaud's photographic "presence" in Wojnarowicz's series, for example, makes him appear not more historical but less, and intentionally so, rupturing traditional narratives of his life, work, and literary reception. As Rimbaud lamented in *A Season from Hell*, "The world marches on! Why shouldn't it turn back?" "Life is the farce we all play. Enough! Here is the punishment—Forward, march!"[73]

In *Camera Lucida* (1980), Barthes argues that history is "a memory fabricated according to positive formulas, a pure intellectual discourse which abolishes mythic Time," in relation to which, "the Photograph is a certain but fugitive testimony; so that everything, today, prepares our race for this impotence: to be no longer able to conceive duration, affectively or symbolically." "Perhaps," he writes,

> we have an invincible resistance to believing in the past, in History, except in the form of myth. The Photograph, for the first time, puts an end to this resistance: henceforth the past is as certain as the present, what we see on paper is as certain as what we touch.[74]

It is in the photograph that Barthes locates "an anterior future," what he elsewhere terms "the return of the dead." He illustrates this painful anachronistic discovery with a photograph by Alexander Gardner of an imprisoned Lewis Payne, the attempted assassin of the United States secretary of state William H. Seward, prior to his hanging in July 1865:

> I read at the same time: this will be and this has been. . . . By giving me the absolute past of the pose (aorist), the photograph tells me death in the future. What pricks me is the discovery of this equivalence.

"In historical photographs," he argues, "there is always a defeat of Time."[75] To the viewer, Payne is simultaneously a ghost, a trace of a person, a memory, and a resolutely present person, returning the camera's look with a defiant, even desiring, stare. Space is problematized too, in Gardner's photograph and in Barthes's reading of it. Payne was held awaiting execution aboard the USS *Saugus*, a monitor ship stationed, by the end of the Civil War, at the Washington, DC, navy yard. Like Wojnarowicz's "Rimbaud," wandering the man-made piers on the derelict New York waterfront, Alexander Payne was, as he awaited death, neither on land nor at sea.

"Payne" was also a pseudonym, misspelt by authorities upon his arrest. As in Wojnarowicz's *Arthur Rimbaud in New York* series, the multiple masked queer bodies were neither wholly Rimbaud nor themselves: "They have their whole lives before them; but also they are dead (today), they are then already dead (yesterday)."[76] The formation of this "fugitive" subject and its "anterior future," composed through a layering of multiple temporalities, each of equal significance, is similarly defined by Jacques Lacan as an intersubjective process in which the Self calls out to the Other, like the anonymous cruiser, uttering "what was only in view of what will be" in order to be named:

> I identify myself in language, but only by losing myself in it like an object. What is realized in my history is not the past definite of what it was, since it is no more, or the present perfect of what it has been in what I am, but the future anterior of what I shall have been for what I am in the process of becoming.[77]

While J. Hillis Miller, in "The Limits of Pluralism" (1977), describes the modern literary text as inhabited "by a long chain of parasitical presences, echoes, allusions, guests, ghosts of previous texts," for Wojnarowicz, the passage of time and the place of the specter was figured through a series of cyclical and cinematographic metaphors, of cold winds, "circling" cars, endlessly flowing rivers, and multiplying bodies.[78] In an early journal entry, Wojnarowicz constructs a detailed image of an itinerant automobile on the waterfront as he describes the ghostly demeanor of a fellow cruiser who eventually propositions him:

> A car came circling in from the highway, a pale face turning towards me behind the window, the eyes of the driver shielded in shadow, lips frozen for a moment in motion as the car makes a swift curve somewhere further down and swings back to envelop me in light.[79]

These framing metaphors of cyclical movement are conveyed later through allusions to photography and cinematography, as in Wojnarowicz's description of the body of a muscular cruising man at the piers multiplying erotically into thousands of desired, ghostly bodies, "like the bleak lit evolution of a Muybridge series."[80] Cinematic metaphors enabled Wojnarowicz to convey the disjointed experience of cruising the derelict waterfront, where broken windows and rotten doors disrupted any clear line of sight; where, in darkness lit only by flashes of matches or the smoking of a cigarette, ordinary vision, like ordinary time, became impossible to track. As Mary Ann Doane argues in *The Emergence of Cinematic Time*, the development of film reflected a twin "obsession with instantaneity and contingency," where "in the face of the increasing rationalization and systemization of time, the lure of the singular instant is that of the free and undetermined moment," holding out "the promise of newness itself," resistant to meaning yet "also always pitted . . . against the reassurance of a meaningful temporal continuity."[81]

For Wojnarowicz, invoking, in his journals, the temporally complex practices of photography and cinema as analogies for autobiographical strategies, highlights the paradox at the heart of both cinematic representation and traditionally chronological biography: how to convey temporal continuity through a succession of still, "frozen" instants. "The effectiveness of the cinematic representation of time," Doane argues, "rests precisely on its unquantifiability. It was necessary to eliminate the temporal specificity of the image in order to produce the experience of time."[82] Wojnarowicz's ghostly cruising figures are represented as spectral to convey both disjointed physical movement and the cruiser's imaginative rejection of traditional time. The waterfront cruiser, his writing suggests, creates not new kinds of space but new kinds of time, moving within a temporal landscape made up of multiple times appropriated from the imagined personal histories of his anonymous partners, past and future. "Traveling," he writes,

> moving in now or pretty much unexperienced environments keeps away the passage of time; times passage—it keeps one unaware of the passage—age becomes irrelevant . . . the animal excitement of the heart in new faces containing great patches of unknown experiences tales revelations and thus always danger danger danger great life excitements in living and present time movement—no . . . past or present reflected future circumstances—one just moves.[83]

Queer space, Jack Halberstam explains in *A Queer Time and Place*, "refers to the place-making practices within postmodernism in which queer people engage," and describes, too, "the new understandings of space enabled by the production of queer counterpublics."[84] In Wojnarowicz's waterfront writing, the abandoned harbor emerges as a queer time-space through both social opposition, that is, the creation of a counterpublic, and appropriation, Wojnarowicz's imaginative engagement with the waterfront's past of sailors, men living itinerant lifestyles, outside traditional familial time, in an erotic sense. Similarly, the cruising individual's desultory search for anonymous, transient, and often multiplicitous, pleasures effects what Ross Chambers terms in his study of London cruising literature, *Loiterature* (1999), "a deliberate rejection of a certain narrative structure that is itself a structuring of history."[85]

Informal but systemic neglect by civic authorities since the late 1950s had separated the Manhattan waterfront from mainstream urban existence, with its ceaseless drive toward economic production. The collapse of the West Side Highway in 1973, cutting off traffic south of Thirty-Fourth Street, reinforced that exclusion. Municipal ineffectiveness had, then, produced a zone ideally suited not only to appropriation as a queer space, but to the production of queer time, inadvertently creating a public space that was always almost not present, always disappearing and reappearing.

In Thomas Mann's novel *The Magic Mountain* (1922), proximity to water heightens these kinds of temporal concerns. For Mann, a "stroll by the shore" provides the occasion for a lengthy consideration of the narrative representation of time. "Can one narrate time," he asks, "time as such, in and of itself? Most certainly not, what a foolish undertaking that would be. The story would go: 'Time passed, ran on, flowed like a mighty stream,' . . . No one with any common sense could call that a narrative."[86] As Halberstam argues in *In a Queer Time and Place*, "a 'queer' adjustment in the way in which we think about time" gives rise, not only to new kind of times, but to "new conceptions of space," a narrative Mann described as having "two kinds of time" and explains through the image of a "temporal hyper-perspective reminiscent of certain anomalous experiences of reality that imply that the sense have been transcended," like the "diaries of opium-eaters."[87] In *The Magic Mountain*, the "blustering wasteland" of the shore is, like the novel itself, "a confusion and obliteration of temporal and spatial distances," where "you walk and walk, and you never get back home on time, because you are lost to time, and it to you."[88]

This confused sense of pastness, generational time, and history is resolutely anti-teleological. In Lee Edelman's conception, nonlinear time is an "appropriately perverse refusal that characterizes queer theory," and linear history a "narrative in which meaning succeeds in revealing itself—as itself—through time."[89] Indeed, Mann concludes his chapter by noting that in this seaside landscape, "time drowns in the unmeasured monotony of space" and must be interpreted as heterogeneous: "Where uniformity reigns, movement from point to point is no longer movement; and where movement is no longer movement, there is no time."[90] Thus, for Wojnarowicz, the abandoned New York waterfront, a postindustrial landscape at once outside of time and weighted with multiple histories and crowded with memories—simultaneously anonymous and subjectively crowded—represents the ideal space for the ghostly queer figure of "Rimbaud" to cruise.

The waterfront's liminal character and indeterminate "magnetic" allure rendered it a popular symbolic space from which a queer literary tradition, from Herman Melville and Walt Whitman to Tennessee Williams, Andrew Holleran, and Wojnarowicz emerged. For each writer, the waterfront was an erotically appealing setting; each was moved by the harbor's rich past lives, by memories of sailors and stevedores, by the eroticism of what Wojnarowicz called "something silent and recalled," by "the sense of age in a familiar place."[91] It was from this multiplicity, this erotic desire for communication and friendship, that the potential for the multigenerational collaboration that Wojnarowicz so keenly explored during his early career, in both personal journals and early publications such as *The Waterfront Journals*, emerged.[92] John Carlin has argued that Wojnarowicz was "closer in spirit to the great nineteenth-century American writers, Emerson and Whitman, than to many of his contemporaries,"[93] and it is likely Wojnarowicz was reading Whitman at the time he conceived of and executed the *Arthur Rimbaud in New York* series. Shortly before returning to New York from Paris in 1979, Wojnarowicz attached a portrait photograph of an older Whitman to the back page of his journal.[94]

In Whitman's poetry, the New York waterfront, most often on the Brooklyn side, appears as a space that plays host, simultaneously, to an entropic disappearance of solid, chronological time and an expanding archive of its uses and inhabitants in the past, present, and future. In the poem "As I Ebb'd with the Ocean of Life," Whitman writes of walking along "the rim, the sediment that stands for all the water and all the land of the globe," where he becomes aware of a "phantom looking down / where we lead, and following me and mine."[95] Elsewhere, he conceives of the waterfront as an intermediate space between the past and the present, the living and the dead. In "Crossing Brooklyn Ferry," the boat journey across the East River to "mast-hemmed Manhattan," along the route later inhabited by the Brooklyn Bridge, inspires broad cross-temporal thoughts: "I am with you, you men and women of a generation, or / ever so many generations hence."[96] A cruising poetics, centered on the waterfront and punctuated by spectral and shadowy symbolism, can also be found in the poetry of Hart Crane, whose lengthy poem "The Bridge" features cruisy references to waiting among the "shadows by the piers" beneath the Brooklyn Bridge. Later in the poem, Crane calls out to "Walt" for his "hand," just as Wojnarowicz cruised his imagined Mayakovsky and Genet on the Hudson River waterfront.[97] Crane, like Wojnarowicz, found in the anonymity of cruising a model for a poetic practice that fostered an active identification with the dead, playing with the distinctions between presence and absence, visibility and invisibility, and expanding the temporal boundaries of cruising's appropriative action.

This practice recalls Allen Ginsberg's notion of a seminal line of "transmission" between himself and Whitman, a literary sensibility transferred, as he saw it, through oral sex, where "the older person made love to the younger person, blew the younger person, and there was the absorption of the younger person's electric vital magnetism." This succession was, he explained in a 1972 interview, "an ancient thing . . . it's very old and very charming for older and younger to make it." Ginsberg put Whitman, and in particular his poem "We Two Boys Together Clinging," at the head of his own canon of influences, and he was eager to join in this neo-Grecian practice, sleeping with Gavin Arthur who "had slept with Edward Carpenter who had slept with Whitman," thus "[receiving] the Whispered Transmission . . . of that love," which Ginsberg in turn passed to Neal Cassady. This transfer is emphatically not chronological. "The main thing is communication," and, Ginsberg argued,

> both profit from the reciprocal exchange. It becomes more than a sexual relationship; it becomes an exchange of strength, an exchange of gifts, an exchange of accomplishments, an exchange of nature-bounties.[98]

In his essay "In the Shadow of the American Dream: Soon All This Will Be Picturesque Ruins," published in *Close to the Knives*, Wojnarowicz imagined the orgasm in similar terms, as outside of traditional temporal markers, "a hyperventilating break through the barriers of time and space and identity," a moment of both "communication" and obliteration:

> the moment where the soul and the weight of flesh disappears in the fracture of orgasm: the sensation of the soul as a stone skipping across the surface of an abandoned lake, hitting blank spots of consciousness.[99]

This moment outside of time, often, though not always or singularly, the culminating point of a cruising encounter, is ghostly, comparable to Wojnarowicz's reanimation of Rimbaud and others, in the sense that it works to "shake all the ropes off, even the ropes of mortality"; "it is in that sense of void—that marriage of body-machine and space—where one should most desire a continuance of life."[100]

In Wojnarowicz's waterfront writing, cruising itself was figured, like the orgasm, as a method for recording a queer history that, as Butler has argued, "is never fully owned."[101] Neil Bartlett, writing about the research process for his book *Who Was That Man? A Present for Oscar Wilde*, which Mark Turner has described as "a kind of ghost story" about the queer experience of cross-temporal cruising, recalled reading "texts with the dogged energy that I usually reserve for cruising; I became excited by the smallest hints; I scrutinized every gesture for significance; sometime I simply stood close and waited for a response."[102] In Wojnarowicz's writing, more important than the performative act of cruising as literary allegory is the symbolism of cruising on the waterfront, this sense of cruising as historical method. The decaying, abandoned nature of the space, its empty rooms and corridors, paralleled the anonymous sexual encounters that Wojnarowicz enjoyed there, that figured the participants as both screen and void, empty and yet brimming with historical and sexual signifiers, and like the warehouses themselves, both "vacant" and "ghostly."[103]

In *Untitled (David Wojnarowicz Project)*, a series of twelve black-and-white photographs produced between 2001 and 2007, the American artist Emily Roysdon donned a mask of Wojnarowicz and posed, as he had in a Rimbaud mask, in bed, in front of shuttered and graffitoed downtown New York stores, and by a wheat-pasted poster depicting a waterfront scene (figures 3.5, 3.6). Viewing the work as a spirited kind of cross-temporal collaboration, the filmmaker Jean Carlomusto noted in an interview with Roysdon that she "assumes Wojnarowicz's subjectivity in a playful cultivation of everyday life. She has him hanging with the gang, even stitches him into bed."[104] Roysdon's series is in part, like *Arthur Rimbaud in New York*, a form of homage. "David," Roysdon notes, "was one of the first people who allowed me to identify as an artist, and it was his everyday life, method, and commitments

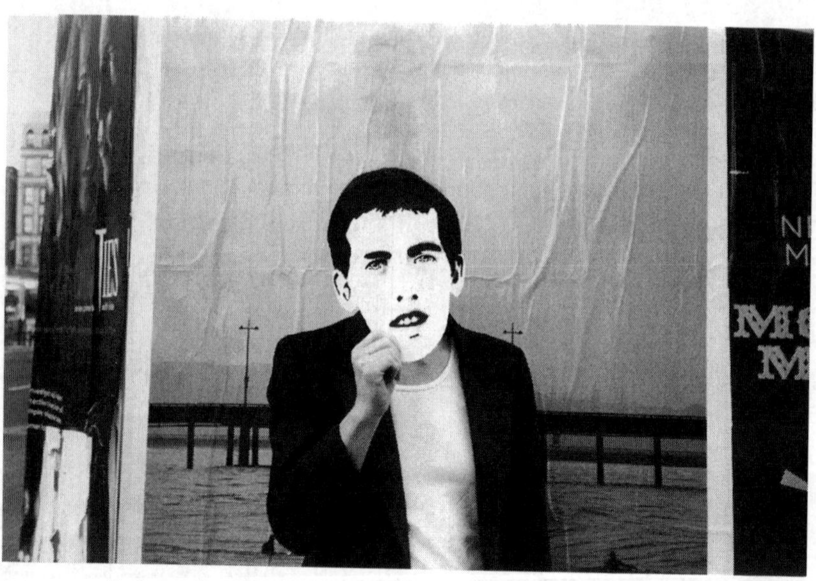

FIGURE 3.5. Emily Roysdon, from *Untitled (David Wojnarowicz project)*, 2001–2007. Courtesy of Emily Roysdon.

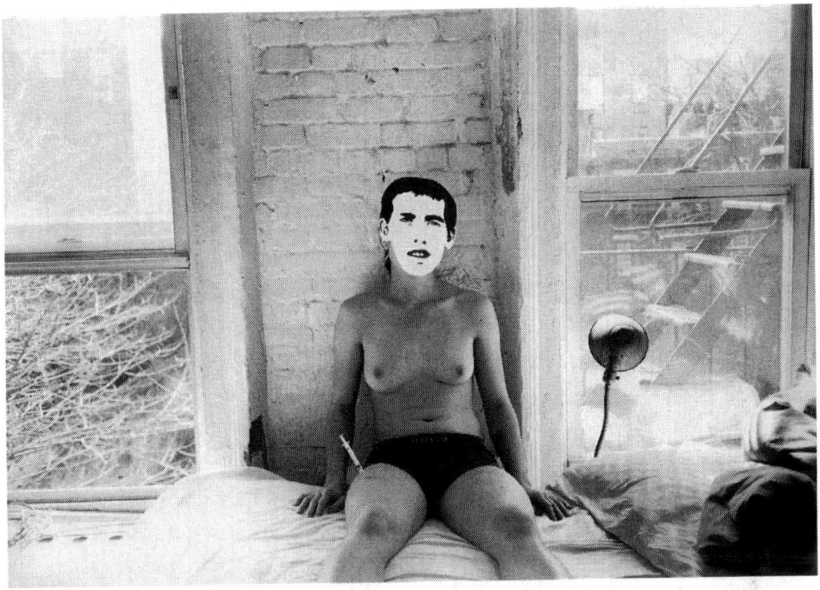

FIGURE 3.6. Emily Roysdon, from *Untitled (David Wojnarowicz project)*, 2001–2007. Courtesy Emily Roysdon.

that spoke to me here. Living life."[105] However, like Wojnarowicz's Rimbaud, Roysdon's Wojnarowicz is a "peer" as well as a queer forbearer.[106] She is a fan and a friend. For Catherine Grant, the figure of the fan—loving, considered, knowledgeable, but distanced from "the object of fascination"—offers a similarly malleable and less teleological way of thinking about influence and creative connection, another "irreverant" mode of thinking about the queer relationship between past and present. Importantly, for Grant, as for Wojnarowicz, reading Rimbaud at the piers and carrying a poster of Rimbaud to Paris, "The figure of the fan . . . combines the reader with the writer, and sees the fan object as a key component in the formation of the fan's own identity."[107]

Roysdon's photographic series, Carlomusto writes, embraces the same temporally complex collaborative spirit as did Wojnarowicz's, in its "desire to re-embody our eccentric and slutty icons, to transport the spirit of our heroes to the present drama of our lives, a drama they somehow inspire anyway." Roysdon frames this cross-temporal connection slightly differently. A "queer relationship to history," she argues, is "in the movement between time and space. . . . Spinning histories wide, looking far and queering all that we can. Mythical as well in the expansive web of our relations and commitments."[108] This is made more complex in Roysdon's series, where, as Grant writes, "a queer female identity is constructed through a masculine gay history," expanding a narrative that is already about "playing with ideas of compression of 'historical time and activity' " to incorporate a play with gender.[109] Roysdon engages with Wojnarowicz directly in the composite time-space of the now; he spends time in her present "not with her but *as* her," Carlomusto writes, traversing boundaries of gender as well as those of time and space.[110]

In an essay written in 2009 as part of the Ecstatic Resistance project, which Royson developed as a model for thinking about future protest practices and activist art making in response to contemporary political challenges for queer people, she writes of the fundamental importance of establishing a nonlinear relationship with the queer past as a model for thinking sustainably about queer existence in the present and future:

> Ecstatic Resistance develops a positionality of the impossible as a viable and creative subjectivity that inverts the vernacular of power. By exposing past impossibilities, the actor of history is thus revealed as the outcast of the contemporary. Ecstatic Resistance works to change this by celebrating the impossible as lived experience and the place from which our best will come. Alongside the vitalization of the impossible life, Ecstatic Resistance asserts the impossible as a model for the political.[111]

Like Wojnarowicz, though she does not invoke him here, Roysdon alludes to sex in her relational model of resistance and impossibility. "The temporality of the ecstatic," she writes, "opens a non-linear experience. . . . It is a personal allowance that once incorporated proliferates the production of alternatives and builds new perspectives from the ruins."[112]

The blackened wooden pilings that line the gentrified West Side waterfront, remnants of the warehouses and piers that collapsed into the Hudson starting in the late 1970s, play a pivotal role in another of Roysdon's works exploring the queer cruising culture of the piers and its legacy. In *West Street*, an artist's book produced in 2010, Roysdon's photographs of the waterfront in the early 2000s share space with Alvin Baltrop's photographs of the same sites in the late 1970s and 1980s: "heavily trafficked cruising areas as well as a diverse array of spaces that were off the legible grid of New York City" before being gentrified and increasingly privatized.[113] The piers, for Roysdon, "are a trace of downtown New York's radical struggles that emerged into an international vanguard of cultural and sexual politics."[114]

Short pieces of text appear across some of Roysdon's images of the piers, ideas "for a public art project that seeks to materialize language in a way that challenges the vernacular of city living." These superimposed phrases—"talk is territorial"—place the space of the harbor and its multiple pasts in dialogue with Roysdon in the present. The "pile fields," as she terms them, "are stunning reminders of a city past. As compared to the monumentality of the [Queensboro] bridge," which also appears in the book and in the public art project she proposes, "the scale here has been anthropomorphized, and thus demands that we acknowledge the physical history of this place, its decay, and the topography of desire that is New York City." Roysdon "asks people to focus on the ethics of communication, the ways in which we move about this city and the speeches we employ. Talk is territorial and speaking is a dance."[115] The nonfunctionality of the pilings, which stand suggestively in the water, no longer supporting a pier or warehouse, and their decaying material status, permit this kind of projection and thus problematize the discourse of "proper use" that Roysdon challenges with this work.[116]

The sense of a space lost or ruined that these suggestive absences project also renders them and the water around them an ideal node from which to commune with Baltrop across time. In an interview in 2011, Roysdon told Carlos Motta that connecting in this direct way with Baltrop's photographic archive was a means of "engaging the way everybody imagines the piers and everything that actually happened down there," of rejecting narratives of the piers that present them as occupied largely by "white men with their pants around their ankles." Wojnarowicz's *Arthur Rimbaud in New York* series and "his welcoming articulation" of the queer space of the piers and its diversity was, she says, a crucial stimulus for the development of the *West Street* project. Roysdon's work, both photographic and textual, reiterates the diversity documented clearly in Baltrop's work but neglected in the present, just as Wojnarowicz sought to reignite Rimbaud's queer poetics in the late 1970s. While the pilings stand, in her photographs, like shadowy figures cruising the now-departed piers, they also act as ghostly sentinels preserving the memory, and underscoring the diversity, of those queer uses. The book's title reinforces that sense of boundary-crossing and exchange:

> West Street is the street you had to cross to get to the piers. I am interested in this choice to cross the street and that sort of boundary, which takes different shapes, and in many ways is not there, except we queers know it is there, and we step over it and we go to a space to find many different things.

Like Wojnarowicz, Roysdon has "one foot in the queer and feminist archives," among old poems, photographs, manifestos, and journals, "and another in [her] lived experience of collectivity," which is understood in both *Untitled (David Wojnarowicz Project)* and *West Street* as material and imaginative.[117] Like Wojnarowicz, Roysdon finds political and personal potential in the characteristic playfulness of the appropriative cruising encounter. Across time, in the archive and in the street, Roysdon generates an active identification with the dead outside traditional genealogy in order to sustain her own queer life in the present and preserve both the possibility for that existence and the potential for cross-generational, cross-temporal queer exchange, inverting heteronormative teleological and linear power dynamics and literal and material gentrification through the queer methodology of ecstatic resistance and the queer space of the piers.

## The Wild Boys on the Waterfront

One of the most profound influences on Wojnarowicz's achronological, collective literary practice was that of the writer William S. Burroughs. While his fascination with Arthur Rimbaud is well documented, the full impact of his long-standing fixation with Burroughs emerges only after a thorough engagement with unpublished archival material. Wojnarowicz planned a film version of Burroughs's novel *The Wild Boys: A Book of the Dead* (1971), a tentative script for which can be found in Wojnarowicz's archive, and an autobiographical novel of his own (large portions of which later appeared in *Close to the Knives*), to be constructed "using ABC method of cut-ups."[118] Wojnarowicz's friend Marguerite van Cook notes that he had written fan mail to Burroughs "since he was a kid," and in 1982 Burroughs provided a short blurb for Wojnarowicz's chapbook *Sounds in the Distance*, an early version of *The Waterfront Journals*, published by the London-based press Aloe Books.[119]

In 1979, just before leaving Paris, Wojnarowicz created a collaged homage, *Bill Burroughs Recurring Dream*, which positioned the writer among a writhing centipede and the dystopian motifs of his writing; proliferating filmic heads, pyramids, and Mayan stone carvings. In an unpublished early manuscript of *The Wild Boys*, Burroughs had written of repressive government agents learning "a simplified picture language derived from the Mayan and Egyptian systems."[120] The dream process suggested by the collage's title was a central motif in the work of both Wojnarowicz and Burroughs. In constructing his imagined cut-up novel, Wojnarowicz planned to "retrieve dreams from notebooks; place approximately within novel structure."[121] In an interview in *The Third Mind*, a collaborative extended exposition of the cut-up, Burroughs emphasizes the significance of dreams in the cut-up process:

> I don't know where fiction ordinarily directs itself but I am quite deliberately addressing myself to the whole area of what we call dreams. Precisely what is a dream? A certain juxtaposition of word and image. . . . In other words, I've been interested in precisely how word and image get around on very, very

> complex association lines . . . ; all of this to see how completely I can project myself back to . . . one point in time.[122]

Elsewhere in *The Third Mind*, Brion Gysin presents "23 stitches," paragraphs explaining the development and uses of the cut-up. The book's history, like that of the cut-up itself, Gysin argues, is "not the history of a literary collaboration but rather the complete fusion in a praxis of two subjectivities," and thereby almost spectral: "it is from this collusion that a new author emerges, an absent third person, invisible and beyond grasp, decoding the silence." In these first cut-up experiments, he writes, "phrases were broken apart, mixed, and combined; the business of disarranging and redistributing the meaning of the message was left to chance. All possibilities of this message were explored." The cut-up was not opposed to narrative form but rejected its insistence on chronology and its teleological demands. "Any narrative passage or any passage," Burroughs asserts, "is subject to any number of variations, all of which may be interesting or valid in their own right."[123]

Gysin is more concerned with maintaining a sense of "the narrative turn" but displays a similar interest in what might be termed its queerness: "Every form of writing will consist of an operation of decoding, of contamination, and of sense perversion. All this because all language is essentially mystification, and everything is fiction."[124] In *The Soft Machine* (1961), the first novel in the cut-up series known as the *Nova Trilogy*, Burroughs describes the cut-up as permitting movement across time and space, dissolving temporal and geographic boundaries:

> Now when I fold today's paper in with yesterday's paper and arrange the pictures to form a time section montage, I am literally moving back to the time when I read yesterday's paper, that is traveling back in time to yesterday—I did this eight hours a day for three months—I went as far as the papers went—I dug out old magazines and forgotten novels and letters—I made fold-ins and composites and I did the same with photos.[125]

This model presented Wojnarowicz with a nonchronological mode through which to explore the contingencies and literary potential of cinematic and queer time. By employing Burroughs and Gysin's techniques, he wrote, "you can achieve semi-surreal beautiful lines but with a method of selection and construction that places those lines in original text without giving the dry cut-up sense."[126]

In *The Wild Boys*, Burroughs depicts a group of violent teenage boys living in homoerotic communes that exist not only outside of convention and the law but outside of time, in a North African desert landscape, "scattered over a wide area from the outskirts of Tangier to the Blue Desert of Silence." They are

> glider boys with bows and laser guns, roller skate boys—blue jockstraps and steel helmets, eighteen-inch bowie knives—naked blowgun boys long hair down their backs a kris at the thigh, slingshot boys, knife throwers, bowmen, bare-hand fighters, shaman boys who ride the wind . . . dream boys who see each other's dreams and the silent boys of the Blue Desert.

The projected image of a smiling Wild Boy spreads the dreamlike desire to join this queer tribe. The narrative moves across time periods and through spectral locations, characterized by relentlessly fragmented architecture, "shattered cities" pieced together from visions of other visits and sights, a kind of cinematic time.[127] "April 3, 1989" in Marrakech, for example,

> looks like an 1890 print from some explorer's travel book. . . . Waves of decoration and architecture have left a series of strata-like exposed geological formations. There isn't a place in the world you can't find a piece of it in Marrakech, . . . a vast film set where the props are continually shifting.

Across these spaces, the Wild Boys, like the trilogy's Nova Mob, are hounded by ruthless government agents, "brave" Americans and their allies seeking victory "over little boys armed with slingshots and scout knives." The boys appear to use temporal fragmentation and filmic collage as a torture device. The descriptions of this paranoid CIA-funded army recall World War II spy films: guards "appear in shots from 1920 gangster films, black Cadillacs careening down city streets," and an agent speaks of having "the uneasy feeling of being in someone else's film set." Burroughs's frequent use of parataxis, a literary device also seen in Wojnarowicz's own writing, adds to this sense of fragmentation and temporal confusion. Quoted speech is interspersed with descriptions of architecture, foreign landscapes, and sexual fantasies. As the Wild Boys close in on the approaching army, the omnipotent screen explodes "in moon craters and boiling silver spots." In this final battle, the boys use their most powerful weapon: "dim jerky stars are blowing away across a gleaming empty sky, the wild boys smile."[128]

Wojnarowicz's script seeks to retain the fragmented mode of the novel and its focus on the deadly mnemonic potential and nonlinear potential of film as a medium. At the beginning of the script he notes that his film is to be set in New York and specifies sites for filming: "from a certain point near bank street," on "bridge structures near jay street." There is to be a dream sequence using the Rimbaud mask at Coney Island, and another among warehouses and "sand dunes along river near canal street." These location shots were to be interspersed with dream visions shot through subway grates and warehouse glory holes. According to one such direction, "Looking through a hole in a wall can permit any view whether of china Africa bronx zoo alligators inferno or interior of any other room." The piers and waterfront warehouses were to be the Wild Boys' "contact point" and would host numerous orgies. In Wojnarowicz's script, the riverside location adds a dystopian urgency to the disturbed form and content of Burroughs's text. Wojnarowicz planned to film the Hudson River before a storm, with "heavy footage of turbulent skies" intimating "the fall of governments." "Phoney news headline[s]" would be "printed up to litter floor with," leading to "shots of wildboys reading communications leaflets." "Use 3 leaflets or portions of those you made," Wojnarowicz wrote, "and send to Burroughs," like the fan letters he had sent to the writer in the early 1970s. One suggestion for the film's final scene focuses on the warehouse "contact point" and its impending demolition: "on floor of pier about to be torn up for fire (shot of it close up—date: 2012—CUT—SHOT OF IT BURNING)."[129] Wojnarowicz's film is an homage but one that pays heed to Gysin's proposition that the cut-up heralds "a negation of the omnipresent and all-powerful author," placing the characters of Burroughs's creation in a landscape specific to Wojnarowicz's psychosexual experience.[130]

Setting the Wild Boys film in this real site, the abandoned New York waterfront, did not calcify the cut-up movement of Burroughs's narrative, which flits between Tangier, Kansas, and Mexico City, but rather mirrored its fragmented character. Wojnarowicz's script directions mention techniques such as splicing and the use of an "accelerated camera sequence," manipulated alongside "twitches manic voiceless screams."[131] Moreover, the warehouse locations recall elements of *The Ticket That Exploded*, the second book in the *Nova Trilogy*, in which anonymous sex in abandoned urban spaces is explored spectrally and more explicitly. In a section entitled "Winds of Time," Burroughs writes of "ghost rectums, spectral masturbating afternoons reflected in the tarnished mirror," in a room situated

> on the roof of a ruined warehouse swept by winds of time through the open window trailing grey veils of curtain sounds and ectoplasmic flakes of old newspapers and newsreels swirling over the smooth concrete floor and under the bare iron frame of the dusty bed—the mattress twisted and molded by absent tenants—[132]

Placing the Wild Boys in the interstitial space of the derelict harbor could, Wojnarowicz suggests, enhance the cut-up quality of the film's structure. As he writes elsewhere in the script, he sought to manufacture "a composite city/mythic city out of manipulation of camera film sequence," echoing Burroughs's assertion that "cut-ups establish new connections between images" and reflecting the feeling of living in New York, which is, he observes, "like living in a series of boxes."[133] In *The Third Mind*, Burroughs and Gysin urge writers to "start thinking in images, without words," suggesting the cut-up's proximity to cinematographic practice. Indeed, Gysin suggests that the cut-up is "the negation of the book as such—or at least the representation of that negation."[134]

In both Burroughs's novel and Wojnarowicz's script, the character of Audrey Carsons, born in Burroughs's hometown of St Louis, serves as a stand-in for the writer, an autobiographical proxy depicted as painfully spectral. "Audrey was a thin pale boy his face scarred by festering spiritual wounds," Burroughs writes. "There was something rotten and unclean about Audrey, an odor of the walking dead."[135] Audrey's spectral identity is explored in one of the novel's "Penny Arcade Peep Show" segments, interludes that function as unifying points in the text, giving background and self-referentially pointing to the filmic structure of the narrative, like the "Camera Eye" portions of John Dos Passos's novel *U.S.A.* (1937).[136] Audrey appears to have been captured by the Wild Boys, who bring him to the peep show, seating him in front of four screens upon which various scenes of an "enigmatic structure" play out, all "at once immediate and spectrally remote in past time."[137]

This sensation of simultaneous presents is echoed in Wojnarowicz's declaration in "Losing the Form in Darkness" that while cruising in downtown Manhattan, he was reminded of his time living as a teenaged hustler in the same spaces: "Old images race back and forth. . . . The streets were familiar more because of the faraway past than the recent past."[138] At the Wild Boys' peep show, Audrey finds himself participating in the images presented on the screens, by way of "narrative sections in which the screens disappear," lending further credence to the character's identification with both Wojnarowicz and Burroughs:

> I experience a series of quite understandable and coherent events as one of the actors. The narrative sequences are preceded by the title on the screen then I am in the film. The transition is painless like stepping into a dream. The structuralized peep show may intersperse the narrative and then I am back in front of the screen and moving in and out of it.[139]

Audrey provides a list of four points that outline the content of the screens, which functions as a guide to the reader through this cut-up, alternate dimension. Movement "in and out of the screen," he observes, elicits "electric sex tingles" and "fragmentary glimpses" of people and spaces are "linked by immediate visual impact," creating "a sensation of speed" as he moves through time.[140]

In one such scene, Audrey is transported through a steel chair to a doctor's surgery, familiar to him from his youth: "Smell of old pain, ether, bandages, sick fear in the waiting room, yes this is Doctor Moor's Surgery in the Lister Building," a physician's office in the West End of St Louis:

> The doctor was a Southern gentleman of the old school. Rather like John Barrymore in appearance and manner he fancied himself as a witty raconteur

> which at times he was. The doctor had charm which Audrey so sadly lacked. No doorman would ever stop him no shopkeeper forget his thank you under eyes that could suddenly go cold as ice. It was impossible for the doctor to like Audrey. "He looks like a homosexual sheep-killing dog" he thought but he did not say this. He looked up from his paper in his dim gloomy drawing room and pontificated "the child is not wholesome."
>
> His wife went further: "It is a walking corpse," she said. Audrey was inclined to agree with her but he didn't know whose corpse he was. And he was painfully aware of being unwholesome.[141]

In Wojnarowicz's script, the scene based on this disturbing, anecdotal memory was to take place inside a waterfront warehouse, further emphasizing the autobiographical significance of both the novel and its filming, and the interstitial qualities of Burroughs's narrative. Eluding wholeness and "never fully owned, but always redeployed, twisted, queered from a prior usage," Audrey is the archetypal queer body, and in Wojnarowicz's film, he functions as a symbolic parallel to the decaying "body" of the waterfront warehouses.[142]

In his own writing, Wojnarowicz used the ideology of the cut-up as an imaginative catalyst, rather than pursuing its syntactic radicalism to total fragmentation or potentially endless rearrangement. As in the *Arthur Rimbaud in New York* series and his phantasmic waterfront cruising of Genet and Mayakovsky in his journals, he continually related the cut-up method to the construction of interpersonal subjectivities through an erotic collage of queer intellectual patrons. The cut-up was one participatory mode in Wojnarowicz's broader spectral practice, but its most autobiographical component. Through the temporal dislocation of Burroughs's cut-up mode and the spectral fraternity of Whitman's riverside ghost, Wojnarowicz himself could be both ghost and flesh, cruising the past and the present in a manner that would accommodate literary homage without compromising his own innovations or sexual experiences, rendering him and his anonymous "toughs" also "unwholesome," multitemporal bodies, ghosts in the queer spaces of this "dead river," and "peers" in this liminal time and place.

# 4
# Protest and Preservation on the Waterfront

In a speech marking the fortieth anniversary of the New York City Planning Commission in January 1979, recently elected mayor Ed Koch remarked, "If there is one thing that I want my administration to be identified with, it is that we brought the harbor back to the city of New York, that we built on our greatest treasure, that we opened the waters to the people of the city."[1] Koch's plans were buoyed by emergent signs of economic recovery; by the end of the 1970s, New York's fiscal condition had rallied, its financial markets were improving, and waterfront redevelopment projects were under way at Battery Park City and the World Financial District. With New York no longer economically dependent on its port, as it had been through the nineteenth and early twentieth centuries, municipal focus moved toward developing its 578 miles of waterfront for commercial investment and public recreation.

As noted in the introduction, in a 1980 study on waterfront development, deputy mayor Robert F. Wagner Jr. wrote euphemistically (in municipal terms, at least) that throughout the 1970s "the least desirable activities were assigned to the waterfront."[2] His and Koch's pronouncements reflected a broader push for waterfront redevelopment across the United States in the late 1970s, seen also in cities including San Francisco, Boston, and Jacksonville. Their comments were symptomatic, too, of a shift in public attitudes toward New York's maritime history, epitomized by the popular tall-ship tours and riverfront festivals held in celebration of the national bicentennial in 1976. In his study, Wagner asserted that New York's vast waterfront "must be viewed as a mosaic, made up of a variety of elements, each of which exists by its own character and strengths and yet are united by their strong ties to the heart of the City."[3] At the same time, he supported the multibillion-dollar Westway project, first proposed in 1974, which would have seen four and a half miles of abandoned piers on the Lower West Side, along with the ruined Miller Highway, destroyed and replaced by 182 acres of landfill, 50 of which were to be zoned for commercial or industrial use. The Westway proposal met with extensive public opposition and struggled with mounting costs and court actions. Campaigners criticized the proposed development on environmental grounds, for preservationist reasons, and because it prioritized highways over local mass transit services.[4] By the time of the bicentennial tall-ships parade in July 1976, the plans were so unpopular that Koch made scrapping Westway a prominent feature of his mayoral campaign, arguing that the federal funds funding it were being misappropriated to provide opportunities for private developers. Once in office, Koch backed down on this early promise, but popular opposition to Westway continued. The project was abandoned in 1985 after a court ruling determined that building a highway over the remaining wharves and ridding the Hudson of its rotting pier footings would destroy an important breeding ground for the striped bass.[5]

Waterfront planning and development in New York in this period was, according to Wagner's report, "hampered by a maze of overlapping and competing government jurisdictions that blur[red] lines of responsibility and accountability and unduly lengthen[ed] project approval processes." Five interstate agencies, four regional authorities, sixteen city agencies, three commissions, two locally elected bodies, fifteen community boards, and five borough boards claimed "some jurisdiction over waterfront development," and were responsible for the issuing of over seventy-four different permits for various uses of the largely postindustrial harbor.[6] Like many previous mayoral administrations, Koch's had sought to determine a homogeneous public function for the waterfront in this midst of this paralyzing bureaucratic mosaic. But the size of the port, the diverse range of municipal and commercial interests with stakes in its redevelopment, and its place in the collective imagination of the city's public made large-scale regeneration difficult to achieve. As Raymond Gastil has noted, although the failure of the Westway project gave a boost to community organizers and local activists, it "delayed the transformation of the waterfront for another fifteen years." Indeed, the most significant piece of waterfront redevelopment on the Lower West Side in the 1980s was the demolition of the Miller Highway in 1989, sixteen years after it had collapsed between Little West Twelfth and Gansevoort Streets under the weight of a dump truck carrying asphalt to be used in its ongoing repairs. But Gastil's assertion that the removal of the Miller Highway left the city "ready to engage with its waterfront again" after decades of exclusion overlooks the fact that gay men had been walking under the collapsed highway on their way to cruise at the piers for years.[7] As Douglas Crimp notes in an article on Alvin

Baltrop's pier photographs, although the highway came to represent a psychic boundary as much as a physical one, "a ghostly barrier between 'civilized' Manhattan and the Hudson River," it did not prevent queer appropriations of the undeveloped waterfront; it encouraged them.[8]

As in this book's earlier chapters, I am interested here in what is cast in relief at the city's edge. Homophobic municipal and federal legislation in the 1970s and early 1980s coincided with the rapid escalation of the gentrification of downtown Manhattan. Redevelopment, as Neil Smith has argued, was framed as positive transformation through a "language of revitalization, recycling, upgrading and renaissance [which] suggests that affected neighborhoods were somehow devitalized or culturally moribund prior to gentrification."[9] "Suffering from years of neglect and divided authority," Manhattan borough president Percy Sutton had lamented in 1966, that the city's waterfront "has too long been regarded as marginal land, a dumping ground for industries, highways, rotting piers, and raw sewage."[10] Here I consider the preservationist efforts of queer writers, artists, and filmmakers in the face of mainstream narratives that tend not only to resist the renewal of existing buildings and landmarks, but to erase minority histories. Cruising, as an illicit appropriation of the city's derelict spaces, was itself a means of preserving them as noncommercial, as spaces for political organizing among gay men and lesbians, and as a home for displaced and at-risk trans people.

Waterfront development on the West Side was rife with bureaucratic complications and underhand tactics. In 1972 the Battery Park City Authority (BPCA) issued a number of "moral obligation" bonds to finance the demolition of several piers and the construction of office buildings on newly created harbor landfill without the usual referendum, on the condition that a proportion of the space be set aside for low-income housing. Despite the fast-track maneuver, the developments were not completed until 1976, by which time the city was on the brink of bankruptcy and "the office market glutted with space."[11] The New York State Urban Development Corporation condemned the site and bought it from the BPCA for a dollar. The BPCA's commitment to low-income housing was scrapped, and architects Alexander Cooper and Stanton Eckstut were commissioned to transform the landfill into a commercially appealing office complex. Their plan, Susan Fainstein notes, claimed to "draw on familiar New York neighborhood images and (assemble) them in a street and block pattern which extend (as view corridors) the Lower Manhattan streets to the waterfront." Yet the finished development was little more than "a recreation zone for the relatively well-to-do," lacking "the spontaneous contrasts of the real twentieth-century metropolis" and appealing to an imagined city public, rather than those citizens who already lived and worked in downtown Manhattan.[12]

The push for commercial and municipal redevelopment of the waterfront—which, with tensions between private and municipal ownership, and public and private use, remained unfunded and unfinished into the mid-1980s—must be read as part of the gentrification being implemented across New York City in the period. This process was a consequence not only of national "Reaganomics" but of decades of poorly managed industrial decline. As Rosalyn Deutsche and Cara Gendel Ryan have argued, urban neglect in New York in the 1970s was largely not a matter of negligence but a considered political strategy, "abandoning buildings, harassing and evicting tenants, and rapidly turning over neighborhood property in order to escalate real-estate values." By 1984, for example, the city had acquired 60 percent of property on the Lower East Side by way of tax defaults and abandonment by incompetent or insolvent landlords. "Contiguous lots" of derelict or neglected housing were "put together to form what is known in the real estate business as 'assemblages' . . . sold for large sums of money at municipal auctions to developers who thus amass entire blocks for the construction of large-scale upper-income housing."[13] Careful management, that is to say perpetuation, of abandoned spaces and empty buildings was key to these municipal strategies of intentional neglect and exclusionary public access and citizenship. One "general public" was being evicted to accommodate another.

Writing in the *New York Times* in 1979, almost contemporaneous with Koch's pledge to "[open] the waters to the people of the city," architecture critic Ada Louise Huxtable bade a bittersweet farewell to the "shabby" East Side harbor, as she criticized the young developer Donald Trump's emergent plans for a commercial restructuring of the still-abandoned riverfront:

> I guess what I am really doing is saying good-bye. Because what will surely be lost is the spirit and identity of the area as it has existed over centuries—something that may only be important to those of us who have loved the small, shabby streets and buildings redolent of time and fish, or shared the cold sunlight of a quiet Sunday morning on the waterfront with the Fulton market cats, when the nineteenth century seemed very much alive.[14]

Huxtable's nostalgic writing acted as a public mourning ritual. Her recollection of "buildings redolent of time" and her sense of personal loss in the face of the material redevelopment of the waterfront reveals the difficulty of reconciling past with present. Sensory memories and descriptions of affective attachments to the harbor imbue Huxtable's valediction with a bodily urgency. While Henri Lefebvre argues that for progressive urban politics to be successful, "the most important thing is to multiply readings of the city," Huxtable's farewell to "the spirit and identity of the area" speaks to municipal and commercial tendencies toward homogenization in renewal and redevelopments efforts as the city recovered from financial crisis in the later 1970s.[15]

Beyond the administrative complexities that shaped waterfront renewal programs, proposals for commercial and municipal waterfront redevelopment in New York in the 1960s, 1970s, and 1980s were dependent on a false narrative of the trajectory of the waterfront's abandonment and a homogeneous, sociopolitically exclusive conception of the identity of the general public—"the people of the city"—whose access to the harbor Koch touted. In 1930 the City's Regional Planning Association had noted in a press release that "it is not within the power of any one body to carry into effect a plan for any proportion of the waterfront of Manhattan."[16] By the mid-1970s, however, the push for a homogenous function, typified by Koch and Wagner's approach, had severely limited public access to the space. Central to these proposals was the production and maintenance of homogeneous narratives asserting that the warehouses and piers along the waterfront were entirely empty, that the public had no access and no use for them, and that a plan for appropriate civic and commercial reuse was required. As Sarah Schulman argues in *The Gentrification of the Mind* (2012), "Gentrification literally replaces mix with homogeneity, it enforces itself through the repression of diverse expression." "Endless crackdowns on cruising and 'public' sex," she writes, are vital components of the gentrification process. Cities are recast as "centers of obedience instead of instigators of positive change," shaped by what she calls "suburban values."[17]

The complex activist politics of the queer cruising and bar scene in and around the waterfront—for example, the appearance of political graffiti at the piers, the establishment of bar owners' organizations to protect managers and customers from continual police raids, and the close connections between activist groups, bars, and sex clubs—have often been obfuscated by a critical tendency to historicize the late 1970s in terms of vague allusions to the Whitmanian democracy of the dark room and the bathhouse, explored in chapter 1, and by singular narratives of the waterfront's abandonment that aimed to bring about regeneration quickly and smoothly.[18] "Key to the gentrification mentality," Schulman argues, "is the replacement of complex realities with simplistic ones."[19] The obscuring of this rich history of the queer waterfront is not only an effect of the contemporaneous process of gentrification; it was one of the means through which that gentrification was effected in the first place. This chapter draws on archival paraphernalia, films, and photographs to trace a political and preservationist history of the piers and of the neighboring queer bar scene that has slipped from view or never been publicly historicized. To Kenneth Jackson, "historic preservation was a preoccupation of social factions that were losing out in the contest to control New York's future."[20] This sense of loss points to a long-standing and deep-rooted view of New York as a city that progresses by destroying what came before, that continually rewrites the story of its own heritage and progress, a practice that gathered pace in the late 1970s with real estate developments, and concomitant tax breaks, designed to attract white-collar labor back to the city it had fled in the 1960s. This city, Gregg Bordowitz has suggested, "is about as archival as a trade paperback whose spine is meant to be broken by mass transit consumption."[21] By focusing on what archival traces remain and on visual records of queer appropriations of the city's piers, I examine the civic battleground of the city's historic waterfront from the perspective of those who were "losing out," exploring the "complex realities" of activism, preservationism, and protest that have been obscured by the gentrification of both the waterfront and its queer history.

## Cruising and preservation

Recording the queer life of the piers appears as an earlier form of Wojnarowicz's later activist aim to "make the *private* into something *public*," an "action that has terrific repercussions" in what he called "the pre-invented world." "Sexuality defined in images," he wrote in the essay "Postcards from America: X-Rays from Hell," "gives me comfort in a hostile world. They give me strength." For Wojnarowicz, this desire to share "diverse representations of 'Reality' on a gallery wall or in a book or a movie" was imbued with a powerful urgency in the midst of the AIDS crisis.[22] This exposure is about preservation as well as publicity. A comparable queer preservationist ethics suffuses Arch Brown's pornographic film *Pier Groups* (1979), in which he documents both queer waterfront culture and the imminent redevelopment of the West Side harbor. Filmed in 1979, the year Koch vowed to restore the city's waterfront "treasure" to the people, *Pier Groups* reflects on the neglect of the piers and emphasizes the urgency of chronicling their queer reuse in the face of emergent gentrification. The film follows a day in the life of Joe, a straight construction worker played by Johnny Kovacs, and his neighbor Rik, played by Keith Anthoni.[23] While Rik wakes up to sex with his lover, Joe, lying quietly in bed with his wife, receives a call from his manager, who informs him of a change of plans. "The city," he says, "is taking bids on the demolition of those rotten piers on the Hudson," the four piers "between 10th and West 12th Street." Their boss, Buzz, "thought that since you lived not far from the piers that you might go over there today . . . and work up a report. . . . They're burned down and rotten, though, so be careful." "Will I see somebody?" Joe asks. "No," his manager replies. "They're abandoned, . . . no-one uses them."

As Joe prepares for his working day at the piers, Rik receives a call informing him that his job for the day has been canceled, leaving him with an unexpected day off. He decides to spend it at "the warehouses" since he "hasn't been there in months." Rik and Joe leave their apartment building at the same time, both dressed in plaid shirts and work boots, neither realizing that the other is also wandering toward the waterfront. The film follows Joe as he inspects the warehouses at Tenth Street, measuring the widths of walls and doorways and scrutinizing the material condition of their corridors, ceilings, and floorboards. As he does so, he encounters men who, unbeknownst to Joe, cruise him as he leans, suggestively it seems, over hard-to-reach portions of the buildings. He soon stumbles across groups of men inside the warehouses themselves, blowing each other in stairwells or fucking inside empty cupboards. Brown underscores the fact that every inch of space in this dilapidated structure is being used for queer erotic ends. He emphasizes the contrast between the bright daylight outside and the permissive darkness inside. The wild dereliction of the piers and warehouses is evident in every frame, as Joe steps over fallen beams and walks through collapsed doors and windows.

The longer Joe spends in the warehouse, the longer he lingers watching these cruising men. We see him peering through a small gap in a steel wall, watching his neighbor Rik with another man. We see him in a darker interior space in the warehouse, framed by a sliver of light, watching while languidly smoking a cigarette. A disembodied voice asks who the guy in the helmet is: "He's hot," another responds. "He looks straight." As Joe moves further inside the building, he overhears snippets of cruising talk. Men direct other men toward pleasurable portions of the warehouse, invite others to rooms catering to particular erotic interests. The film's climax shows Joe watching, from above, an orgy in a large, vaulted space inside one of the warehouses, in which Rik is strung up by his wrists from a beam in the ceiling, surrounded by three, then four, other men. Joe and Rik acknowledge each other's presence in the pier, but Joe does not join in; he only watches. The film culminates with Rik and Joe returning, separately, to their apartment building, where Joe is welcomed home by his wife, and Rik, intrigued, lingers in the stairway as Joe shuts his door without looking back.

While the primary value of Brown's film is the unembellished view it presents into the cruising scene at the piers in the late 1970s, it also offers an evocative impression of the tensions between corporate redevelopment and creative erotic reuse of the waterfront. While, clearly, Brown is keen to address the misconception that "no-one uses them," recording their appropriation as a cruising space, the prospective demolition that Joe is recruited to assist with casts a shadow over the film. *Pier Groups* captures a cruising scene at risk of disappearance as the piers are threatened with demolition and the surrounding waterfront area with redevelopment. Like Gordon Matta-Clark's cutting work *Day's End*, which appears in the film, it chronicles the scene's "historical passage into outmodedness, illuminating the twilight of the pier itself."[24] Brown uses the erotic longing that the film invariably generates strategically, arousing in the viewer both a straightforward sense of sexual desire and, like Rik standing perplexed in the stairwell as Joe walks back into his apartment with his wife, a melancholy impression of the cruising culture that would be lost were the piers demolished. This dual effect evokes David Wojnarowicz's contemporaneous concern with documenting the cruising cultures of the piers, recording "not just sexuality, but the slow disintegration of these architectural structures" and "visions of people that appear out of darkness and disappear into darkness."[25] Later, in the text "Biographical Dateline," he recalled a sense of urgency in recording "the gradual decline of these places as . . . poverty spread throughout the country" in the years preceding Ronald Reagan's election to the presidency in November 1980.[26]

For Wojnarowicz, as for Brown, preserving the queer sexual culture of the piers through word and image as they became the subject of the gentrifying gaze of municipal forces was as much political as it was personal. In a similar way, Ivan Galietti's film *Pompeii New York* sought to "preserve" and "visually document the graffiti, murals, ravage, ravish, lust et al. of this womb of alternative life-styles and 'unnatural' acts" as Pier 46 faced imminent demolition.[27] This queer preservation, enacted through writing and image-making, did not stem from a concern for maintaining the buildings themselves, or for preserving them in any normative material or economic sense. The failure of municipal preservation efforts, their industrial and material collapse, was in fact one of the conditions that made their queer reuse possible. Documenting and preserving details of these creative queer appropriations, however, "serves as a dismantling tool against the illusion of" what Wojnarowicz calls the "ONE-TRIBE NATION."[28]

For both Wojnarowicz and Brown, creative preservationist work like this was motivated by a desire to record queer appropriations of New York's ruins and to preserve at least the conditions for the existence of sites where the city's heteronormative functionality was compromised or became unsustainable after abandonment, places where the ideological homogeneity of the city was itself abandoned. As an illicit appropriative occupation of the city's derelict spaces and a mode of being in the city that is discontinuous, fragmentary, and economically nonproductive, cruising can in itself be seen a form of preserving these sites as noncommercial spaces and as places for queer association and community. Queer records like Wojnarowicz's and Brown's posit equally fragmentary, discontinuous, and original forms of recording and sharing these histories, while further challenging the false municipal narrative of the waterfront's utter abandonment and ideal civic reuse. As Wojnarowicz himself acknowledged, an important aspect of his waterfront writing was the act and process of bearing witness to the "decline" of the harbor, to "the architectures' exposure to elements and fires," and to those who cruised this decaying space.[29] If historic preservation in New York was, as Kenneth Jackson argues, the "preoccupation of social factions that were losing out in the contest to control New York's future," then this waterfront writing had a distinctly preservationist agenda.[30] "Soon," Wojnarowicz observed as he wrote about the cruising space of the derelict piers, "all this will be picturesque ruins."[31]

Ruins, Rebecca Solnit writes, "are evidence not only that cities can be destroyed but that they survive their own destruction, are resurrected again and again." They "stand as reminders." "To erase the ruins," she argues, "is to erase the visible public triggers of memory; a city without ruins and traces of age is like a mind without memories." The "ruins themselves, like other traces, are treasures: our links to what came before, our guide to situating ourselves in a landscape of time."[32] The image and experience of the ruin as ephemeral, temporally complex, and resistant to homogeneous historicization is central to Wojnarowicz's queer preservationism. The history of the ruin is a history of power. Creating a fiction of total abandonment in the 1970s, writing out the ruined harbor's unsanctioned social and sexual appropriations, was a municipal strategy of social exclusion. Wojnarowicz's waterfront writing works, in part, to resist and redirect this process of renewal and gentrification through the disclosure of personal erotic experiences. But memory, Solnit reminds us, "is always incomplete, always imperfect, always falling into ruin."[33] Wojnarowicz's focus on the erotic and political potential of the waterfront ruins in his late 1970s art and writing was one among many efforts to resist this totalizing renewal of lower Manhattan by recording its queer erotic appropriations. The "larger the range of representations," he wrote later, "the more I feel there is room in the environment for my existence, that not the entire environment is hostile."[34] In *The Gentrification of the Mind*, Schulman similarly stresses the importance of sharing diverse narratives as itself "an antigentrification process," an "individuation of perception."[35] If we "lift the curtains for a brief peek," Wojnarowicz asserts, "the term 'general public' disintegrates."[36]

## Safety, gentrification, and the politics of pier cruising

While the number of bathhouses, gay bars, and sex clubs on Manhattan's Lower West Side expanded rapidly in the early 1970s, safeguarding a distinctly queer presence along West Street and the waterfront, anti-queer violence perpetrated by both citizens and police was a continuing problem. In a 1975 article for *Our Town*, John Turcott describes the piers as "a mugger's paradise."[37] Both Wojnarowicz and John Hall, chatting in December 1980, share their fear of being mugged or stabbed while cruising at the piers.[38] In *Rushes*, John Rechy writes that "haunted male figures lurk for nightsex in the burnt-out rooms" of waterfront warehouses, while "in recurring forays with sticks, slashed bottles, knives, guns, crowbars, packs of gaunt young marauders also prowl those areas, for 'queers.'" The quiet is disrupted by "the crunch of assaulted flesh—and the filthy floors are bloodied."[39]

Wojnarowicz's first book, *The Waterfront Journals* (1982)—a series of monologues drawing on conversations with strangers collected during his journeys across the United States in the late 1970s and early 1980s—captures the homophobic violence that undercut the queer pleasures the piers permitted and the institutional disinterest of law enforcement officials in the routine nature of gay bashing on the waterfront. In "Man on Second Avenue, 2:00 am," the narrating subject remarks casually to Wojnarowicz that "kids come around all the time throwin bottles and screaming *Queer* and then takin off." One evening, however, after sharing a beer in a harborside bar, this man and a friend were walking down West Street when "this car from Jersey . . . cruised by real slow and some kid leans out the window saying Suck my dick and my friend gives him the finger and said something." The narrator's friend is subjected to an aggressive beating, with "five kids" stomping "on his head and chest," breaking ribs and leaving him lying on West Street, "his face just a puddle of blood":

> the kids chased after him but he ran faster and faster through the streets and outta the neighborhood and he kept running until he collapsed somewhere on some street . . . later he woke up in the hospital and found out he had been out for about five or six days. The doctors told him he was found by the cops unconscious on West Street surrounded by a bunch of guys . . . apparently he had hallucinated the whole thing of getting up and running away.

The kids from New Jersey, the narrator concludes, "got away" without retribution or legal charges.[40] As Wojnarowicz's writings make clear, attacks like this and fear of them were an everyday experience for men cruising the piers and patronizing the bars by the waterfront in the mid- to late 1970s.

Throughout New York, muggings and murders were on the increase as poverty rates increased and the city's law enforcement agencies and other municipal bodies failed to respond effectively to increased crime and public disorder. Between 1960 and 1968, robberies in New York had increased more than eightfold and burglaries had more than quadrupled.[41] The number of homicides in New York tripled between 1965 and 1975.[42] Between August 1976 and August 1977, the city was in thrall to the serial killer David Berkowitz, known by the self-assigned moniker "Son of Sam," who murdered six people, all women, and wounded seven others, sparking an extensive police manhunt and equally expansive press coverage. In the midst of this spiraling violence and continued urban neglect, the safety of queer New Yorkers was additionally compromised by homophobic policing, epitomized by the many raids on gay and lesbian bars, which continued after Stonewall into the 1970s, and by limited civil rights legislation. Beginning in 1971 the Gay Activists Alliance (GAA) sought to challenge New York's continued failure to protect its gay, lesbian, and transgender citizens from violence and discrimination by sponsoring a bill in the city council, titled Intro. 554, to extend the prohibition of "discrimination in employment, housing or public accommodations based on race, religion or sex" to include that based on sexuality.[43] The bill did not pass until 1986.

In the summer of 1975, Jim Ryan, a West Village resident and, by then, retired pier cruiser, began producing a safety-oriented newsletter about the waterfront cruising scene, which he distributed each weekend throughout the Village, printing between 2,500 and 3,000 copies and leaving them "next to Kellers hanging on the gates of the caterer also next to the Underground and tied on the fence in Christopher Park." Distribution points in the warehouses appear in some of Leonard Fink and Alvin Baltrop's photographs (figure 4.1). The anonymously written newsletter identified muggers and other troublemakers active on the waterfront and detailed recent muggings and homophobic attacks, as well as documenting "the dangerous physical conditions of the ruined buildings." In the first issue, published in August 1975, the lead headline told of a fire that had destroyed a section of Pier 48, likely sparked by a "SMOLDERING CIGARETTE." Another article ran with news that "ROBBERIES AND ASSAULTS CONTINUE ON PIERS AND IMMEDIATE PIER AREA," noting that on August 17 "5 YOUNGSTERS" had been challenged by cruisers in relation to the spate of attacks. These youngsters "did not venture out to the far end of the pier, but did have in their hands pipes and sticks." "DAY TIMERS ON [Pier] 48," Ryan observed, ignored "WARNINGS TO STAY OFF." The September issue carried news of a "WAVE OF SERIOUS STICK-UPS WITH GUNS & KNIVES ON PIER 48 & 49." "NITE TIME IS PRIME TIME FOR MUGGERS ON BOTH PIERS," Ryan warned: "WATCH YOUR BACK WHEN CRUISING 48–49."[44]

Other articles detailed the continued risk of fire "ON ALL PIERS" and news of a young man "killed instantly" by a truck on West Street one Thursday afternoon. The protective aims of Ryan's newsletter were seen also in

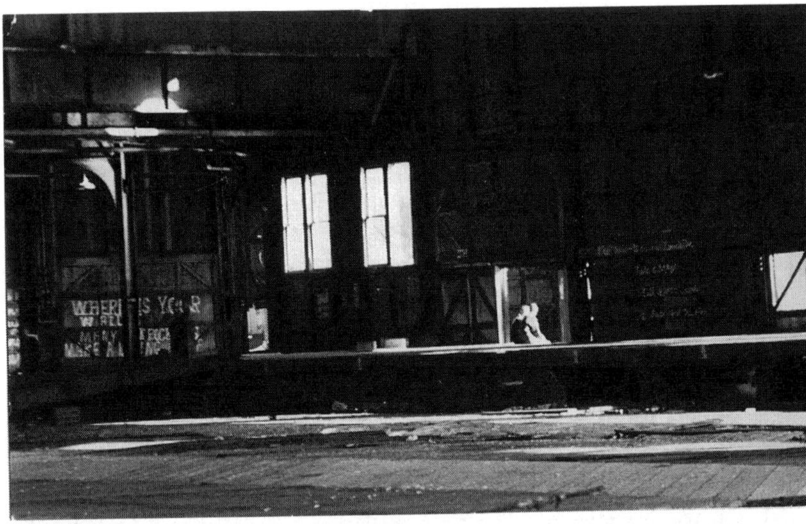

FIGURE 4.1. Alvin Baltrop, *Piers (two men sitting in window, graffiti on wall "Free Pier Warehouse Newsletter, take a copy, tell your friends the truth about the piers")*, n.d. (1975–1986). Silver gelatin print. Photograph courtesy of the Alvin Baltrop Trust. 

the spray-painted safety messages that appeared on warehouse walls in the mid-1970s, intended for nighttime cruisers. "Pickpocket paradise area," read one: "they work in teams every night, be careful." "Muggers and gay bashers operate here," warned another. Graffiti at the piers was not, however, limited to messages of personal security. Some of Fink's photographs document the façade of a rotting riverside building emblazoned with graffiti urging readers to "STOP ANITA," a reference to the efforts of former beauty queen Anita Bryant in 1977 to repeal an ordinance in Dade County, Florida, outlawing discrimination on the basis of sexual orientation. Others advocated "queer youth" power and unity, and another, on an upper-level warehouse window, urged pier cruisers to help "BEAT WESTWAY."

In his newsletter, Ryan urged men to stay out of the crumbling piers, in no uncertain terms. "It is a hell of a thing to print, say, or even think," he asserted,

> but every last one of you guys who goes into Pier 48 deserves what happens to you because you have all been warned, experienced others being ripped-off, know positively that things occur there, many of the pier regulars know the muggers on sight, and yet continue to go there.

"Are you guys so bent on sucking cock," Ryan admonished his readers, "that you can't read or comprehend what you read in print? Is the scent of ass so overwhelming that your reading ability or common sense won't prevent you from going to the Pier at nite?" If "taking the chance of being confronted with a gun, knife or whatever instead of being confronted with a cock is your 'stick,'" Ryan wrote, failing to recognize the erotic appeal of the dangerous cruising space,

> then go ahead—it is your life to do with what you will. If getting ripped off, stabbed and held up at gun point is a way of getting your rocks off that satisfies your desires, Pier 48 is just the place for you. Perhaps you should wave a sign in front of you or something equivalent so the muggers won't have to waste time looking for you and you can all get thing off for effeciently and in less time so the muggers can move on to their next victum. STAY OUT OF THE PIERS AT NIGHT—ALL OF THEM!!!!!!!![45]

Ryan was particularly critical of cruising men who were reluctant or refused to file police complaints about muggings and assaults, and of those who declined to get involved when they witnessed them. "The apathy shown by the majority is pathetic!" he wrote:

> If half of the readers who have commented to me in a positive way about the effects of the NEWSLETTER, would get up off their pathetic, apathetic asses most of the problems we have in or near the West Street Pier Area would be solved. But NO—everyone complains, but no one ever bothers himself to lift a hand to help someone out.

Outside his writing for the pier newsletter, however, Ryan was very clear about the "catch-22" situation in which men attacked at the piers found themselves, with many feeling unable to report assaults or muggings to homophobic and otherwise hostile police officers. "It's against the Waterfront act" to go out onto the piers, he noted in an interview with John Turcott for *Our Town* in 1975, "and if caught one could be charged with a misdemeanor. Invariably the cops will ask someone reporting a crime on the piers questions like, 'What the hell are you doing on the pier in the first place?'"[46] "When a spokesperson from Ports and Terminals was asked about the piers," Turcott wrote, "he said that there was considerable discussion about the problem and that no solution could be found at the present time. 'We've tried boarding them up, people rip it open again,' the spokesperson said. 'We have found the placement of a security guard is unsatisfactory.'"[47] The spokesperson acknowledges that "plans were formulated to demolish the piers and build recreation areas on the sites this fall [1975], but with this financial crunch that's out. Maybe we can find federal funds for it, I can't say. I believe the only answer is to knock them down."[48]

On the question of why violent assaults and muggings occured at the piers with such frequency, Ryan writes, "Many claim, and I am inclined to agree, that the methadone boat that used to be docked at the foot of Christopher Street drew many undesirable people to the area." The boat was managed by the New York City Methadone Maintenance Treatment Program, run through the Health Department and Health Services Administration, and docked at the city-owned Pier 45. It served around 550 former addicts and, in 1971 at least, was guarded by a police officer twenty-four hours a day.[49] "Originally," Ryan argued in the September 27–28 edition of the pier newsletter,

> the boat was to despence methadone only to addicts who lived in the West Village area. Gradually as other centers closed for lack of funds their clients were told to come to the Boat for their medicine. As a result, addicts from uptown, crosstown, downtown and wherever began streeming into the Village. The summer of '75 saw our area become "heavy" with many undesirable visitors. Muggers and pick-pockets work openly and brazenly in the Piers at night and a few of them have caused serious problems for people in the pier area during the daylight hours. Literally hundreds of people have fallen victim to these scum types.[50]

Although ostensibly an attempt to raise awareness among cruising gay men of the increasing number of assaults and muggings at the piers, Ryan's diatribe is a critique of the creative mixed use of the derelict waterfront that privileges one sort of appropriation and asserts a right to safe association and protection from violence shaped by a discriminatory attitude with regard to class and race. Christina B. Hanhardt has noted that in neighborhoods like Chelsea and the West Village in the mid- to late 1970s, "the departure and displacement of racially diverse working-class communities from dilapidated housing stock was followed by an influx of middle- and upper-income whites who refurbished homes and businesses." She adds that this same area was, of course, "also home to the majority of New York's gay leather and S/M bars, courtesy of its emptying industrial spaces and proximity to the popular public sex spot of the piers along the West Side."[51] The gentrification of the area can be gauged in part, Hanhardt suggests, by tracking the growing hostility of its white gay male residents toward teenaged people of color in the neighborhood, and their efforts to formalize it.

Ryan's pier newsletter can be seen, then, as part of a broader neighborhood effort to protect gay men in the area from assault, and to "increase police presence and a neighborhood wide recognition that antigay violence was unacceptable."[52] It was followed in 1976 by the foundation of the Society to Make

America Safe for Homosexuals (SMASH), a "vigilante" group formed "by a small group of new gay residents of the gentrifying neighborhood." Hanhardt notes that SMASH patrolled the piers and neighboring streets with the intent of "rousing" anti-queer violence in order to document and publicize the threat.[53] Although the threat of homophobic violence on the piers was a very real one, resistance efforts like Ryan's newsletter and SMASH's nighttime patrols relied on the stoking of racial tensions and class antagonisms. They suggest a rejection of solidarity between the white queer people moving into the Village in the 1970s and members of the poor black and Latinx communities who had been resident there for many years, regardless of the extent to which both groups were impacted by poor policing, exclusionary municipal rights legislation, and discriminatory private policies affecting access to housing and employment. SMASH, Hanhardt writes, predominantly patrolled areas "that were largely home to low-income people of color" and failed to recognize and deal with the racialization of urban poverty and the correlations often made publicly between racialized poverty and violence.[54] Ryan's evocative image of "scum types" infiltrating the Village by way of the city-run methadone boat presents the presumed perpetrators of violence against cruising gay men as infectious agents attacking the body of the proper citizenry, despite the fact that, as the ambivalence of many cruising men toward the police suggests, it was the readers of the pier newsletter, not those making use of the methadone boat, whose appropriation of this urban interzone was illegal, while the police, through continued bar raids and cruising crackdowns, were often the perpetrators of violence.[55]

Ryan's vision of the piers under threat from "undesirable visitors" also suggests the appropriation of the derelict waterfront and neighboring portions of the West Village by other marginalized groups, and the antagonism between the different groups who appropriated these ruined spaces. In an interview with Benjamin Shepard, Adonis Baugh, a homeless person from Brooklyn who lived at the West Side piers in the 1970s and 1980s, remembers that in 1981 the piers were a populous utopian space where "you [could] go, no matter what age you were, and be you. . . . Drag queens, transgenders. . . . Everybody not considered the norms could go there and be themselves and not looked at any other way."[56] In 1971 activists Sylvia Rivera and Marsha P. Johnson formed Street Transvestite Action Revolutionaries (STAR), the first political organization dedicated to fostering and supporting the rights of trans people in the United States (figure 4.2). Their primary objective was to give food and shelter to the growing numbers of young, homeless trans people, many of whom were, like Rivera and Johnson, low-income people of color, who lived out on the West Side piers. They established a residence in "a parked trailer truck in an outdoor parking lot in Greenwich Village," where up to two dozen kids would sleep every night. STAR House existed in two locations, in the trailer near the piers and then at a building on Second Avenue on the Lower East Side, for two years. "We fed people and clothed people," Rivera said of STAR's work, and "we kept the building going. We went out and hustled the streets. We paid the rent. We didn't want the kids out in the streets hustling. They would go out and rip off food."[57] The same qualities of empty space and a lack of thorough policing that first appealed to cruising gay men in the late 1960s made the waterfront a popular spot for sex work through the 1970s. Its proximity to New Jersey roadways and, later, to the financial district, appeared to make West Street and the Meatpacking District an ideal place to hustle suburban commuters. Efrain John Gonzalez, who worked in and around the area in the late 1970s and 1980s, sometimes as a cab driver, documented the lives of sex workers in the area in a series of black-and-white photographs, which were exhibited at the Bureau of General Services Queer Division bookshop in New York's LGBT Center in 2015 (figure 4.3).

Commercial and noncommercial sexual communities overlapped at the piers, much like the contemporaneous sex scene around Forty-Second Street, where, as Samuel Delany has written, "peep shows, sex shops, adult video stores and dirty magazine stores, massage parlors—and porn theaters" occupied the same space as "a flourishing trade in female street-walkers, drugs, and hustlers":

> The population was incredibly heterogeneous—white, black, Hispanic, Asian, Indian, Native American, and a variety of Pacific Islanders. In the Forty-second Street area's sex theaters specifically, since I started frequenting them in the summer of 1975, I've met playwrights, carpenters, opera singers, telephone repair men, stockbrokers, guys on welfare, guys with trust funds, guys on crutches, on walkers, in wheelchairs, teachers, warehouse workers, male nurses, fancy chefs, guys who worked at Dunkin Donuts, guys who gave out flyers on street corners, guys who drove garbage trucks, and guys who washed windows on the Empire State Building. As a gentile, I note that this is the only place in a lifetime's New York residency I've had any extended conversation with some of the city's Hasidim.[58]

In pre-gentrified Times Square, these "two orders of sexual relationship," cruising for sex and hustling for sex work, Delany wrote, "sat by one another in the sex movie theaters, drank shoulder to shoulder in the same bars, walked down the same streets, and lingered by the same shop windows to make themselves available for conversation in the afternoons and evenings." At the piers this

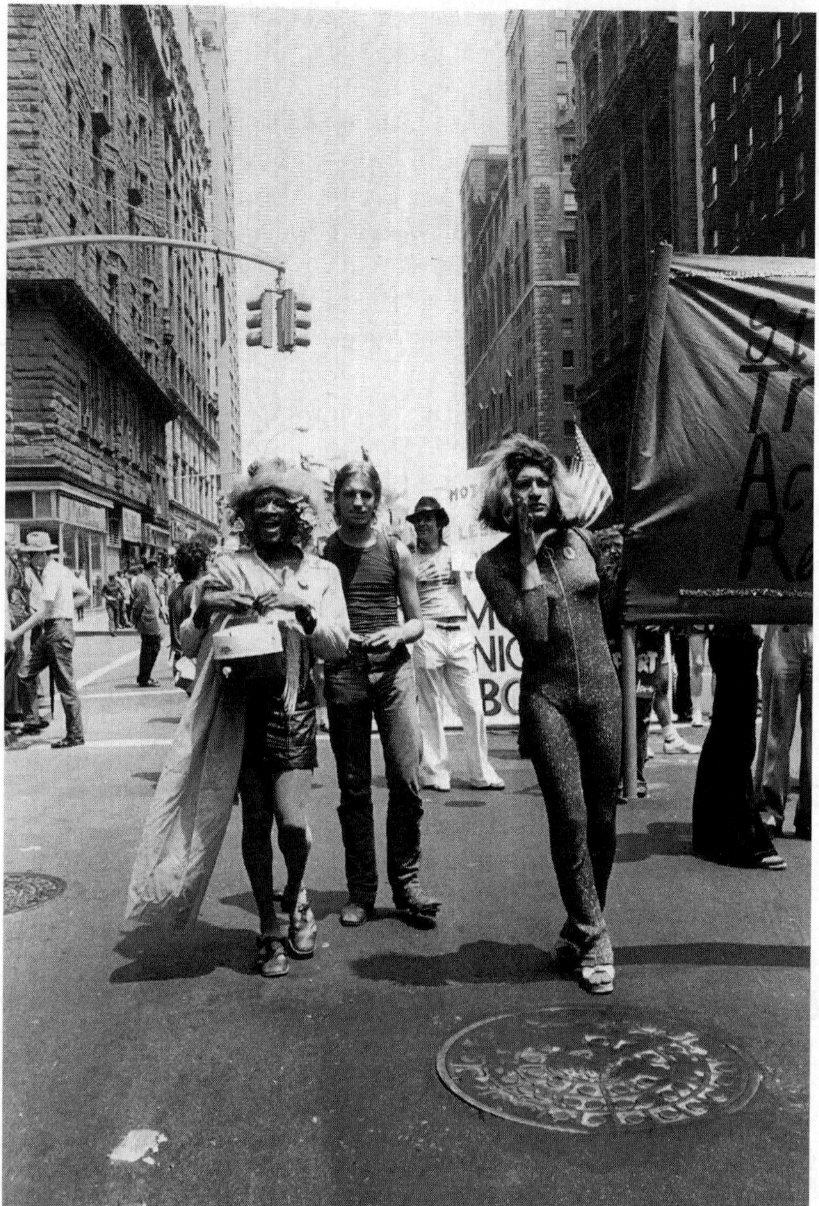

FIGURE 4.2. Sylvia Rivera (holding banner) and Marsha P. Johnson (far left) at the Christopher Street Gay Liberation Day Parade, New York, June 24, 1973. Photograph by Leonard Fink. © The LGBT Community Center National History Archive.

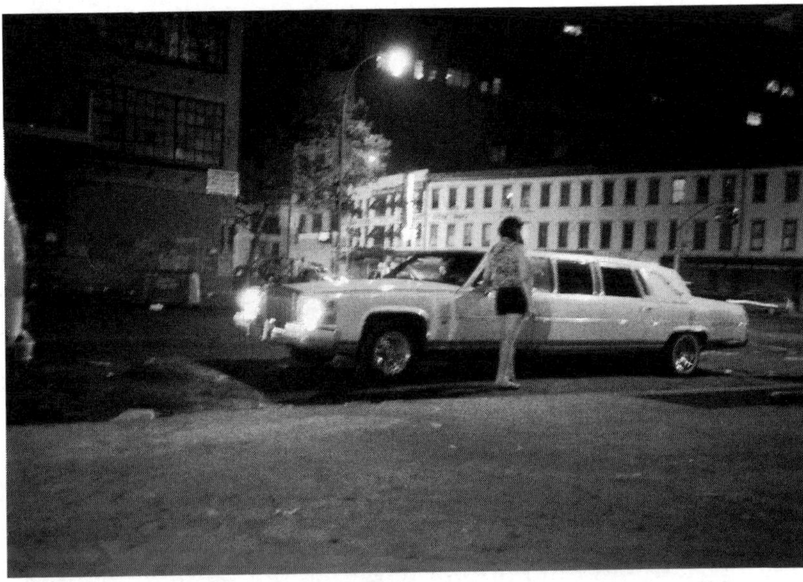

FIGURE 4.3. Photograph by Efrain John Gonzalez, ca. 1979. © Efrain John Gonzalez.

confluence of erotic uses often sparked tensions between these two groups, themselves diverse and heterogeneous, and, as Delany noted of Times Square, there were "occasionally intense" confrontations.[59] While in the early 1990s, Wojnarowicz dedicated *Close to the Knives* to, among others, the "drag queens along the Hudson River and their truly revolutionary states," in his early writing, he demonstrated an unsympathetic indifference toward the trans people and drag queens with whom he shared this riverside space.[60] In a journal entry from July 1979, he wrote that on "getting out of the pier we walked back along the highway towards Christopher Street, [where] against a doorway were five transvestites all yakkin' away done up in their personal glories with makeup and low-cut blouses and silicone shots or hormone tits and John was awed that they were really transvestites." Similarly, in a journal entry from August 1980, he described hearing an assault in one of the warehouses:

> out of one the side rooms that once had been a loading dock there was a series of hysterical high-pitched screams and in all of that gathered darkness a figure of light flew out, speed motions with arms and legs pumping, propelling it towards the far wall, blur lines of movement, an abject silence following in the wake of screams, and I immediately thought to myself: stupid queen.[61]

Sylvia Rivera left New York in 1973, having broken with the Gay Activists Alliance in 1972 after the group moved to eliminate references to trans people from its proposals for a municipal antidiscrimination bill. Protest actions like the Stonewall riots, in which Rivera played a central role, had demonstrated the need for direct action in demanding safe spaces for queer people, but continued institutional homophobia had left gay groups like the GAA supportive of relative assimilation. After drag queens testified before the first city council hearing in 1971, Toby Marotta recalled that the "confusion between transvestism and homosexuality" among council members "played a significant role in the bill's defeat." In 1974 GAA activists permitted an amendment to the bill excluding "transvestism from the definition of sexual orientation."[62] In an essay for a 2013 collection of writings by and interviews with Rivera and Johnson, former STAR activist Ehn Nothing argued that "the resistance that STAR faced as a multi-racial group of revolutionary street queens illuminates the wider dynamics of the gay liberation movement" in the 1970s: "Revolutionary street queens of color were an impediment to the goal of assimilation into the white straight capitalist world."[63]

The presence of a community of trans people of color at the piers has largely slipped from view, even as popular awareness of the creative reuse of the waterfront as a gay cruising space has increased through the publication of numerous memoirs of gay life in New York in the 1970s. The limited visibility of this queer history of the piers reflects the persistent exclusion of this trans community from many of the predominantly gay spaces and activist groups in the West Village at the time. "These forces of gay normativity and revolutionary management," Nothing wrote, "marginalized, erased, and silenced those whose bodies, histories, or ethical orientations refused dominant models."[64] This is a gentrification, as Sarah Schulman has argued, of the mind, which has alienated "people who did not have rights, who were not represented, who did not have power," and who were perceived to be "undesirable" occupants of even the most marginal city spaces.[65] Like the false history of abandonment that underpinned municipal harbor redevelopment efforts in the 1970s, this gentrification "enforces itself through the repression of diverse expression" and the obscuring of diverse histories of alternate use. Like the GAA's earlier rejection of trans inclusion in the city council antidiscrimination bill, this gentrification "literally replaces mix with homogeneity."[66] In the context of these obscured histories of trans occupation of the waterfront, the partial recovery of this narrative in the present elucidates the unexpectedly diverse gentrifying forces that have shaped New York's physical redevelopment, its material gentrification and the gentrification of its history in Schulman's terms, and have determined which of its queer reuses remain visible in the present.

## Queer organizing in the bars

While Jim Ryan's newsletter provides useful documentation of the kinds of violence gay men cruising the abandoned waterfront experienced in the mid-1970s, his singular focus on the dangers of the piers and warehouses fails to address the continued risks faced by patrons of the gay bars and sex clubs along West Street. Both Ryan and John Turcott failed to acknowledge the continued targeting of gay clubs and bars near the waterfront by the New York Police Department, which shaped queer experience of the area and helped foster the cruising scene at the piers. In March 1970 police raided the Snake Pit, a gay bar on West Tenth Street, just before dawn, led by Deputy Inspector Seymour Pine, who had overseen the raid on the Stonewall the previous year. Police removed 167 people from the bar and arrested them for disorderly conduct, though these charges were later dismissed. The raid received public attention after Diego Vinales, an Argentine national living in the United States, feared his homosexuality might be exposed, making his possession of a visa illegal under the 1950 McCarran Act, which prohibited homosexuals from entering the country.[67] Vinales jumped out of a window at the police station and impaled himself on a railing below. He was taken to St. Vincent's Hospital in the Village, where he was later charged with resisting arrest. The recently formed GAA took up the cause and organized a march through the Village to the police station and a vigil outside the hospital. Months later, police conducted two further raids on gay bars in the area, again pushing patrons out into the street, making them visible to passersby. In these raids police used crowbars and "other implements of destruction in a 'search' for drugs and whiskey," causing more than twenty thousand dollars' worth of property damage.[68]

In December 1975, the *New York Post* ran an article detailing a predawn police raid at the Anvil, a gay bar on West Fourteenth Street near Eleventh Avenue, with the headline "Bust 5 at Swinging Gay Soiree." It describes the bar as an "an unlicensed homosexual cabaret in the wholesale meat district which allegedly featured a sado-masochist show in which a nude masked man swung from chains while sex acts were performed on him." Five men were arrested on liquor law and obscenity charges, the article notes, by "10 infiltrators, one of whom was dressed all in leather." The bar had been operating without a liquor license since September, according to Captain Lawrence Hepburn, part of the NYPD Public Morals Division, who led the raid. Hepburn said that the place had two nude bartenders, two nude male dancers on the bar, and two others on side stages. In another room, "homosexual films were shown, and in a darkened kitchen, individuals took turns performing private homosexual acts 'for no charge,' Hepburn said." Police seized 180 cases of beer, 25 cases of liquor, $400 in receipts, and, the article concluded, "sadomasochist apparatus, including two black leather jackets with Police Dept. patches on them and an assortment of whips."[69]

In the mid- to late 1970s, many of the bars around the waterfront were seen to be considerably safer than the piers in terms of homophobic attacks or muggings. However, though an article in the *New York Post* in December 1977 suggested, unconvincingly, that "gays bars have won grudging acceptance in Manhattan," the Anvil, the Mineshaft, and the Eagle were all raided by police as late as 1979 for liquor law violations, among other offenses. At a raid on the Fifteenth Street club Crisco Disco in August 1979, fourteen people were arrested. Police rejected suggestions that the raids were motivated by homophobia. "We don't care that they're gay bars, straight bars, or any other kind of bars," Sergeant Tambasco, of the Public Morals Division, told the *Post*. "Each of the raided bars calls itself a 'private club' not falling under the state's liquor laws," Tambasco continued, "All admit the general public and are not private clubs." In 1980 Jack Modica, one of the owners of the Mineshaft, suggested that the raided bars "incorporate as a non-profit organization" to protect themselves against the ongoing threat of raids. "It's time we organized a tavern guild," Modica wrote in a letter to local bar owners: "there are still laws on the books against us; 'It's against the law for a gay person to own a bar,' and 'It's against the law for homosexuals to congregate.' We still experience prejudice and harassment."

Modica's suggestion exemplified a growing political consciousness among both owners and patrons of the gay bar scene in the West Village and the Meatpacking District in the 1970s. In June 1973 the Mineshaft held an "Emergency Benefit" for those affected by the deadly fire at the Everard Baths, in conjunction with the Metropolitan Community Church. "Money is needed," a flyer for the event read, "to help guys now in hospital for future treatment." The growth of political engagement at the bars was by generated by the work of the GAA and driven by the challenges faced by city council representatives seeking ratification of Intro. 554. The archives of the Eagle, the legendary leather bar on West Twenty-Eighth Street near the West Side Highway, include a letter from Arthur J. Katzman, the Democratic city councilman for the Twenty-Second District, from the mid-1970s, thanking the Eagle for a benefit it held for his reelection campaign. "It is my hope and belief," Katzman wrote in the letter, "that justice and decency will ultimately prevail, and that Intro 554, the Gay Civil Rights Bill, will pass into the City Council. Your efforts will certainly help to assure that goal." A "Picket the Bigots" rally organized by the GAA in the mid-1970s was advertised at Badlands, the self-proclaimed "Baddest Bar in the Village," on the corner of Christopher and West Streets. A flyer read, "Your privacy or the public morals squad! . . . While hospitals close and the West Side loses its subway service, the Public Morals Squad grows. FIGHT BACK." The GAA urged Manhattan's queer bar community to protest against cops "who brutally harass and arrest Lesbians, Gays, Transpeople, Single Women and Youth; who are organizing and funding middle-class 'protection' squads against us." The rally took place on the same night as a benefit at Badlands for the Gay Switchboard. And the political engagement of gay bar and sex club patrons reached beyond the bars themselves. In 1978, for example, the downtown bathhouse Man's Country hired two billboards above Village Cigars at the intersection of Christopher Street and Seventh Avenue. One read "GAY RIGHTS," the other "REGISTER & VOTE."

Political engagement in the bars and around the cruising areas on the waterfront gathered momentum in the later 1970s as activists organized, first, for the March on Washington for Lesbian and Gay Rights in October 1979 and, second, in response to the negative portrayal of the Village gay bar scene in William Friedkin's feature film *Cruising*, filmed in the summer of 1979 and released in February 1980. In the early 1970s, clients of the leather bars and sex clubs along West Street had been implicated in a series of murders of members of their own community. The popular media made much of the seeming irony of men engaged with sadomasochism being victims of very real and unanticipated physical violence. Writing in the *New York Times* in January 1973, Grace Lichtenstein reported that "three similarly violent murders in three weeks in lower Manhattan involving men the police said were part of the 'leather bar' scene have sent waves of rumors and fear through the area's homosexual community." "The dead men," she wrote, "had been known as patrons of 'leather' bars, which cater to homosexuals who dress in leather jackets and dungarees. They are said by some homosexuals to be synonymous with the 'S and M'—sado-masochist—scene," and she named the Eagle's Nest as a favorite of the three victims.[70] The murders, and others like them, were covered with a more sympathetic eye by the openly gay journalist Arthur Bell in the *Village Voice*. All bore similarities to the plot of the 1970 novel *Cruising*, written by a *New York Times Magazine* editor, Gerard Walker. Friedkin's film drew on the salacious title and popular appeal of Walker's novel, but Friedkin claims to have "spun a completely original film out of it based on Arthur Bell's articles in the *Village Voice*."[71] Friedkin's *Cruising* stars Al Pacino as Steve Burns, a New York City police officer investigating a series of murders, believed to be perpetrated by a serial killer who picks up men at downtown leather bars and dumps their mutilated bodies in the Hudson River. Horrified by the homophobic brutality of the investigating police officers, Burns agrees to go undercover, is drawn into the world of the bars, and befriends a number of its residents. The film ends ambiguously as a major suspect is shown to be innocent, and Burns returns to his girlfriend uptown, who, in the film's final scene, tries on the peaked cap he wore as part of his leather "disguise."

*Cruising* met with extensive criticism from gay audiences across the United States, not least from Bell, who, having read a leaked copy of the script, described it as "the most oppressive, ugly, bigoted look at homosexuality ever presented on the screen, . . . the worst possible nightmare of the most uptight straight."[72] In his *Village Voice* column on July 16, 1979, he urged Village residents to "give Friedkin and his production crew a terrible time if you spot them in your neighborhoods." In response to Bell's very public concerns about the violent image of queer life being presented in Friedkin's film, activists organized protests that attempted to halt filming at sites in Greenwich Village. They pointed "mirrors at the shoot to interfere with the lighting, and surrounded the set blasting whistles and air horns."[73] That more than five hundred local gay men were hired as extras for the film's club and bar scenes, many of which were filmed on location in leather bars by the waterfront, appeared to lend weight to Friedkin's assertion that his depiction of the early 1970s waterfront and leather scene was authentic. Declarations of the film's realism were key to its success, and Bell's rejection of the legitimacy of its perspective was problematic given Friedkin's reliance on his *Village Voice* writings. When the film was released, it was preceded by a disclaimer: "This film is not intended as an indictment of the homosexual world." Friedkin described the addition as "a sap to organized gay rights groups" who had protested the shooting the previous year.[74]

As the disclaimer suggests, activists' critiques centered on what they perceived as the film's totalizing effects, its positing of a singular narrative of the bar and club scene around the waterfront as not only violent, but homicidal toward its own. In an article for the *Village Voice* in August 1979, John Rechy responded to the swell of activist energy around the film, criticizing the support for censorship implicit in the protests. "By insisting doggedly on presenting a so-called 'positive' image—often a euphemism for heterosexual imitation," he writes, we deny "the enriching spectrum of our experience, including an abundant sexuality, which needs no apology."[75] For Rechy, the challenges to gay liberation presented by the film hinged upon questions of diversity and narrative multiplicity. Why, he asked, "does every homosexual film or book—unlike heterosexual films or books—have to represent our entire world, each and every one of us, when we have so many rich and diverse voices?"[76] Beyond the issue of censorship, then, Rechy was concerned that only one vantage point on the cruising culture and bar scene along the West Side Highway in the late 1970s might be preserved. His defense of the film's merits was, however, short-lived. In early 1980, he was invited by Friedkin to view the film's final cut, shortly before it was released. "The original first images of the film," he recalled, "were these":

> On a graffiti-scrawled wall was splashed the slogan of gay liberation at the time: WE ARE EVERYWHERE. There then occurred a quick-cut to the murdered homosexual, being pulled out of the river. The film was opening in New York the following week, and there was no time for major editing. This much was possible: On the telephone I told Friedkin that the juxtaposition was appalling; I suggested that the shot of the wall be deleted, and a disclaimer inserted to indicate that what was depicted was a small segment of a vast world. He deleted the offensive shot and included a revision of the disclaimer.[77]

One of *Cruising*'s most prominent supporters had, upon seeing the film's troubling juxtaposition of gay liberation and antigay violence, felt it necessary to demand explicit affirmation of the partial nature of its content.

Later in the year, two gay bars along West Street were the scene of a very real homicidal attack. The violence was wrought not from inside, as in *Cruising*, but from without. On November 19, 1980, Ronald Crumpley, a former Transit Authority officer in his late thirties, opened fire with a stolen Uzi rifle on men waiting outside the Ramrod and Sneakers, a gay dive bar further along the block. Two men were killed, six others wounded. According to articles in the *New York Daily News* and the *New York Times*, Crumpley referred to men walking around West Street as "ghosts" and "apparitions"[78] "I'll kill them all—the gays," he was reported to have said on his arrest: "they ruin everything."[79] The murders sparked expansive protests. Two thousand people marched by candlelight, in silence, from Christopher Street to the Ramrod on West Street, directly opposite the Christopher Street Pier. In front of the bar, in a patriotic appeal for protection, protestors sang "The Battle Hymn of the Republic."[80] At trial a year later, Crumpley was found not responsible for the attack "by reason of mental disease or defect."[81]

The filmmaker Jim Hubbard recorded the protests against the filming of *Cruising* on Super 8 film, using the material in a short film he titled *(Stop the Movie) Cruising* (1980; figure 4.4). Hubbard's film switches between footage of street protests in the West Village, aiming to disrupt the filming of *Cruising*, and voyeuristic recordings of extras on the set, chatting, laughing, and dancing inside the waterfront leather bars in which Friedkin filmed. Recorded without sound, it becomes difficult to tell how these two animated crowds relate. By filming the extras from outside the bars, peering in, Hubbard utilizes

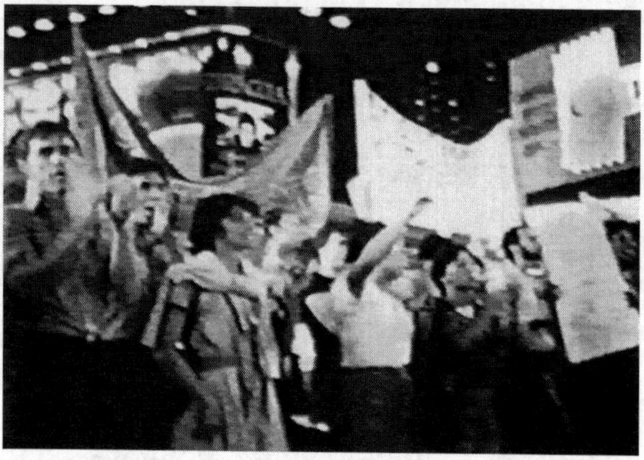

FIGURE 4.4. Jim Hubbard, *(Stop the Movie) Cruising*, 1980 (still). Courtesy of Jim Hubbard.

the vantage point of cruising, and the representations of the leather bar scene in the Village acquire an unanticipated kind of realism. It is clear that the set locations are real bars, well-established sites in the queer landscape of the Lower West Side. As Hubbard moves between the club and the street, between inside and outside, he sets up clear parallels between the multiple queer bodies congregating, fictionally, in the bars and the crowds of gay and lesbian activists rallying against the film in the streets of the Village. Rather that emphasize the differences between these gatherings, Hubbard plays with the thin line between fact and fiction that Friedkin made use of in his own work. Hubbard's vision of efforts to "stop the movie" is complex and nuanced, and has an archival bent. In juxtaposing scenes of real protest and of fictional queer congregation in the bars, (*Stop the Movie*) *Cruising* does not reject the suggestion that the dramatized bar scene is realistic but, instead, underscores its totalizing narrative effects. The confusing proximity of fact and fiction stresses the risk that the breadth of queer life in the Village in the 1970s was being obscured by the violent vision presented in *Cruising*. Like the street protests it records, and like Arch Brown's earlier, queerly preservationist film *Pier Groups*, Hubbard's work has a distinctly preservationist agenda, resisting at a structural level the viability of Friedkin's singular narrative of queer life in Manhattan in the late 1970s and documenting collective efforts to reject it.

### Sane recreation: The waterfront after the 1970s

Through the 1980s and into the 1990s, the future of Manhattan's harbor remained a point of mayoral concern. In the summer of 1998, echoing Percy Sutton's and Ed Koch's calls for waterfront renewal over twenty years earlier,

New York City mayor Rudolph Giuliani signed the Hudson River Park Act into law, empowering a state-owned corporation to transform the still largely derelict West Side waterfront into a series of public parks and sports venues, "replacing a once unsightly and deteriorating waterfront with . . . a five-mile riverfront esplanade that will be enjoyed by New Yorkers and tourists alike." State governor George Pataki echoed Giuliani's grand claims with nationalistic hyperbole, celebrating it as a "public" city space integral to the country's democratic claims. The river park, he argued, "is in every sense a renewal of New York's commitment to open space, the Hudson shoreline and the very history of our state and nation."[82]

This Hudson River Park legislation came after almost five years of a rigorous "quality of life" campaign that saw an increased and increasingly aggressive police presence throughout Manhattan, and numerous antivagrancy and public order laws ushered in under Giuliani's mayoralty. Brutal police crackdowns on loitering, unlawful assembly, and public urination, along with strongly enforced curfews, continued to push unwelcome guests out of the near-ghetto of the waterfront, whose queer hospitality had been fostered by decades of municipal neglect of the city's perimeter. The push for a safe space for queer youth, particularly queer youth of color, was especially urgent given the closure of Keller's in 1991 and the Two Potato, a gay bar on the corner of Christopher and Greenwich Street and "a 'legendary' gathering place for queer and transgender people of color," particularly during the AIDS crisis, in 2004.[83]

The queer activist groups Sex Panic! and FIERCE (Fabulous Independent Educated Radicals for Community Empowerment) have battled with wealthy neighborhood associations like Residents in Distress (RID) and the Christopher Street Patrol against police harassment and racial profiling of waterfront visitors.[84] Former FIERCE leader Jay Dee Melendez accused these residents' associations of "putting water, piss and garbage out of their windows onto the youth" during a "Save Our Space" rally in October 2002.[85]

These protests drew on earlier anti-gentrification actions by local queer community groups. In a 1994 *New York Times* report on "the new world near West Street" and the tensions it had begun to generate, Randy Kennedy wrote:

> In the last six years, the area west of Washington Street on Christopher, including parts of West Street, West 10th Street and tiny Weehawken Street—long a hustling and cruising area—has attracted a much younger crowd from outside Manhattan. The growing population became noticeable enough by 1992 that Community Board 2 began to talk about how to control it, said Maurice Engler, the site director for a community youth center, the Neutral Zone, that grew out of those discussions. "I think the neighborhood was freaked

> out, plain and simple," Mr. Engler said. "In place of the 20- and 30-something mostly white gays, there was a growing number of 'fem' and 'banjee,' black and Latino teen-agers."[86]

At the Lesbian and Community Center in the West Village in September 1997, the historian Allan Bérubé presented a slideshow of images showing queer reuses of the waterfront in the 1960s, 1970s, and 1980s and gave a talk on the multiple erotic, social, and activist appropriations of the site, the histories of which were in danger of being lost entirely as municipal regeneration efforts gathered pace in the mid-1990s. Afterward, Sex Panic! led the audience toward the piers and held a rally there. The combination of academic lecture and demonstration recalled Bérubé's article "The History of Gay Bathhouses," which was, in part, a protest against the forced closure of bathhouses in the mid-1980s as part of a nationwide crackdown on supposed "routes of transmission" for HIV, with no regard for their value as sites for queer community building and the sharing of safe-sex practices and AIDS education. "Public policy regarding bathhouses," Bérubé writes, "has been criticized as being based on political expediency rather than on medical or social science."[87] The removal of spaces where supposedly private activities—sex, political and social dissent—could be performed in public and where communities could develop was and is a key regulatory tactic in waterfront renewal, urban renewal, and social exclusion in New York more broadly. This process of neoliberal gentrification began in the ruins of the 1970s. As the city faced bankruptcy toward the end of the decade, Sarah Schulman writes, "the remaining poor, working-class, and middle-class residents simply did not provide a wide enough tax base to support the city's infrastructure," and "city policy began to be developed with the stated goal of attracting wealthier people back to the city in order to pay the municipal bills." "We now know," she concludes, "that real estate profit was a motive" for tax breaks and legislative support for converting old industrial buildings into condominiums.[88]

Waterfront anti-gentrification campaigns by queer activist groups gathered pace in the early 2000s in the light of attacks on LGBT young people in the area. In May 2003 Sakia Gunn, a fifteen-year-old black lesbian, was murdered on her way home to New Jersey after a night on the pier. Her killer was sentenced to twenty years for aggravated manslaughter, arguing that Sakia ran into his knife.[89] In 2006 four lesbian teenagers, also from New Jersey, were sentenced to between three and a half and eleven years in prison for attempted murder for defending themselves against a homophobic knife attack that took place near the Christopher Street pier. A working group appointed by the Hudson River Park Trust Advisory Council was advised by local community groups to "expand both the recreational spaces and income-generating uses, and provide more park space and increased revenue, without large-scale private development."[90] Since 2007, as part of its Safe Space campaign, FIERCE has been agitating for a twenty-four-hour LGBT youth drop-in center on Pier 40. The organization interviewed close to three hundred LGBT youth from across New York City to determine what services are needed: a covered space in the winter, space to produce art, access to healthy foods, mental health and emotional support, GED training, provision of clothes, HIV testing, and safe-sex education from a "transgender-sensitive medical staff." "A successful LGBT youth center," states FIERCE's initial proposal, "would work in unison with the Hudson River Park's own mission to create a park that is available for all of New York to enjoy." "We propose," they stress, "not only to maintain but to re-emphasize Pier 40 as community and recreation space."[91]

The present zoning of the pier, however, presents major limitations for this proposal. As a M-2/3 zoned area, or "medium manufacturing district"—which these parts of the waterfront have not been for over forty years—but a legally required "passive and active open space" under the Hudson River Park Act, "drug and alcohol counseling services, HIV testing services, or mental health counseling" are not permitted. Gardening and the growing of vegetables would violate the River Park Trust's rules against keeping gardening tools "to plant, prune, maintain, fertilize, or interfere . . . with any vegetation in any area under the jurisdiction of the Trust."[92] Not-for-profit medical services are zoned to be allowed only in residential districts, meaning the LGBT youth who frequent the piers are pushed out by residents' associations, "quality of life" legislation, and commercial zoning regulations simultaneously.

This rhetoric of renewal and exclusive access is essential to the success of present-day development of the waterfront and characterizes contemporary popular literature on the topic. In newspapers and in public discourse, the history of the space is rewritten as one of desperate and accidental neglect, its regeneration a moral imperative. Nathan Ward's history of organized crime on the waterfront, *Dark Harbor* (2010) was heralded by an op-ed piece in the *New York Times* in which Ward praised the development of spaces for "sane recreation" at the harbor under Giuliani and his successor as mayor, Michael Bloomberg. While in *Dark Harbor*, Ward muses on there being "a forlorn beauty to the slow dilapidation" of the space, in the more public space of the *New York Times* he praises "former Williamsburg beer plants . . . reborn as luxury condos; and Brooklyn's old Pier 6, where many a sailor once stepped ashore, . . . now filled with playing children." The city, he argues, "has celebrated the reclamation of the waterfront. But the effort, laudable though it is, obscures a not-so-insignificant historical misunderstanding: we are in fact *claiming* the waterfront, not *reclaiming* it."[93] Like Koch's proclamation to open "the waters to the people of the city" in the late 1970s, Ward's support for the work of the River Park Trust is based on a false conception of the extent of the waterfront's abandonment and a misunderstanding of the city's attitudes to its harbor and its rich past. Oblivious to the multiple "mis-uses" of the waterfront as an unregulated public space and sexual interzone, Ward's description of the postindustrial harbor as "a place most people never wanted to be" is part of the long-running misrepresentation of the long-standing queer appropriation of New York's piers that has been essential to constructing the contemporary waterfront as a space for "sane recreation."[94]

As contemporary conflicts over the piers demonstrate, the gentrified waterfront remains the setting for a bitter battle over the permissibility of queer space, the preservation of supposedly public space, the meaning of open access, and the limits of public and private citizenship. To continue to tell the stories of these queer appropriations, to document their persistence and their struggle in the present, to resist, like Schulman, the elimination of complex narratives of its use, might, as Wojnarowicz's waterfront writing did, serve "as a dismantling tool against the illusion of the ONE-TRIBE NATION," preserving a historical heterogeneity, shaping the way we record the past lives of this queer space, and a material one, shaping how we occupy it in the present and continue to relate to its liminal and littoral form in the future.[95]

CONCLUSION

# Rising into Ruin

Wojnarowicz's vision of the Hudson and its piers and warehouses as a "dead river" acquired unanticipated prescience and poignancy in the context of the HIV/AIDS epidemic, which came to define queer experience in New York after the final demolition of the abandoned waterfront warehouses in the mid-1980s. In 1984, as the members-only River Club on West Street held its closing party, remarking on a flyer for the event that "times change . . . tastes change . . . the end of an era is now at hand," small pieces of memorializing graffiti were appearing on the surfaces of the remaining walls and stone piers.[1] The waterfront's abandoned warehouses became something of "an informal archive," both of what David Román has called the "pre-AIDS moment" and of the later queer dead.[2] The queer space of the derelict waterfront was reshaped into "a memorial site" that marked the disappearance of a sexual culture and a historic city space as much as the death of the individuals who participated in it.[3] As the decade progressed, the decline of the gay cruising space of the piers was one disappearance among many, as the city's gay bathhouses and sex clubs faced closure under new legislation in the New York State Sanitary Code. By 1986 over half of Manhattan's bathhouses had shut down completely. There had been 28,712 cases of AIDS reported and 24,559 deaths. Peter Hujar died in November the following year, Paul Thek in August 1988. Wojnarowicz himself died in July 1992, the same year as Leonard Fink.

As we follow Wojnarowicz, Hujar, Fink, Alvin Baltrop, John Rechy, Andrew Holleran, and Arch Brown as they trace their own histories of the piers' queer reuses in the midst of plans for their redevelopment in the late 1970s and very early 1980s, our contemporary knowledge haunts these texts, photographs, and films. We are aware of the HIV/AIDS epidemic that devastated many of the queer communites who used the piers and warehouses. It shapes our reading of these decaying spaces. Both buildings and bodies appear ephemeral, the latter unwittingly. This sense of death-to-come is doubled, at least, in a photograph of the Ward Line warehouse by Andreas Sterzing, taken in 1983. Behind the ruined harbor in the foreground stand the Twin Towers of the World Trade Center. While Sterzing aimed to set up a clear contrast between the decaying warehouse and the robust construction of the World Trade Center, to a contemporary viewer the towers, as the artist Robert Smithson might have it, appear to "rise into ruin."[4] They have also since disappeared from the architectural landscape of lower Manhattan. It becomes difficult to establish or to maintain a linear temporal connection between the piers and the towers, and a past and present viewer, to imagine a time before.

The late 1970s can appear now as a moment filled with a tragic viral momentum, as an epidemic always on the cusp of development. The prevalence of the ruin in the downtown Manhattan landscape in this period appears to make this connection literal. For Tim Edensor, ruins are "symbolic of the inevitability of life passing, of a future in which obsolescence was certain and the inexorable processes of nature dispassionately took their toll of all things." Ruins, he argues, prefigure "imminent degeneration and collapse."[5] The prevalence of a visual culture of ruins in queer art and writing in the late 1970s is complicated by the frequency with which the gay liberation movements and cruising cultures of the period were cast in popular conservative discourse as excessive and self-destructive, and often likened to the last days of Rome. Fundamentalist Christian evangelists like Tim LaHaye, Jerry Falwell, and Pat Robertson decried the proliferation of gay cruising cultures in the 1970s as symptomatic of impending apocalypse, literalized in vindicatory fashion by the appearance of HIV/AIDS in the early 1980s.[6] Where once the piers recalled the pleasures of Pompeii, these conservative accounts evoked its destruction. Indeed, the ill-fated Roman town occupied a special position in the popular American imagination of the mid-1980s. In the introduction to the popular television miniseries *The Last Days of Pompeii* (1984), based on Edward Bulwer-Lytton's 1834 novel, a voiceover proclaims Pompeii a "byword for excess and indulgence, and dedication to the pursuit of pleasure . . . renowned for its works of art, its thriving commerce, but notorious for its licentiousness."[7] In an interview with *Playboy* magazine the same year, the actress Joan Collins drew similar connections: "Herpes and AIDS have come as the great plagues to teach us all a lesson. It's like the Roman Empire. Wasn't everybody running around just covered in syphilis? And then it was destroyed by the volcano."[8] For the conservative gay writer Andrew Sullivan, writing in the mid-1990s, this was "the Faustian bargain of the pre-AIDS closet."[9]

The value of the metaphor of the ruin for thinking through the queer cruising cultures on Manhattan's derelict waterfront in the late 1970s is, of course, not that it provides us with a metaphor for thinking about the ruination of diseased bodies or that it underscores a heterosexist image of an earlier queer sexual culture in supposedly evitable decay. In their queer ruination and in the temporal complexity this ruination generates, these ruins provide us with a means of visualizing sexual liberation beyond a homophobic causal relation between cruising and the development of HIV/AIDS. Normative distinctions between time periods and generations, between past and present, had, as Wojnarowicz observed in his early visits to the piers, become "irrelevant," unmoored from a normative linear connection that the waterfront cruising scene drew upon and enhanced.[10]

Writing in the midst of the HIV/AIDS epidemic, Douglas Crimp argued, famously, for the affective and activist value of promiscuity and cruising as a way of life. It is a complex "psychic preparation," he wrote, "that will save us." "Promiscuity," he argued,

> taught us many things, not only about the pleasures of sex, but about the great multiplicity of those pleasures. . . . Gay male promiscuity should be seen instead as a positive model of how sexual pleasures might be pursued by and granted to everyone if those pleasures were not confined within the narrow limits of institutionalized sexuality.[11]

Seen in this way, the erotically and historically promiscuous practice of waterfront cruising in ruins in the "pre-AIDS moment" of the late 1970s emerges as a model for the production of queer memory and the experience of queer time in a hostile environment. Through the act of cruising, through the experience of engaging in multiplicitious, anonymous sexual encounters, across and through time, but against teleology, the men who had wandered the piers developed numerous ways with which to deal with this "epidemic of signification."[12] Thinking through the queer matter of the ruin provides us with the means to reject causality and teleology in the pursuit of making fully visible these liberatory archival traces of a queer past. Viewed in this way, Wojnarowicz's work on ruins, along with Brown's, Rechy's, Baltrop's, Fink's, Roysdon's, and Hujar's, rids the "pre-AIDS moment" of the viral momentum and impression of imminent tragedy that often inhibits the contemporary viewer. It stimulates instead the pleasures of looking back, of cruising the derelict spaces and "abandoned sets of futures" of the late 1970s.[13] Writing of the graffiti memorials that appeared on the waterfront in the mid-1980s, Robert Sember argues that recollections of the cruising space of the piers, whether photographic, literary, filmic, or spoken, "do not constitute an official history of the site." Indeed, they cannot. Instead, "they offer glimpses, like those grabbed in the flash of light across water, of presences that ghost through our current intimacies."[14]

In much the same way, the story of the queer cruising culture of the abandoned Manhattan waterfront in the 1970s is not simply one of a queerly appropriated harbor, but is a story of the impossibility and undesirability of creating or sustaining singular narratives of the past. It is a story about the practice of queer history itself, of creating space for stories that exceed or contradict heteronormative narratives of the life of the city, of how to make use of the traces that remain, stubbornly and promiscuously, in the "vacant" and "ghostly"[15] gaps in the once "unhemmed"[16] fabric of the gentrifying city, not as a memorial, but as a demonstration.

# *Acknowledgments*

This book would not exist without the support of staff in the many archives in which work by David Wojnarowicz, Peter Hujar, Alvin Baltrop, Leonard Fink, and others now resides. I am so fortunate to have had the support of Lisa Darms, Marvin Taylor, Brent Phillips, Rachel Greer, and many others at the Fales Library and Special Collections at New York University over the past ten years. It has been a pleasure and an honor to work with them. Andreas Sterzing helped me immeasurably as I began work on this project in 2008, sharing his time, his photographs, and his memories of the Ward Line pier project over coffees in Vauxhall. Rich Wandel at the Lesbian, Gay, Bisexual & Transgender Community Center's National History Archive was the perfect guide to Leonard Fink's diverse collection of photographs. Thanks also to Caitlin McCarthy. Stephen Koch, the director of the Peter Hujar Archive, generously shared with me his memories of Hujar, Wojnarowicz, and Paul Thek over a number of years. Amy DiPasquale and Hedi Sorger kindly provided me access to the Peter Hujar Archive's vast collection of photographs. I am grateful to Yona Backer at Third Streaming for access to Alvin Baltrop's photographs. I am very grateful also to Emily Roysdon, Liz Ligon, Xaviera Simmons, Jill Magid, Efrain Gonzalez, Richard Hell, and Stanley Stellar for sharing their work with me. Thank you to the staff at the New York Public Library, particularly those engaged with the International Gay Information Center archive and the Berg Collection, and to Electronic Arts Intermix, the Carnegie Museum of Art, and David Zwirner Gallery. The Faculty of Humanities and Social Sciences at Newcastle University provided essential funding for the reproduction of these images.

In New York, I am thankful for the generosity and good conversation of John Fekner, Shelley Seccombe, Jim Hubbard, Sarah Schulman, Ted Bonin,

Anneliis Beadnell, and Jonathan VanDyke. I am grateful to Ivan Galietti, who shared his work and his memories of Wojnarowicz with me so openly. Thanks also to Cynthia Carr, Sur Rodney (Sur), and Richard Hell. Jonathan D. Katz and André Dombrowski hosted me generously in Philadelphia. I am very grateful to Jonathan for his long-standing support for my work and for his advice on preparing this book. All of this primary research was generously supported by funding from the Arts and Humanities Research Council and the Terra Foundation for American Art. Thank you to Karen Lamberti (my Mrs. Madrigal in Manhattan), and to Manuel Betancourt and Josh Gang for their friendship and good queer conversation.

This book has benefited immeasurably from the hard work, humor, and support of Mark Turner and John Howard. Adrian Rifkin and Michael Bibler were exemplary early reviewers. Mignon Nixon shaped my art historical thinking (and still does). I'm fortunate to have been able to develop this project in conversations with Bob Mills, Richard Maguire, Ben Nichols, Victoria Carroll, Skyler Hijazi, and so many others through Queer@King's. Our queer network was a unique source of intellectual, personal, and political pleasure and encouragement. We knew it then and I feel it now. Colleagues at the University of York, especially Jason Edwards, Michael White, and Emanuele Lugli, and the University of Edinburgh (Halle O'Neal, Vicky Coltman, Richard Williams, Carol Richardson, and Neil Cox especially) were kind and encouraging as I began preparing the manuscript and negotiating the strange and difficult terrain of postdoctoral life. I am grateful to so many inspiring students at both institutions. I also have greatly enjoyed sharing this research with staff and students at galleries and universities, including Tate Modern, the Royal Academy of Arts, Nottingham University, Carleton College, and the University of Oxford. I am lucky to spend most of my time in the company of artists. Colleagues and students at Newcastle University have been incredibly supportive and inspiring in sometimes unexpected ways. Thanks especially to Richard Talbot, Giles Bailey, Vee Pollock, Nadia Hebson, and Paul Becker. My CRUSEV family—especially Glyn Davis, Laura Guy, Nat Raha, and Benny Nemerofsky Ramsay—have supported this research and this researcher in productive and generous ways. Thank you to Matt Carter and the team at LUX Moving Image for sharing our vision of cruising as a method. I am so grateful to Jo Applin for her guidance on the book writing process. James Toftness, Joel Score, and many others at the University of Chicago Press deserve particular thanks for their commitment to this project.

Huw Lemmy introduced me to David Wojnarowicz's work over lukewarm lagers at a party in London in 2006. I bought *Close to the Knives: A Memoir of Disintegration* from Gay's the Word the next day, and it changed my life. As I've cruised this material since, this project has been shaped by friendships, chance conversations, unexpected discoveries in second-hand bookshops, casual and not-so-casual relationships, drinks receptions, serendipitous library visits, and gallery trips, and by roads not taken. I am grateful to so many friends and peers for their support of this work, including Catherine Grant, Amy Tobin, Conal McStravick, Victoria Horne, Harry Weeks, James Bell, Sam Ashby, Marko Ilić, Iggy Cortez, Lauren Porter, Lucy and Oli Hazzard, Felicity and Sam Wilkinson, Julian Smith-Newman, Niall Hodson, Malia Vella, Kyung An, Christopher Griffin, Fiontán Moran, Tom Scutt, Lucy Bradnock, Lottie Cantle, and many members of the Anderson, Paterson, and Moore families. James Boaden deserves a sentence of his own, for being a brilliant art historian and an even better friend. Greg Normand has supported and inspired me throughout—thank you for listening, and thank you for reading.

# *Notes*

### Introduction

1. David Wojnarowicz Papers, series 3, subseries A, box 5, folder 142, Fales Library and Special Collections, New York University Libraries.

2. Hart Crane, "The Bridge," in *The Complete Poems of Hart Crane* (Garden City, NY: Doubleday, 1958), 4.

3. Edmund White, *Nocturnes for the King of Naples* (London: Picador, 1984), 135.

4. White, *Nocturnes*, 137.

5. Robert F. Wagner Jr., "New York City Waterfront: Changing Land Use and Prospects for Redevelopment," in *Urban Waterfront Lands*, Committee on Urban Waterfront Lands (Washington, DC: National Academy of Sciences, 1980), 78, 80.

6. M. Christine Boyer, *The City of Collective Memory: Its Historical Imagery and Architectural Entertainments* (Cambridge, MA: MIT Press, 1994), 465.

7. Barry Blinderman, "The Compression of Time: An Interview with David Wojnarowicz," in *David Wojnarowicz: Tongues of Flame*, ed. Blinderman (New York: D.A.P., 1989), 54.

8. Wojnarowicz Papers, series 1, box 1, folder 11.

9. Wayne Hoffmann, "The Great Gay Way: A Brief History of Christopher Street," *Village Voice*, June 15, 2004, accessed November 8, 2015, http://www.villagevoice.com/news/the-great-gay-way-6406854.

10. David Wojnarowicz, "Biographical Dateline," in Blinderman, *David Wojnarowicz*, 118.

11. John Rechy, *Rushes* (New York: Grove, 1979), 13.

12. Andrew Holleran, "Nostalgia for the Mud," in *The View from Christopher Street: Journalism from America's Leading Gay Magazine*, ed. Michael Denneny, Charles Ortleb, and Thomas Steele (London: Chatto and Windus, 1983), 68.

13. Georg Simmel, "The Ruin," in *Ruins*, ed. Brian Dillon (Cambridge, MA: MIT Press, 2011), 23.

14. Laud Humphreys, *Tearoom Trade: Impersonal Sex in Public Places* (Chicago: Aldine, 1975), 48.

15. Sarah Schulman, *The Gentrification of the Mind: Witness to a Lost Imagination* (Berkeley: University of California Press, 2012), 36.

16. Christopher Reed and Christopher Castiglia, *If Memory Serves: Gay Men, AIDS, and the Promise of the Queer Past* (Minneapolis: University of Minnesota Press, 2011), 39.

17. Max Page, *The Creative Destruction of Manhattan, 1900–1940*, Chicago: University of Chicago Press, 1999), 2, 5, 15.

18. Michel de Certeau, *The Practice of Everyday Life* (Berkeley: University of California Press, 1984), 91.

19. Page, *Creative Destruction of Manhattan*, 15.

20. Jane Jacobs, *The Death and Life of Great American Cities* (Harmondsworth: Penguin, 1965), 200.

21. Jacobs, *Death and Life*, 202.

22. Schulman, *Gentrification of the Mind*, 28, 36.

23. Amy Scholder, ed., *In the Shadow of the American Dream: The Diaries of David Wojnarowicz* (New York: Grove, 1999), 206.

## Chapter One

1. Amy Scholder, ed., *In the Shadow of the American Dream: The Diaries of David Wojnarowicz* (New York: Grove, 1999), 33.

2. David Wojnarowicz Papers, series 1, box 1, folder 15 (Journals, Aug 1980–1981, Paris, NY), Fales Library and Special Collections, New York University Libraries.

3. Barry Blinderman, "The Compression of Time: An Interview with David Wojnarowicz," in *David Wojnarowicz: Tongues of Flame*, ed. Blinderman (New York: D.A.P., 1989), 54.

4. Blinderman, "Compression of Time," 54.

5. Wojnarowicz Papers, series 1, box 1, folder 14 (Journals [1980]).

6. John Rechy, *Rushes* (New York: Grove, 1979), 13.

7. Andrew Holleran, "Nostalgia for the Mud," in *The View from Christopher Street: Journalism from America's Leading Gay Magazine*, ed. Michael Denneny, Charles Ortleb, and Thomas Steele (London: Chatto and Windus, 1983), 68.

8. Scholder, *In the Shadow of the American Dream*, 145.

9. Wojnarowicz Papers, series 1, box 1, folder 11 (Journals NYC, 1979).

10. Dolores Hayden, *The Power of Place: Urban Landscape as Public History* (Cambridge, MA: MIT Press, 1997), 13.

11. Scholder, *In the Shadow of the American Dream*, 145; emphasis added.

12. David Wojnarowicz, *Close to the Knives: A Memoir of Disintegration* (New York: Vintage, 1991), 16, 12–13.

13. Mark Turner, *Backwards Glances: Cruising Queer Streets in London and New York* (London: Reaktion, 2003), 9–10.

14. Tim Dean, *Unlimited Intimacy: Reflections on the Subculture of Barebacking* (Chicago: University of Chicago Press, 2009), 181.

15. David Carter, *Stonewall: The Riots That Sparked a Gay Revolution* (New York: St. Martin's Press, 2004), 36.

16. Samuel Delany, *The Motion of Light in Water* (New York: Arbor House, 1988), 225.

17. Ira Tattelman, "Staging Sex and Masculinity at the Mineshaft," *Men and Masculinities* 7, no. 3 (January 2005): 302.

18. Delany, *Motion of Light in Water*, 215, 216. Carter (*Stonewall*, 36) reports up to three hundred men cruising the area on weekends.

19. Delany, *Motion of Light in Water*, 226.

20. Delany, *Motion of Light in Water*, 226–27.

21. Carter, *Stonewall*, 29, 36.

22. Burton W. Peretti, *Nightclub City: Politics and Amusement in Manhattan* (Philadelphia: University of Pennsylvania Press, 2007), 167.

23. Mary Virginia Lee Badgett, *Money, Myths and Change: The Economic Lives of Lesbians and Gay Men* (Chicago: University of Chicago Press, 2003), 105.

24. Jacquin Lait and Lee Mortimer, *New York: Confidential!* (New York: Crown, 1951).

25. Martin Duberman, *Stonewall* (New York: Plume, 1994), 184.

26. Carter, *Stonewall*, 115.

27. Wayne Hoffmann, "The Great Gay Way: A Brief History of Christopher Street," *Village Voice*, June 15, 2004. David Carter notes that, while "the NYPD had ceased entrapping homosexual men, the Transit Police, who were not controlled by the mayor's office, continued the practice." Carter, *Stonewall*, 115.

28. Carter, *Stonewall*, 115. The Mattachine Society was a homophile "service and welfare organization" founded in 1951 by Harry Hay, "devoted to the protection and improvement of Society's Androgynous Minority" across New York and, later, other major cities throughout the United States. Will Roscoe with Harry Hay, *Radically Gay: Gay Liberation in the Words of Its Founder* (Boston: Beacon, 1996), 63.

29. Carter, *Stonewall*, 116.

30. Carter, *Stonewall*, 115.

31. Perry Brass, "Lost Gay New York: Truckin' at the Trucks," August 3, 2010, accessed July 10, 2011, http://queernewyorkblog.blogspot.com/2010/08/perry-brass-lost-gay-new-york-truckin.html.

32. Jeff Auer, "Bette at the Bathhouse," *Gay and Lesbian Review* 15, no. 3 (May–June 2008), accessed July 10, 2011, http://www.glreview.com/article.php?articleid=59.

33. Maer Roshan, "Larry Kramer: Queer Conscience," *New York*, March 30, 1998, accessed July 10, 2011, http://nymag.com/nymetro/news/people/features/2423/.

34. Carter, *Stonewall*, 116.

35. John Rechy, *City of Night* (London: Panther, 1968), 56.

36. Rechy, *City of Night*, 60.

37. Rechy, *City of Night*, 182, 60.

38. Rechy, *City of Night*, 60.

39. Rechy, *Rushes*, 22.

40. George Chauncey, *Gay New York: The Making of the Gay Male World, 1890–1940* (London: Flamingo, 1995), 208.

41. Allan Bérubé, "The History of Gay Bathhouses," in *Policing Public Sex*, ed. Dangerous Bedfellows and Ephen Glenn Colter (Boston: South End Press, 1996), 193. An earlier version of the essay was later published in *Journal of Homosexuality* 44, nos. 3–4 (2003): 33–53.

42. Edmund White, *States of Desire: Travels in Gay America* (London: Pan Books, 1986), 269, 266. In August 1971, Christopher's End was the site of an anti-Mafia protest, organized by the Gay Activists' Alliance. http://digitalcollections.nypl.org/items/510d47e3-57e7-a3d9-e040-e00a18064a99. Accessed October 4, 2015.

43. White, *States of Desire*, 266.

44. Roshan, "Larry Kramer: Queer Conscience."

45. Larry Kramer, *Faggots* (London: Minerva, 1990), 173.

46. Tattelman, "Staging Sex and Sexuality," 302.

47. Delany, *Motion of Light in Water*, 225.

48. "Ephemera: Bars," International Gay Information Center archive, New York Public Library.

49. Tattelman, "Staging Sex and Sexuality," 302.

50. Kramer, *Faggots*, 228.

51. Tattelman, "Staging Sex and Sexuality," 302.

52. Gordon Brent Ingram, Anne-Marie Bouthillette, and Yolanda Retter, eds., *Queers in Space: Communities–Public Spaces–Sites of Resistance* (Seattle, WA: Bay Press, 1997), 391.

53. Tattelman, "Staging Sex and Sexuality," 302; emphasis added.

54. Tattelman, "Staging Sex and Sexuality," 302.

55. "Ephemera: Bars," International Gay Information Center archive, New York Public Library.

56. "Ephemera: Bars," International Gay Information Center archive, New York Public Library.

57. "Ephemera: Bars," International Gay Information Center archive, New York Public Library.

58. Ingram, Bouthillette, and Retter, *Queers in Space*, 402.

59. Edmund White, *City Boy: My Life in New York during the 1960s and '70s* (London: Bloomsbury, 2011), 238.

60. Rodney Lofton, *No More Tomorrows: Two Lives, Two Stories, One Love* (Largo, MD: Strebor Books, 2009), 69.

61. Dennis Altman, *The Homosexualization of America: The Americanization of the Homosexual* (New York: St. Martin's Press, 1982), 206.

62. John Paul Ricco, *The Logic of the Lure* (Chicago: University of Chicago Press, 2002), 19.

63. Bérubé, "History of Gay Bathhouses," 191.

64. Aaron Betsky, *Queer Space: Architecture and Same-Sex Desire* (New York: William Morrow, 1997), 142, 190.

65. Michel Foucault, "Of Other Spaces," *Diacritics* 16, no. 1 (Spring 1986): 24.

66. Betsky, *Queer Space*, 147.

67. Dianne Chisholm, *Queer Constellations: Subcultural Space in the Wake of the City* (Minneapolis: University of Minnesota Press, 2004), 75.

68. Ricco, *Logic of the Lure*, 19.

69. Rechy, *Rushes*, 131.

70. Rechy, *Rushes*, 15–16.

71. Wojnarowicz, "Biographical Dateline," 118. City journalists were also somewhat unresponsive to the discrimination that characterized much of the violence on the waterfront. As Pamela Lee notes, while many "complained of the growing crime that took place around the piers, a 'mugger's paradise' as one writer called it, they implicitly (and homophobically) criminalized the victim's behavior." Lee, *Object to Be Destroyed: The Work of Gordon Matta-Clark* (Cambridge, MA: MIT Press, 1999), 120.

72. White, *City Boy*, 77.

73. Jim Ryan, untitled pier newsletter, International Gay Information Center archive, New York Public Library.

74. Douglas Crimp, "Alvin Baltrop: Pier Photographs, 1975–1986," *Artforum*, February 2008, 269. In 2015 a selection of Baltrop's photographs of the piers was included in the group show *Greater New York* at MoMA PS1, for which Crimp was one of four curators.

75. Carlos Motta, "An Interview with Emily Roysdon," *We Who Feel Differently*, April 15, 2011, accessed June 6, 2018, http://wewhofeeldifferently.info/interview.php?interview=112.

76. Alvin Baltrop, quoted in Crimp, "Alvin Baltrop," 269.

77. Douglas Crimp, *Before Pictures* (Chicago: University of Chicago Press, 2016), 190.

78. Wojnarowicz Papers, series 1, box 1, folders 14 [journal entry], 12 (Journals NY, 1979–80) ["Dream"], and 5 (New York–France, 1978) ["End Street"].

79. Rechy, *Rushes*, 133.

80. Macaulay, "A Note on New Ruins," in *Ruins*, ed. Brian Dillon (Cambridge, MA: MIT Press, 2011), 27.

81. Hayden, *Power of Place*, 13.

82. Scholder, *In the Shadow of the American Dream*, 146–47.

83. Wojnarowicz, *Close to the Knives*, 42.

84. Scholder, *In the Shadow of the American Dream*, 146–47.

85. Blinderman, "Compression of Time," 54.

86. Scholder, *In the Shadow of the American Dream*, 146–47.

87. Denis Diderot, "Salon of 1767," in *Ruins*, ed. Brian Dillon (Cambridge, MA: MIT Press, 2011), 22.

88. Wojnarowicz Papers, series 1, box 1, folder 13 (Journals NY 1980 Feb 2–Apr 3).

89. Wojnarowicz Papers, series 1, box 1, folder 13 (Journals NY 1980 Feb 2–Apr 3).

90. Wojnarowicz Papers, series 1, folder 11 (NYC Journals 1979). The film Wojnarowicz describes was never made.

91. Wojnarowicz Papers, series 1, box 1, folder 15 (Journals, Aug 1980–1981, Paris, NY); emphasis added. Wojnarowicz lived in Paris and Brittany for a number of months between 1977 and 1978.

92. Michael Trask, *Cruising Modernism: Class and Sexuality in American Literature and Social Thought* (Ithaca, NY: Cornell University Press, 2003), 129.

93. Jack Halberstam, *In a Queer Time and Place: Transgender Bodies, Subcultural Lives* (New York: New York University Press, 2005), 2.

94. Wojnarowicz Papers, series 1, box 1, folder 11 (Journals NYC, 1979).

95. Trask, *Cruising Modernism*, 128.

96. Wojnarowicz Papers, series 1, box 1, folder 11 (New York—June 6, 1979 to August 28, 1979).

97. Wojnarowicz Papers, series 1, box 1, folder 15 (Journals, Aug 1980–1981, Paris, NY); emphasis added.

98. Jean Genet, *The Thief's Journal*, trans. Bernard Frechtman (New York, Grove Press, 1964), 29 (emphasis added), 45.

99. Wojnarowicz Papers, series 1, box 1, folder 14 (Journals 1980).

100. Wojnarowicz Papers, series 1, box 1, folder 11 (New York—June 6, 1979 to August 28, 1979).

101. White, *City Boy*, 77.

102. Tim Dlugos, "Chez Jane," in *A Fast Life: The Collected Poems of Tim Dlugos*, ed. David Trinidad (Callicoon, NY: Nightboat Books, 2011), 246.

103. Dlugos, "Chez Jane," 247.

104. Kramer, *Faggots*, 125, 137, 125–26, 137, 138.

105. Émile Augier, *Le mariage d'Olympe* (Paris: Calmann Lévy, 1881), 5.

106. Tom Wolfe, "Radical Chic: That Party at Lenny's," *New York*, June 8, 1970, accessed November 8, 2015, http://nymag.com/news/features/46170/.

107. Holleran, "Nostalgia for the Mud," 68–69.

108. Seth Koven, *Slumming: Sexual and Social Politics in Victorian London* (Princeton, NJ: Princeton University Press, 2004), 9. See also Chad Heap, *Slumming: Sexual and Racial Encounters in American Nightlife, 1885–1940* (Chicago: University of Chicago Press, 2009)

109. Holleran, "Nostalgia for the Mud," 70, 69, 68, 70.

110. Holleran, "Nostalgia for the Mud," 70.

111. Henry Miller, "The Ghetto (N.Y.)," from *Sexus*, in *The Henry Miller Reader*, ed. Lawrence Durrell (New York: New Directions, 1959), 72.

112. Holleran, "Nostalgia for the Mud," 69.

113. Turner, *Backwards Glances*, 9.

114. Scholder, *In the Shadow of the American Dream*, 135.

## Chapter Two

1. Giuliana Bruno, *Atlas of Emotion: Journeys in Art, Architecture, and Film* (New York: Verso, 2002), 103.

2. Timothy Corrigan, *The Essay Film: From Montaigne, after Marker* (Oxford: Oxford University Press, 2011), 106.

3. Gordon Matta-Clark, "Work with Abandoned Structures" (ca. 1975), in *Gordon Matta-Clark: Works and Collected Writings*, ed. Gloria Moure (Barcelona: Ediciones Poligrafa, 2006), 141.

4. Scholder, *In the Shadow of the American Dream*, 117.

5. John Rechy, *Rushes* (New York: Grove, 1979), 12.

6. Scholder, *In the Shadow of the American Dream*, 117.

7. Scholder, *In the Shadow of the American Dream*, 117–18.

8. Scholder, *In the Shadow of the American Dream*, 119.

9. Mark Turner, *Backward Glances: Cruising Queer Streets in London and New York* (London: Reaktion, 2003), 9.

10. David Wojnarowicz Papers, series 8, subseries A, media ID 092.0530 (John/David conversation, 12/31/1980, Part 2), Fales Library and Special Collections, New York University Libraries.

11. Barry Blinderman, "The Compression of Time: An Interview with David Wojnarowicz," in *David Wojnarowicz: Tongues of Flame*, ed. Blinderman (New York: D.A.P., 1989), 54.

12. Wojnarowicz Papers, series 1, box 1, folder 13.

13. Wojnarowicz, *In the Shadow of the American Dream*, 119.

14. Wojnarowicz Papers, series 9, subseries A [2], box 31, folder 16, envelope 16 (Peter Hujar at pier [early 80s], Don Rodan with plane).

15. Titles given to works by Stephen Koch, executor of Hujar's estate and archive. According to Koch, Hujar tended to leave his landscape photographs untitled. Interview with Stephen Koch, August 2014.

16. Walker Evans, "The Auto Junkyard," *Fortune*, April 1962, 132, 133.

17. Gayle S. Rubin, "Thinking Sex: Notes for a Radical Theory of the Politics of Sexuality," in *Deviations: A Gayle Rubin Reader* (Durham, NC: Duke University Press, 2011), 151.

18. Robert Smithson, "A Tour of the Monuments of Passaic, New Jersey," in *Robert Smithson: The Collected Writings*, ed. Jack Flam (Berkeley: University of California Press, 1996), 71.

19. Smithson, "Tour of the Monuments," 71, 72.

20. Smithson, "Tour of the Monuments," 74; Scholder, *In the Shadow of the American Dream*, 135.

21. Gene R. Swenson, "Beneath the Skin: Interview with Paul Thek (1966)," in *Paul Thek: Artist's Artist*, ed. Harald Falckenberg and Peter Weibel (Cambridge, MA: MIT Press, 2009), 348.

22. Michael Fried, "Art and Objecthood," in *Art and Objecthood: Essays and Reviews* (Chicago: University of Chicago Press, 1998), 155.

23. "Paul Thek and His Circle in the 1950s," accessed August 4, 2016, https://www.leslielohman.org/exhibitions/2013/paul-thek-and-his-circle-3.html.

24. Paul Thek, letter to Peter Harvey (no date), in *Paul Thek and His Circle in the 1950s*, exh. cat. (Leslie-Lohman Museum of Gay and Lesbian Art, 2013), 18.

25. Paul Thek, letter to Peter Harvey (no date), 19.

26. Susan Sontag, "Introduction," in Peter Hujar, *Portraits in Life and Death* (New York: Da Capo, 1976).

27. Swenson, "Beneath the Skin," 348.

28. Wojnarowicz Papers, series 8, subseries A, media ID 092.0514 (interview with Peter Hujar, pt 2).

29. Robert Smithson, "Entropy and the New Monuments," in ed. Jack Flam, *Robert Smithson: The Collected Writings* (Berkeley: University of California Press, 1996), 10, 11.

30. Smithson, "Entropy and the New Monuments," 11.

31. Smithson, "Entropy and the New Monuments," 16; William S. Burroughs, *Nova Express* (New York: Grove, 1964), 95.

32. Smithson, "Entropy and the New Monuments," 10

33. Nancy Foote, "The Apotheosis of the Crummy Space," *Artforum* (October 1976), 30.

34. Foote, "Apotheosis of the Crummy Space," 30, 29.

35. Martin Beck, "Alternative Space," in *Alternative Art, New York, 1965–1985: A Cultural Politics Book for the Social Text Collective, the Drawing Center, New York*, ed. Julie Ault (Minneapolis: University of Minnesota Press, 2002), 256.

36. Beck, "Alternative Space," 251.

37. Jacki Apple and Mary Delahoyde, *Alternatives in Retrospect: An Historical Overview, 1969–1975* (New York: New Museum, 1981), 15.

38. Beck, "Alternative Space," 260.

39. Beck, "Alternative Space," 262. Beck quotes Reesa Greenberg's feminist criticisms of the appropriation of industrial spaces in the 1970s and foundation of AIR Gallery in 1972. Greenberg argued that "the move to factory exhibition spaces can be seen as a reclaiming of the spaces of and for work as masculine." She cites AIR Gallery as countering this masculine dominance by addressing "the pressing and obvious need for more exhibition space given over to the work of women artists" and for "models and encouragement which a greater body of women artists' work would provide."

40. Richard J. Williams, *After Modern Sculpture* (Manchester: Manchester University Press, 2000), 111.

41. Douglas Crimp, *On the Museum's Ruins* (Cambridge, MA: MIT Press, 1993), 150.

42. Martha Buskirk, *The Contingent Object of Contemporary Art* (Cambridge, MA: MIT Press, 2003), 133.

43. Crimp, *On the Museum's Ruins*, 151.

44. Buskirk, *Contingent Object*, 132.

45. Mario Garcia Torres, *9 at Leo Castelli* (San Juan, PR: Instituto de Cultura Puertorriqueña, 2009), 8.

46. Torres, *9 at Leo Castelli*, 9.

47. Lynne Cooke and Douglas Crimp, with Kristin Poor, eds., *Mixed Use, Manhattan: Photography and Related Practices, 1970s to the Present* (Cambridge, MA: MIT Press; Museo Nacional Centro de Arte Reina Sofia, 2010), 37.

48. Cooke and Crimp, *Mixed Use, Manhattan*, 37.

49. Cooke and Crimp, *Mixed Use, Manhattan*, 41.

50. Kate Linker, *Vito Acconci* (New York: Rizzoli, 1994), 41.

51. Molly Nesbitt, "Bright Lights, Big City: The '80s without Walls," *Artforum*, April 2003, 186, 245.

52. Vito Acconci, "Public Space in a Private Time," *Critical Inquiry* 16, no. 4 (1990): 901.

53. Acconci, "Public Space in a Private Time," 910.

54. Joan Jonas with Rosalind Krauss, "Seven Years," *The Drama Review: TDR* 19, no.1 (March 1975): 13. (Krauss's name was misspelled Krause in the journal.)

55. Crimp, "Action around the Edges," in Cooke and Crimp, *Mixed Use, Manhattan*, 117.

56. Crimp, "Action around the Edges," 125.

57. Jonas and Krauss, "Seven Years," 13.

58. Crimp, "Action around the Edges," 127.

59. Pamela M. Lee, *Object to Be Destroyed: The Work of Gordon Matta-Clark* (Cambridge, MA: MIT Press, 1999), 120.

60. Lee, *Object to Be Destroyed*, 121.

61. Lee, *Object to Be Destroyed*, 127.

62. Thomas Crow, *Modern Art in the Common Culture* (New Haven, CT: Yale University Press, 1996), 135.

63. Matta-Clark, quoted in Cooke and Crimp, *Mixed Use, Manhattan*, 104.

64. Lee, *Object to Be Destroyed*, 127.

65. Lee, *Object to Be Destroyed*, 121.

66. Gordon Matta-Clark, "Splitting the Humphrey Street Building" (interview with Liza Bear, May 21, 1974), *Avalanche*, December 1974, 34.

67. Lee, *Object to Be Destroyed*, 127.

68. Juan A. Suárez, "Styles of Occupation: Manhattan in Experimental Film and Video from the 1970s to the Present," in Cooke and Crimp, *Mixed Use, Manhattan*, 137.

69. "Gordon Matta-Clark: The Making of Pier 52, an Interview with Liza Bear, March 11, 1976," in Moure, *Gordon Matta-Clark*, 217. Quoted in Crimp, "Action around the Edges," 108.

70. Gordon Matta-Clark, "My Understanding of Art" (typewritten statement ca. 1975), in Moure, *Gordon Matta-Clark*, 204. Quoted in Crimp, "Action around the Edges," 114.

71. Baltrop, quoted in Crimp, "Action around the Edges," 83.

72. Lee, *Object to Be Destroyed*, 121.

73. Crimp, "Action around the Edges," 114.

74. Matta-Clark, "Work with Abandoned Structures," 141.

75. Anney Bonney and Mike Bidlo, "Mike Bidlo," *BOMB* 45 (Fall 1993), accessed July 20, 2010, http://bombsite.com/issues/45/articles/1693.

76. Sylvere Lotringer, ed., *David Wojnarowicz: A Definitive History of Five or Six Years on the Lower East Side* (New York: Semiotext(e), 2006), 29.

77. Wojnarowicz Papers, series 6, subseries D, box 10, folder 78B (Artist file: Wojnarowicz bios).

78. Cynthia Carr, *A Fire in the Belly: The Life and Times of David Wojnarowicz* (London: Bloomsbury, 2012), 141.

79. Fiona Anderson, "Notions of the Collaborative in the Work of David Wojnarowicz," *Papers of Surrealism*, Spring 2010, 7.

80. Blinderman, "Compression of Time," 54.

81. Carr, *Fire in the Belly*, 225.

82. Anderson, "Notions of the Collaborative," 7.

83. Blinderman, "Compression of Time," 56.

84. Carr, *Fire in the Belly*, 194.

85. Wojnarowicz Papers, series 6, subseries D, box 10, folder 78B (Artist file: Wojnarowicz bios).

86. Wojnarowicz Papers, series 6, subseries D, box 10, folder 78B (Artist file: Wojnarowicz bios).

87. Interview with Andreas Sterzing, October 2008.

88. Interview with Andreas Sterzing, October 2008.

89. Lotringer, *David Wojnarowicz*, 31.

90. Blinderman, "Compression of Time," 56.

91. James Wines (SITE), *De-Architecture* (New York: Rizzoli, 1987), 107.

92. Interview with John Fekner, February 2009.

93. Carr, *Fire in the Belly*, 225.

94. See Peter Hujar, *Animals and Nudes* (Sante Fe, NM: Twin Palms, 2001).

95. Mysoon Rizk, "Reinventing the Pre-Invented World," in *Fever: The Art of David Wojnarowicz*, ed. Dan Cameron et al. (New York: Rizzoli, 1999), 48.

96. Wojnarowicz Papers, series 3, subseries H, box 6, folder 299 (reviews of Ivan Galietti's "Pompeii New York").

97. Wojnarowicz Papers, series 3, subseries H, box 6, folder 299 (reviews of Ivan Galietti's "Pompeii New York").

98. Andreas Sterzing, interview with the author, October 2008.

99. Robert Sember, "In the Shadow of the Object: Sexual Memory in the AIDS Epidemic," *Space & Culture* 6, no. 3 (August 2003): 218.

100. Wojnarowicz Papers, series 6, subseries D, box 10, folder 78B (Artist file: Wojnarowicz bios).

101. Smithson, "Tour of the Monuments," 72.

102. Wojnarowicz Papers, series 6, subseries D, box 10, folder 78B (Artist file: Wojnarowicz bios).

103. Various Artists, Pier 54. The High Line, accessed August 17, 2017, http://art.thehighline.org/project/pier54/.

## Chapter Three

1. David Wojnarowicz Papers, series 1, box 1, folder 10 (Journals France 1979/NY Ocean), Fales Library and Special Collections, New York University Libraries.

2. Amy Scholder, ed., *In the Shadow of the American Dream: The Diaries of David Wojnarowicz* (New York: Grove, 1999), 147; emphasis added.

3. Scholder, *In the Shadow of the American Dream*, 127, 169, 147.

4. Jacques Derrida, *Spectres of Marx* (London, Routledge, 1994), xix, 4.

5. Derrida, *Spectres of Marx*, 6; Wojnarowicz Papers, series 1, box 1, folder 5 (New York–France, 1978).

6. Scholder, *In the Shadow of the American Dream*, 142, 141.

7. Jack Halberstam, *In A Queer Time and Place: Transgender Bodies, Subcultural Lives* (New York: New York University Press, 2005), 2.

8. Elizabeth Freeman, *Time Binds: Queer Temporalities, Queer Histories* (Durham, NC: Duke University Press, 2010), 95.

9. Penny Arcade, "On David Wojnarowicz's *In the Shadow of the American Dream* (1999)," in Dan Cameron et al., *East Village USA* (New York: New Museum, 2004), 110.

10. Roland Barthes, "The Death of the Author," in *Image/Music/Text*, trans. Stephen Heath (London: Fontana, 1977), 148, 147.

11. Wojnarowicz Papers, series 8, subseries A, media ID 092.0487 (Keith Davis interview [no date, ca. 1983]).

12. Michel Foucault et al., "Friendship as a Way of Life," in *Michel Foucault: Ethics, Subjectivity and Truth*, ed. Paul Rabinow (Paris: Editions G, 1997), 138, 136.

13. Catherine Grant, "Fans of Feminism: Re-Writing Histories of Second-Wave Feminism in Contemporary Art," *Oxford Art Journal* 34, no. 2 (2011): 271, 286, 274.

14. Freeman, quoted in Grant, "Fans of Feminism," 274.

15. Freeman, *Time Binds*, 95.

16. Judith Butler, *Bodies That Matter* (New York: Routledge, 1993), 228.

17. Derrida, *Spectres of Marx*, 4.

18. Wojnarowicz Papers, series 1, box 1, folder 11 (Journals NYC, 1979).

19. Wojnarowicz, "Biographical Dateline," 118.

20. Wojnarowicz Papers, series 1, box 1, folder 4.

21. Henry Miller, *The Time of the Assassins: A Study of Rimbaud* (New York: New Directions, 1962), preface, vi.

22. Arthur Rimbaud, "Bad Blood," in *A Season in Hell*, in *Rimbaud: Complete Works, Selected Letters*, trans. Wallace Fowlie (Chicago: University of Chicago Press, 1966), 175; David Wojnarowicz, *Close to the Knives: A Memoir of Disintegration* (New York: Vintage, 1991), 3.

23. Rimbaud, "Bad Blood," 177.

24. Miller, *Time of the Assassins*, 43.

25. Arthur Rimbaud, *I Promise to Be Good: The Letters of Arthur Rimbaud*, trans. Wyatt Mason (New York: Modern Library, 2003), 33.

26. Sylvere Lotringer, ed., *David Wojnarowicz: A Definitive History of Five or Six Years on the Lower East Side* (New York: Semiotext(e), 2006), 219. The statements were part of Wojnarowicz's court testimony against Reverend Donald Wildmon, executive director of the American Family Association (AFA). Wojnarowicz was looking to halt the publication of a pamphlet by the AFA, in which portions of his *Sex Series (for Marion Scemama)* (1988–1989) were reproduced without context, and seeking damages based upon claims of copyright infringement, defamation, and violations of the New York Artists' Authorship Rights Act. Wojnarowicz's lawsuit was successful and he was awarded one dollar in damages.

27. Lotringer, *David Wojnarowicz*, 217.

28. Freeman, *Time Binds*, 95.

29. Leo Bersani, quoted in Lee Edelman, *Homographesis: Essays in Gay Literary and Cultural Theory* (London: Routledge, 1994), 107.

30. Wojnarowicz Papers, series 1, box 1, folder 10 (Journals France 1979/NY Ocean).

31. Marjorie Perloff, *The Poetics of Indeterminacy: Rimbaud to Cage* (Evanston, IL: Northwestern University Press, 1981), 53, 3.

32. Perloff, *Poetics of Indeterminacy*, 45.

33. Marjorie Perloff, *Frank O'Hara: Poet among Painters* (New York: George Braziller, 1977), 144.

34. Frank O'Hara, "In Memory of My Feelings," *The Collected Poems of Frank O'Hara*, ed. Donald Allen (Berkeley: University of California Press, 1995), 255.

35. Carrie Jaurés Noland, "Rimbaud and Patti Smith: Style as Social Deviance," *Critical Inquiry* 21, no. 3 (Spring 1995): 582.

36. Richard Hell, "I Is Another" (review of Edmund White's Rimbaud biography, *The Double Life of a Rebel*), *New York Times*, October 15, 2008, BR8.

37. Wallace Fowlie, *Rimbaud: The Myth of Childhood* (Chicago: University of Chicago Press, 1965), 58.

38. Richard Hell Papers, series 3R, box 13, folder 933 (Artifact, first draft w/corrections), Fales Library and Special Collections, New York University Libraries.

39. Benjamin H. D. Buchloh, "Allegorical Procedures: Appropriation and Montage in Contemporary Art," *Artforum*, September 1982, 52.

40. Richard Hell Papers, series 3R, box 13, folder 934 (early draft, Unrequited Narcissism).

41. Tennessee Williams, *Moise and the World of Reason* (London: W. H. Allen, 1976), 114, 150.

42. Wojnarowicz Papers, series 1, box 1, folder 10.

43. Wojnarowicz Papers, series 1, box 1, folder 7.

44. Wojnarowicz Papers, series 1, box 1, folder 5.

45. Gregory Corso, "Paris," in *Poems for Architects: An Anthology*, ed. Jill Stoner (San Francisco: William Stout, 2003), 75.

46. Corso, "Paris," 75.

47. William S. Burroughs, "Paris Please Stay the Same," in *The Adding Machine: Selected Essays* (New York: Arcade, 1993), 106, quoting Arthur Rimbaud, "Novel," in *Rimbaud: Complete Works*, 51.

48. Wojnarowicz Papers, series 1, box 1, folder 10.

49. Dennis Cooper, ed., *Little Caesar*, no. 5, "Rimbaud Issue," Dennis Cooper Papers, series VI, box 11, folder 85, Fales Library and Special Collections, New York University Libraries. Also at http://www.dennis-cooper.net/littlecaesar/lc05.htm (accessed July 27, 2017).

50. Daniel Kane, *Do You Have a Band? Poetry and Punk Rock in New York City* (New York: Columbia University Press, 2017), 210.

51. Cooper, *Little Caesar* #5.

52. Wojnarowicz Papers, series 1, box 1, folder 10.

53. Guillaume Apollinaire, "Zone," in *Alcools: Poems*, trans. Donald Revell (Hanover, NH: University Press of New England, 1995), 9.

54. Apollinaire, "Zone," 11; Wojnarowicz Papers, series 3, subseries A, box 4, folder 94.

55. Stéphane Mallarmé, "The Tomb of Edgar Poe," trans. Daisy Aldan, in *An Anthology of French Poetry from Nerval to Valéry in English Translation*, ed. Angel Flores (Garden City, NY: Doubleday, 1958), 157.

56. Marian Zwerling Sugano, *The Poetics of the Occasion: Mallarmé and the Poetry of Circumstance* (Stanford, CA: Stanford University Press, 1992), 104.

57. T. S. Eliot, "Tradition and the Individual Talent," in *Modernism: An Anthology*, ed. Lawrence Rainey (Oxford: Blackwell, 2005), 153–54.

58. Barthes, "Death of the Author," 145.

59. T. S. Eliot, "Burnt Norton," in *Collected Poems: 1909–1962* (London: Faber and Faber, 1963), 189, 190.

60. Eliot, "Tradition and the Individual Talent," 153.

61. Penny Arcade, "On David Wojnarowicz's *In the Shadow of the American Dream* (1999)," 110.

62. Derrida, *Spectres of Marx*, 39.

63. Harold Bloom, *Anxiety of Influence: A Theory of Poetry* (Oxford: Oxford University Press, 1997), 5.

64. Bloom, *Anxiety of Influence*, 141.

65. Eliot, "Tradition and the Individual Talent," 147, 15, 152.

66. Wojnarowicz, "Biographical Dateline," 118.

67. Bloom, *Anxiety of Influence*, 15.

68. Wojnarowicz Papers, series 3, subseries A, box 4, folder 94.

69. Derrida, *Spectres of Marx*, 40; Bloom, *The Anxiety of Influence*, 141.

70. Eliot, "Tradition and the Individual Talent," 153.

71. Derrida, *Spectres of Marx*, 40.

72. Roland Barthes, *Camera Lucida: Reflections on Photography*, trans. Richard Howard (London: Flamingo, 1984), 16, 87.

73. Arthur Rimbaud, "Bad Blood," in *Rimbaud: Complete Works*, 174.

74. Barthes, *Camera Lucida*, 93, 87.

75. Barthes, *Camera Lucida*, 96, 10, 96.

76. Barthes, *Camera Lucida*, 96.

77. Jacques Lacan, *Écrits* (London: Tavistock, 1977), 86.

78. J. Hillis Miller, "The Limits of Pluralism, III: The Critic as Host," *Critical Inquiry*, Spring 1977, 446; Scholder, *In the Shadow of the American Dream*, 136.

79. Scholder, *In the Shadow of the American Dream*, 136.

80. Wojnarowicz Papers, series 1, box 1, folder 13.

81. Mary Ann Doane, *The Emergence of Cinematic Time* (Cambridge, MA: Harvard University Press, 2002), 214.

82. Doane, *Emergence of Cinematic Time*, 214.

83. Wojnarowicz Papers, series 1, box 1, folder 5 (New York–France, 1978).

84. Halberstam, *In a Queer Time and Place*, 6.

85. Ross Chambers, *Loiterature* (Omaha: University of Nebraska Press, 1999), 77.

86. Thomas Mann, *Magic Mountain* (London: Everyman, 2005), 641.

87. Halberstam, *In a Queer Time and Place*, 6; Mann, *Magic Mountain*, 641.

88. Mann, *Magic Mountain*, 647.

89. Lee Edelman, *No Future: Queer Theory and the Death Drive* (Durham, NC: Duke University Press, 2004), 4.

90. Mann, *Magic Mountain*, 648.

91. Scholder, *In the Shadow of the American Dream*, 138,

92. Herman Melville, *Moby-Dick; or, The Whale* (1851; London: Penguin, 2009), 3.

93. John Carlin, "David Wojnarowicz: As the World Turns," in *David Wojnarowicz: Tongues of Flame*, ed. Barry Blinderman (New York: D.A.P., 1989), 29.

94. Wojnarowicz Papers, series 1, box 1, folder 5.

95. Walt Whitman, "As I Ebb'd with the Ocean of Life," in *Complete Poems* (London: Penguin, 2004), 281, 283.

96. Whitman, "Crossing Brooklyn Ferry," in *Complete Poems*, 194, 191.

97. Hart Crane, "The Bridge," in *The Complete Poems of Hart Crane* (Garden City, NY: Doubleday, 1958), 4, 42.

98. Allen Young, "Interview with Allen Ginsberg," in *Gay Sunshine Interviews*, vol. 1, ed. Winston Leyland (San Francisco: Gay Sunshine Press), 107, 106.

99. Wojnarowicz, *Close to the Knives*, 57.

100. Wojnarowicz, *Close to the Knives*, 41.

101. Butler, *Bodies That Matter*, 228.

102. Mark Turner, *Backward Glances: Cruising Queer Streets in London and New York* (London: Reaktion, 2003), 48; Bartlett, quoted in Chambers, *Loiterature*, 78.

103. Andrew Holleran, *Dancer from the Dance* (New York: Harper Perennial, 1978), 79–80.

104. Jean Carlomusto, and Emily Roysdon, "Radiant Spaces: An Introduction to Emily Roysdon's Photograph Series *Untitled*," *GLQ: A Journal of Lesbian and Gay Studies* 10, no. 4 (2004): 671.

105. Carlomusto and Roysdon, "Radiant Spaces," 672.

106. Wojnarowicz Papers, series 8, subseries A, media ID 092.0487 (Keith Davis interview [no date, ca. 1983]).

107. Grant, "Fans of Feminism," 274, 271.

108. Carlomusto, "Radiant Spaces," 671, 674.

109. Grant, "Fans of Feminism," 276.

110. Carlomusto, "Radiant Spaces," 671.

111. Emily Roysdon, "Ecstatic Resistance," *C Magazine*, no. 104 (2009), 17.

112. Roysdon, "Ecstatic Resistance," 21.

113. Carlos Motta, "An Interview with Emily Roysdon," *We Who Feel Differently*, April 15, 2011, accessed June 6, 2018, http://wewhofeeldifferently.info/interview.php?interview=112.

114. Emily Roysdon, *West Street* (New York: Printed Matter, 2010), n.p.

115. Roysdon, *West Street*, n.p.

116. Motta, "Interview with Emily Roysdon."

117. Roysdon, "Ecstatic Resistance," 15.

118. Wojnarowicz Papers, series 3, subseries B, box 5, folder 206 (mss., "scenes for a novel").

119. Lotringer, *David Wojnarowicz*, 108.

120. William S. Burroughs Papers, folio 59, box 14, folder 31 (The *Wild Boys* transcripts), Berg Collection, New York Public Library.

121. Wojnarowicz Papers, series 3, subseries B, box 5, folder 206 (mss., "scenes for a novel"); emphasis added.

122. William S. Burroughs and Brion Gysin, *The Third Mind* (London: J. Calder, 1979), 1.

123. Burroughs and Gysin, *Third Mind*, 9, 14, 3.

124. Burroughs and Gysin, *Third Mind*, 15.

125. William S. Burroughs, *The Soft Machine* (New York: Grove, 1966), 82.

126. Burroughs and Gysin, *Third Mind*, 15.

127. William S. Burroughs, *The Wild Boys: A Book of the Dead* (London: Penguin, 2008), 147, 101.

128. Burroughs, *Wild Boys*, 50, 128, 126, 128, 184.

129. Wojnarowicz Papers, series 3, subseries F, box 6, folder 273 (film script notes, loose adaptation of Burroughs's *Wildboys*).

130. Burroughs and Gysin, *Third Mind*, 18.

131. Wojnarowicz Papers, series 3, subseries F, box 6, folder 273 (film script notes, loose adaptation of Burroughs's *Wildboys*).

132. William S. Burroughs, *The Ticket That Exploded* (London: Fourth Estate, 2010), 5.

133. Wojnarowicz Papers, series 3, subseries F, box 6, folder 273 (film script notes, loose adaptation of Burroughs's *Wildboys*).

134. Burroughs and Gysin, *Third Mind*, 2, 18.

135. Burroughs, *Wild Boys*, 32.

136. Burroughs makes this comparison in Burroughs and Gysin, *Third Mind*, 3.

137. Burroughs, *Wild Boys*, 42.

138. Wojnarowicz, *Close to the Knives*, 13.

139. Burroughs, *Wild Boys*, 42.

140. Burroughs, *Wild Boys*, 41.

141. Burroughs, *Wild Boys*, 40.

142. Butler, *Bodies That Matter*, 228.

## Chapter Four

1. Ann L. Buttenwieser, *Manhattan Water-bound: Planning and Developing Manhattan's Waterfront from the Seventeenth Century to the Present* (New York: New York University Press, 1987), 205.

2. Robert F. Wagner Jr., "New York City Waterfront: Changing Land Use and Prospects for Redevelopment," in *Urban Waterfront Lands*, Committee on Urban Waterfront Lands (Washington, DC: National Academy of Sciences, 1980), 78.

3. Wagner, "New York City Waterfront," 204, 96.

4. See William W. Buzbee, *Fighting Westway: Environmental Law, Citizen Activism, and the Regulatory War That Transformed New York City* (Ithaca, NY: Cornell University Press, 2014).

5. Raymond W. Gastil, *Beyond the Edge: New York's New Waterfront* (New York: Princeton Architectural Press, 2002), 42.

6. Wagner, "New York City Waterfront," 96.

7. Gastil, *Beyond the Edge*, 43.

8. Douglas Crimp, "Alvin Baltrop: Pier Photographs, 1975–1986," *Artforum*, February 2008, 269.

9. Neil Smith, *The New Urban Frontier: Gentrification and the Revanchist City* (London: Routledge, 1996), 30.

10. Buttenwieser, *Manhattan Water-bound*, 203.

11. Susan S. Fainstein, *The City Builders: Property Development in New York and London, 1980–2000* (Lawrence: University Press of Kansas, 2001), 165.

12. Fainstein, *City Builders*, 166.

13. Rosalyn Deutsche and Cara Gendel Ryan, "The Fine Art of Gentrification," *October*, no. 31 (Winter 1984), 96, 95.

14. Buttenwieser, *Manhattan Water-bound*, 206.

15. Henri LeFebvre, *Writings on Cities* (Oxford: Blackwell, 1996), 159.

16. Buttenwieser, *Manhattan Water-bound*, 210.

17. Sarah Schulman, *The Gentrification of the Mind: Witness to a Lost Imagination* (Berkeley: University of California Press, 2012), 28, 27.

18. See Dennis Altman, *The Homosexualization of America: The Americanization of the Homosexual* (New York: St. Martin's Press, 1982), 206, and John Paul Ricco, *The Logic of the Lure* (Chicago: University of Chicago Press, 2002), 19.

19. Schulman, *Gentrification of the Mind*, 36.

20. Randall Mason, *The Once and Future New York: Historic Preservation and the Modern City* (Minneapolis: University of Minnesota Press, 2009), xiii.

21. Gregg Bordowitz, *The AIDS Crisis Is Ridiculous and Other Writings* (Cambridge, MA: MIT Press, 2004), 180.

22. David Wojnarowicz, *Close to the Knives: A Memoir of Disintegration* (New York: Vintage, 1991), 120, 121.

23. Buttenwieser, *Manhattan Water-Bound*, 205.

24. Pamela M. Lee, *Object to Be Destroyed: The Work of Gordon Matta-Clark* (Cambridge, MA: MIT Press, 1999), 127.

25. Barry Blinderman, "The Compression of Time: An Interview with David Wojnarowicz," in *David Wojnarowicz: Tongues of Flame*, ed. Blinderman (New York: D.A.P., 1989), 54.

26. Wojnarowicz, "Biographical Dateline," 118.

27. "Ephemera—Bars," International Gay Information Center archive, New York Public Library.

28. Wojnarowicz, *Close to the Knives*, 121.

29. Wojnarowicz, "Biographical Dateline," 118.

30. Mason, *Once and Future New York*, xiii.

31. Wojnarowicz, *Close to the Knives*, 24.

32. Rebecca Solnit, "The Ruins of Memory" (2007), in *Ruins*, ed. Brian Dillon (Cambridge, MA: MIT Press, 2011), 151.

33. Solnit, "Ruins of Memory," 151.

34. Wojnarowicz, *Close to the Knives*, 121.

35. Schulman, *Gentrification of the Mind*, 17.

36. Wojnarowicz, *Close to the Knives*, 121.

37. John Turcott, "The Village Piers: A Mugger's Paradise?" *Our Town* (New York), November 14, 1975, 1.

38. David Wojnarowicz Papers, series 8, subseries A, media ID 092.0530 (John/David conversation, 12/31/1980, Pt 2), Fales Library and Special Collections, New York University Libraries.

39. John Rechy, *Rushes* (New York: Grove, 1979), 13.

40. David Wojnarowicz, "Man on Second Avenue 2:00 am," in *The Waterfront Journals* (New York: Grove, 1996), 104.

41. Laura L. Finley, ed., *Encyclopedia of Juvenile Violence* (Westport, CT: Greenwood Press, 2007), 166.

42. Daniel J. Flannery, Alexander T. Vazsonyi, and Irwin D. Waldman, eds., *The Cambridge Handbook of Violent Behavior and Aggression* (Cambridge: Cambridge University Press, 2007), Kindle edition.

43. Ira Glasser, "The Yellow Star and the Pink Triangle," *New York Times*, September 10, 1975, 45.

44. Jim Ryan, untitled pier newsletter, International Gay Information Center archive, New York Public Library.

45. Ryan, untitled pier newsletter.

46. Ryan, untitled pier newsletter.

47. Ryan, untitled pier newsletter.

48. Ryan, untitled pier newsletter.

49. Kenneth Brodney, "A Methadone Ferry in Village Waters," *Village Voice*, August 19, 1971, 3.

50. Ryan, untitled pier newsletter.

51. Christina B. Hanhardt, *Safe Space: Gay Neighborhood History and the Politics of Violence* (Durham, NC: Duke University Press, 2013), 110.

52. Hanhardt, *Safe Space*, 110.

53. Hanhardt, *Safe Space*, 109.

54. Hanhardt, *Safe Space*, 112.

55. Ryan, untitled pier newsletter.

56. Benjamin Shepard and Greg Smithsimon, *The Beach beneath the Streets: Contesting New York City's Public Spaces* (New York: State University of New York Press, 2011), 110.

57. Leslie Feinberg, "Lavender and Red 73: Street Action Transvestite Revolutionaries," *Workers' World*, September 26, 2006, accessed August 31, 2016, http://www.workers.org/2006/us/lavender-red-73/.

58. Samuel Delany, *Times Square Red, Times Square Blue* (New York: New York University Press, 1999), 15–16.

59. Delany, *Times Square Red*, 146.

60. Amy Scholder, ed., *In the Shadow of the American Dream: The Diaries of David Wojnarowicz* (New York: Grove, 1999), 169.

61. Scholder, *In the Shadow of the American Dream*, 120, 169.

62. David Paternotte and Manon Tremblay, eds., *Ashgate Research Companion to Lesbian and Gay Activism* (London: Routledge, 2016), 95.

63. Ehn Nothing, "Introduction: Queens against Society," in *Street Transvestite Action Revolutionaries: Survival, Revolt, and Queer Antagonist Struggle* (New York: Untorelli Press, 2013), 5, 6.

64. Nothing, "Queens against Society," 6.

65. Schulman, *Gentrification of the Mind*, 14.

66. Schulman, *Gentrification of the Mind*, 28.

67. Rachel Kranz and Tim Cusick, *Gay Rights* (New York: Facts on File, 2000), 36.

68. Karla Jay and Allen Young, eds., *Out of the Closets: Voices of Gay Liberation* (New York: New York University Press, 1992), 12.

69. "Ephemera—Bars," International Gay Information Center archive, New York Public Library. The following two paragraphs also rely on documents in this file.

70. Grace Lichtenstein, "Homosexuals in 'Village' Fearful after Series of Similar Killings," *New York Times*, January 18, 1973, 88.

71. William Friedkin, interviewed in Linda Williams, *The Erotic Thriller in Contemporary Cinema* (Bloomington: Indiana University Press, 2005), 135.

72. Nathan Lee, "Gay Old Time," *Village Voice*, August 28, 2007, accessed August 24, 2016, http://www.villagevoice.com/film/gay-old-time-6419214.

73. Lee, "Gay Old Time."

74. Williams, *Erotic Thriller*, 138.

75. John Rechy, *Beneath the Skin: The Collected Essays* (New York: Carroll & Graf, 2004), 80.

76. Rechy, *Beneath the Skin*, 81.

77. Rechy, *Beneath the Skin*, 81–82.

78. "Ephemera—Bars," International Gay Information Center archive, New York Public Library.

79. David W. Dunlap, "New York's Own Anti-Gay Massacre, Now Barely Remembered," *New York Times*, June 16, 2016, A18.

80. Thomas L. Long, *AIDS and American Apocalypticism: The Cultural Semiotics of an Epidemic* (New York: State University of New York Press, 2005), 107.

81. Dunlap, "New York's Own Anti-Gay Massacre," A18.

82. "Governor, Mayor Recommend Head of Hudson River Park Trust," June 16, 1999, accessed July 16, 2012, http://www.nyc.gov/html/om/html/99a/pr235-99.html.

83. Benjamin Shepard, "Sylvia and Sylvia's Children: A Battle for a Queer Public Space" in *That's Revolting! Queer Strategies for Resisting Assimilation*, ed. Sycamore [Mattilda Bernstein] (New York: Soft Skull, 2004), 145.

84. See Rickie Manazala, "The FIERCE Fight for Power and the Preservation of Public Space in the West Village," *S & F Online* 10, nos. 1–2 (Fall 2011/Spring 2012), http://sfonline.barnard.edu/a-new-queer-agenda/the-fierce-fight-for-power-and-the-preservation-of-public-space-in-the-west-village/. Accessed 14 July 2017.

85. Shepard, "Sylvia and Sylvia's Children,"103.

86. Randy Kennedy, "Neighborhood Report: West Village. The Young: Risk and Refuge: The New World Near West Street," *New York Times*, June 19, 1994, accessed July 14, 2017, http://www.nytimes.com/1994/06/19/nyregion/neighborhood-report-west-village-young-risk-refuge-new-world-near-west-street.html.

87. Allan Bérubé, "History of Gay Bathhouses," *Journal of Homosexuality* 44, nos. 3–4 (2003): 33.

88. Schulman, *Gentrification of the Mind*, 25.

89. Mick Meenan, "Sakia Gunn's Killer Pleads Guilty," *Gay City News* 4, no. 10 (March 10–16, 2005), accessed July 14, 2017, http://gaycitynews.nyc/gcn_410/sakiagunnskiller.html.

90. Arthur Z. Schwartz, "Recommendation of the Pier 40 Working Group of the Hudson River Park Advisory Council regarding the Development Proposals for Pier 40" (June 28, 2007), 5, accessed August 24, 2016, http://www.gvshp.org/documents/pier40wkggrprecs.htm.

91. FIERCE, with the Urban Justice Center, "LGBT Youth Center: Pier 40 Recommendation" (January 29, 2008), 10, 8, 14; accessed August 24, 2016, http://www.fiercenyc.org/sites/default/files/resources/2889_Pier40Proposal.pdf.

92. Hudson River Park Rules and Regulations, quoted in FIERCE and Urban Justice Center, "LGBT Youth Center," 12, 13.

93. Nathan Ward, "Take Me to the River, Finally," *New York Times*, July 4, 2010, A17.

94. Ward, "Take Me to the River, Finally," A17.

95. Wojnarowicz, *Close to the Knives*, 121.

## Conclusion

1. "Ephemera—Bars," International Gay Information Center archive, New York Public Library.

2. Robert Sember, "In the Shadow of the Object: Sexual Memory in the AIDS Epidemic," *Space & Culture* 6, no. 3 (August 2003): 217; David Román, *Acts of Intervention: Performance, Gay Culture, and AIDS* (Bloomington: Indiana University Press, 1998), 100.

3. Sember, "In the Shadow of the Object," 219.

4. Robert Smithson, "A Tour of the Monuments of Passaic, New Jersey," in *Robert Smithson: The Collected Writings*, ed. Jack Flam (Berkeley: University of California Press, 1996), 71.

5. Tim Edensor, *Industrial Ruins: Space, Aesthetics, and Materiality* (Oxford: Berg, 2005), 11.

6. Thomas L. Long, *AIDS and American Apocalypticism: The Cultural Semiotics of an Epidemic* (New York: State University of New York Press, 2012), 6, 2.

7. Quoted in Victoria C. Gardner Coates, Kenneth Lapatin, and Jon L. Seydl, eds. *The Last Days of Pompeii: Decadence, Apocalypse, Resurrection* (Los Angeles: Getty Publications, 2012), 87.

8. Jon L. Seydl, "Decadence, Apocalypse, Ressurection," in Gardner Coates et al., *Last Days of Pompeii*, 21.

9. Andrew Sullivan, "When Plagues End: Notes on the Twilight of an Epidemic," *New York Times Magazine*, November 10, 1996, 61–62.

10. Amy Scholder, ed., *In the Shadow of the American Dream: The Diaries of David Wojnarowicz* (New York: Grove, 1999), 135.

11. Douglas Crimp, "How to Have Promiscuity in an Epidemic," *October*, no. 43 (October 1987), 253.

12. Paula Treichler, *How to Have Theory in An Epidemic: Cultural Chronicles of AIDS* (Durham, NC: Duke University Press, 1999), 11.

13. Smithson, "Tour of the Monuments," 71.

14. Sember, "In the Shadow of the Object," 217.

15. Andrew Holleran, *Dancer from the Dance* (New York: Harper Perennial, 1978), 79–80.

16. M. Christine Boyer, *The City of Collective Memory: Its Historical Imagery and Architectural Entertainments* (Cambridge, MA: MIT Press, 1994), 465.

# *Bibliography*


Acconci, Vito. "Public Space in a Private Time." *Critical Inquiry* 16, no. 4 (1990): 900–918.

Altman, Dennis. *The Homosexualization of America: The Americanization of the Homosexual.* New York: St. Martin's Press, 1982.

"Anarchitecture." *Flash Art*, June 1974, 36–37.

Apollinaire, Guillaume. *Alcools: Poems*. Translated by Donald Revell. Hanover, NH: University Press of New England, 1995.

Apple, Jacki, and Mary Delahoyd. *Alternatives in Retrospect: An Historical Overview, 1969–1975.* New York: New Museum, 1981.

Augier, Émile. *Le mariage d'Olympe*. Paris: Calmann Lévy, 1881.

Badgett, Mary Virginia Lee. *Money, Myths, and Change: The Economic Lives of Lesbians and Gay Men.* Chicago: University of Chicago Press, 2003.

Barthes, Roland. *Camera Lucida: Reflections on Photography.* Translated by Richard Howard. London: Flamingo, 1984.

———. "The Death of the Author." In *Image/Music/Text*. Translated by Stephen Heath. London: Fontana, 1977.

Bartlett, Neil. *Who Was That Man? A Present for Mr. Oscar Wilde*. London: Serpent's Tail, 1988.

Beck, Martin. "Alternative Space." In *Alternative Art New York, 1965–1985: A Cultural Politics Book for the Social Text Collective, the Drawing Center, New York*. Edited by Julie Ault. Minneapolis: University of Minnesota Press, 2002.

Bersani, Leo. "Is the Rectum a Grave?" *October*, no. 43 (1987), 197–222.

Betsky, Aaron. *Queer Space: Architecture and Same-Sex Desire*. New York: William Morrow, 1997.

Blinderman, Barry, ed. *David Wojnarowicz: Tongues of Flame*. New York: D.A.P., 1989.

Bloom, Harold. *The Anxiety of Influence: A Theory of Poetry*. Oxford: Oxford University Press, 1997.

Bonney, Anney, and Mike Bidlo. "Mike Bidlo." *BOMB*, no. 45 (1993), 22–27. http://bombsite.com/issues/45/articles/1693.

Bordowitz, Gregg. *The AIDS Crisis Is Ridiculous and Other Writings*. Cambridge, MA: MIT Press, 2004.

Boyer, M. Christine. *The City of Collective Memory: Its Historical Imagery and Architectural Entertainments*. Cambridge, MA: MIT Press, 1994.

Bravmann, Scott. *Queer Fictions of the Past: History, Culture and Difference*. Cambridge: Cambridge University Press, 1997.

Brodney, Kenneth. "A Methadone Ferry in Village Waters." *Village Voice*, August 19, 1971.

Bruno, Giuliana. *Atlas of Emotion: Journeys in Art, Architecture, and Film*. New York: Verso, 2002.

Buchloh, Benjamin H. D. "Allegorical Procedures: Appropriation and Montage in Contemporary Art." *Artforum*, September 1982, 43–56.

Burroughs, William S. *The Soft Machine*. New York: Grove, 1966.

———. *The Ticket That Exploded*. London: Fourth Estate, 2010.

———. *The Wild Boys: A Book of the Dead*. London: Penguin, 2008.

Burroughs, William S., and Brion Gysin. *The Third Mind*. London: J. Calder, 1979.

Buskirk, Martha. *The Contingent Object of Contemporary Art*. Cambridge, MA: MIT Press, 2003.

Butler, Judith. *Bodies That Matter*. London: Routledge, 1993.

Buttenwieser, Ann L. *Manhattan Water-bound: Planning and Developing Manhattan's Waterfront from the Seventeenth Century to the Present*. New York: New York University Press, 1987.

Buzbee, William W. *Fighting Westway: Environmental Law, Citizen Activism, and the Regulatory War That Transformed New York City*. Ithaca, NY: Cornell University Press, 2014.

Cameron, Dan, et al. *East Village USA*. New York: New Museum, 2004.

———, ed. *Fever: The Art of David Wojnarowicz*. New York: Rizzoli, 1999.

Carlomusto, Jean, and Emily Roysdon. "Radiant Spaces: An Introduction to Emily Roysdon's Photograph Series Untitled." *GLQ: A Journal of Lesbian and Gay Studies* 10, no. 4 (2004): 671–79.

Carr, Cynthia. *A Fire in the Belly: The Life and Times of David Wojnarowicz*. London: Bloomsbury, 2012.

Carter, David. *Stonewall: The Riots that Sparked a Gay Revolution*. New York: St. Martin's Press, 2004.

Certeau, Michel de. *The Practice of Everyday Life*. Translated by Steven Rendal. Berkeley: University of California Press, 1984.

Chambers, Ross. *Loiterature*. Lincoln: University of Nebraska Press, 1999.

Chisholm, Dianne. *Queer Constellations: Subcultural Space in the Wake of the City*. Minneapolis: University of Minnesota Press, 2004.

Clunis, D. Merilee, et al. *Lives of Lesbian Elders: Looking Back, Looking Forward*. New York: Haworth Press, 2005.

Cooke, Lynne, and Douglas Crimp, with Kristin Poor, eds. *Mixed Use, Manhattan: Photography and Related Practices, 1970s to the Present*. Cambridge, MA: MIT Press; Museo Nacional Centro de Arte Reina Sofia, 2010.

Corrigan, Timothy. *The Essay Film: From Montaigne, after Marker*. Oxford: Oxford University Press, 2011.

Corso, Gregory. "Paris." In *Poems for Architects: An Anthology*, ed. Jill Stoner. San Francisco: William Stout, 2003.

Crane, Hart. *The Complete Poems of Hart Crane*. Garden City, NY: Doubleday, 1958.

Crimp, Douglas. "Action around the Edges." In Cooke and Crimp, *Mixed Use, Manhattan*.

———. "Alvin Baltrop: Pier Photographs, 1975–1986." *Artforum*, February 2008, 262–73.

———. *Before Pictures*. Chicago: University of Chicago Press, 2016.

———. "How to Have Promiscuity in an Epidemic." *October*, no. 43 (1987), 237–71.

———. *On the Museum's Ruins*. Cambridge, MA: MIT Press, 1993.

Crow, Thomas. *Modern Art in the Common Culture*. New Haven, CT: Yale University Press, 1996.

Dean, Tim. *Unlimited Intimacy: Reflections on the Subculture of Barebacking*. Chicago: University of Chicago Press, 2009.

Delany, Samuel R. *The Motion of Light in Water*. New York: Arbor House, 1988.

———. *Times Square Red, Times Square Blue*. New York: New York University Press, 1999.

Derrida, Jacques. *Spectres of Marx*. Translated by Peggy Kamuf. London: Routledge, 1994.

Deutsche, Rosalyn, and Cara Gendel Ryan. "The Fine Art of Gentrification." *October*, no. 31 (Winter 1984).

Dillon, Brian, ed. *Ruins*. Documents of Contemporary Art. Cambridge, MA: MIT Press, 2011.

Dinshaw, Carolyn, Lee Edelman, et al. "Theorizing Queer Temporalities: A Roundtable Discussion." *GLQ: A Journal of Lesbian and Gay Studies* 13, nos. 2–3 (2007): 177–95.

Dlugos, Tim. *A Fast Life: The Collected Poems of Tim Dlugos*. Edited by David Trinidad. Callicoon, NY: Nightboat Books, 2011.

Doane, Mary Ann. *The Emergence of Cinematic Time*. Cambridge, MA: Harvard University Press, 2002.

Duberman, Martin. *Stonewall*. New York: Plume, 1994.

Dunlap, David W. "New York's Own Anti-Gay Massacre, Now Barely Remembered." *New York Times*, June 16, 2016.

Edelman, Lee. *Homographesis: Essays in Gay Literary and Cultural Theory*. London: Routledge, 1994.

———. *No Future: Queer Theory and the Death Drive*. Durham, NC: Duke University Press, 2004.

Eliot, T. S. *Collected Poems: 1909–1962*. London: Faber and Faber, 1963.

———. "Tradition and the Individual Talent." In *Modernism: An Anthology*, ed. Lawrence Rainey. Oxford: Blackwell, 2005.

Fainstein, Susan S. *The City Builders: Property Development in New York and London, 1980–2000*. Lawrence: University of Kansas Press, 2001.

Feinberg, Leslie. "Lavender and Red 73: Street Transvestite Action Revolutionaries." *Workers' World*, September 26, 2006.

Finley, Laura L., ed. *Encyclopedia of Juvenile Violence*. Westport, CT: Greenwood Press, 2007.

Flannery, Daniel J., Alexander T. Vazsonyi, and Irwin D. Waldman, eds. *The Cambridge Handbook of Violent Behavior and Aggression*. Cambridge: Cambridge University Press, 2007.

Foote, Nancy. "The Apotheosis of the Crummy Space." *Artforum*, October 1976, 26–36.

Foucault, Michel. "Of Other Spaces." *Diacritics* 16, no. 1 (Spring 1986): 22–27.

Foucault, Michel, René de Ceccatty, Jean Danet, and Jean Le Bitoux. "Friendship as a Way of Life." In *Michel Foucault: Ethics, Subjectivity and Truth*, edited by Paul Rabinow. Paris: Editions G, 1997.

Fowlie, Wallace. *Rimbaud: The Myth of Childhood*. Chicago: University of Chicago Press, 1965.

Freeman, Elizabeth. *Time Binds: Queer Temporalities, Queer Histories*. Durham, NC: Duke University Press, 2010.

Genet, Jean. *Querelle of Brest*. Translated by Gregory Steatham. London: Faber, 1973.

———. *The Thief's Journal*. Translated by Bernard Frechtman. New York: Grove, 1964.

Glasser, Ira. "The Yellow Star and the Pink Triangle." *New York Times*, September 10, 1975.

Gove, Ben. *Cruising Culture: Promiscuity, Desire and American Gay Literature*. Edinburgh: Edinburgh University Press, 2000.

Grant, Catherine. "Fans of Feminism: Re-Writing Histories of Second-Wave Feminism in Contemporary Art." *Oxford Art Journal* 34, no. 2 (2011): 265–86.

Halberstam, Jack. *In a Queer Time and Place: Transgender Bodies, Subcultural Lives*. New York: New York University Press, 2005.

Hanhardt, Christina B. *Safe Space: Gay Neighborhood History and the Politics of Violence*. Durham, NC: Duke University Press, 2013.

Hayden, Dolores. *The Power of Place: Urban Landscape as Public History*. Cambridge, MA: MIT Press, 1997.

Heap, Chad. *Slumming: Sexual and Racial Encounters in American Nightlife, 1885–1940*. Chicago: University of Chicago Press, 2009.

Hoffman, Wayne. "The Great Gay Way: A Brief History of Christopher Street." *Village Voice*, June 15, 2004.

Holleran, Andrew. *Dancer from the Dance*. New York: Harper Perennial, 1978.

———. "Nostalgia for the Mud." In *The View from Christopher Street: Journalism from America's Leading Gay Magazine* ed. Michael Denneny, Charles Ortleb, and Thomas Steeled (London: Hogarth Press, 1984).

Hujar, Peter. *Animals and Nudes*. Sante Fe, NM: Twin Palms, 2001.

———. *Portraits in Life and Death*. New York: Da Capo, 1976.

Humphreys, Laud. *Tearoom Trade: Impersonal Sex in Public Places*. Chicago: Aldine, 1975.

Ingram, Gordon Brent, Anne-Marie Bouthillette, and Yolanda Retter, eds. *Queers in Space: Communities–Public Spaces–Sites of Resistance*. Seattle, WA: Bay Press, 1997.

Jacobs, Jane. *The Death and Life of Great American Cities*. Harmondsworth: Penguin, 1965.

Jay, Karla, and Allen Young, eds. *Out of the Closets: Voices of Gay Liberation*. New York: New York University Press, 1992.

Kane, Daniel. *Do You Have a Band? Poetry and Punk Rock in New York City*. New York: Columbia University Press, 2017.

Kennedy, Randy. "Neighborhood Report: West Village. The Young: Risk and Refuge: The New World Near West Street." *New York Times*, June 19, 1994.

Koch, Stephen, et al. *Peter Hujar*. New York: Grey Art Gallery and Study Center, New York University, 1990.

Koven, Seth. *Slumming: Sexual and Social Politics in Victorian London*. Princeton, NJ: Princeton University Press, 2004.

Kramer, Larry. *Faggots*. London: Minerva, 1990.

Kranz, Rachel, and Tim Cusick. *Gay Rights*. New York: Facts on File, 2000.

Lacan, Jacques. *Écrits*. Translated by Alan Sheridan. London: Tavistock, 1977.

Lee, Nathan. "Gay Old Time." *Village Voice*, August 28, 2007.

Lee, Pamela M. *Object to Be Destroyed: The Work of Gordon Matta-Clark*. Cambridge, MA: MIT Press, 1999.

———. *Writings on Cities*. Translated by Eleonore Kofman and Elizabeth Lebas. Oxford: Blackwell, 1996.

Linker, Kate. *Vito Acconci*. New York: Rizzoli, 1994.

Lippard, Lucy, et al. *Brushfires in the Social Landscape*. New York: Aperture Foundation, 2015.

Lofton, Rodney. *No More Tomorrows: Two Lives, Two Stories, One Love*. Largo, MD: Strebor Books, 2009.

Long, Thomas L. *AIDS and American Apocalypticism: The Cultural Semiotics of an Epidemic*. New York: State University of New York Press, 2005.

Lotringer, Sylvere, ed. *David Wojnarowicz: A Definitive History of Five or Six Years on the Lower East Side*. New York: Semiotext(e), 2006.

Mallarmé, Stéphane. "The Tomb of Edgar Poe." Translated by Daisy Aldan. In *An Anthology of French Poetry from Nerval to Valéry in English Translation*, edited by Angel Flores. Garden City, NY: Doubleday, 1958.

Manazala, Rickie. "The FIERCE Fight for Power and the Preservation of Public Space in the West Village." *S & F Online* 10, nos. 1–2 (Fall 2011/Spring 2012).

Mann, Thomas. *The Magic Mountain*. Translated by John E. Woods. London: Everyman, 2005.

Mason, Randall. *The Once and Future New York: Historic Preservation and the Modern City*. Minneapolis: University of Minnesota Press, 2009.

Meenan, Mick. "Sakia Gunn's Killer Pleads Guilty." *Gay City News* 4, no. 10 (March 10–16, 2005).

Melville, Herman. *Moby-Dick; or, The Whale*. 1851; London: Penguin, 2009.

Miller, Henry. "The Ghetto (N.Y.)," from *Sexus*. In *The Henry Miller Reader*, edited by Lawrence Durrell. New York: New Directions, 1959.

———. *The Time of the Assassins: A Study of Arthur Rimbaud*. New York: New Directions, 1946.

Motta, Carlos. "An Interview with Emily Roysdon." *We Who Feel Differently*, April 15, 2011.

Moure, Gloria, ed. *Gordon Matta-Clark: Works and Collected Writings*. Barcelona: Ediciones Poligrafa, 2006.

Nesbitt, Molly. "Bright Lights, Big City: The '80s without Walls." *Artforum*, May 2003, 184–89, 245–48.

O'Hara, Frank. "In Memory of My Feelings." In *The Collected Poems of Frank O'Hara*. Ed. Donald Allen. Berkeley: University of California Press, 1995.

Page, Max. *The Creative Destruction of Manhattan, 1900–1940*. Chicago: University of Chicago Press, 1999.

Paternotte, David, and Manon Tremblay, eds. *The Ashgate Research Companion to Lesbian and Gay Activism*. London: Routledge, 2016.

Peretti, Burton W. *Nightclub City: Politics and Amusement in Manhattan*. Philadelphia: University of Pennsylvania Press, 2007.

Perloff, Marjorie. *Frank O'Hara: Poet among Painters*. New York: George Braziller, 1977.

———. *The Poetics of Indeterminacy: Rimbaud to Cage*. Evanston, IL: Northwestern University Press, 1981.

Picano, Felice. *The Lure*. New York: Dell, 1979.

Rechy, John. *Beneath the Skin: The Collected Essays*. New York: Carroll & Graf, 2004.

———. *City of Night*. London: Panther, 1968.

———. *Rushes*. New York: Grove, 1979.

Reed, Christopher, and Christopher Castiglia. *If Memory Serves: Gay Men, AIDS, and the Promise of the Queer Past*. Minneapolis: University of Minnesota Press, 2011.

Ricco, John Paul. *The Logic of the Lure*. Chicago: University of Chicago Press, 2002.

Rimbaud, Arthur. *I Promise to Be Good: The Letters of Arthur Rimbaud*. Translated by Wyatt Mason. New York: Modern Library, 2003.

———. *Rimbaud: Complete Works, Selected Letters*. Translated by Wallace Fowlie. Chicago: University of Chicago Press, 1966.

Román, David. *Acts of Intervention: Performance, Gay Culture, and AIDS*. Bloomington: Indiana University Press, 1998.

Roscoe, Will, with Harry Hay. *Radically Gay: Gay Liberation in the Words of Its Founder*. Boston: Beacon, 1996.

Roth, Andrew, ed. *Rimbaud in New York 1978–1979*. New York: PPP Editions, 2004.

Roysdon, Emily. *West Street*. New York: Printed Matter, 2010.

Scholder, Amy, ed. *In the Shadow of the American Dream: The Diaries of David Wojnarowicz*. New York: Grove, 1999.

Schulman, Sarah. *The Gentrification of the Mind: Witness to a Lost Imagination*. Berkeley: University of California Press, 2012.

Seccombe, Shelley. *Lost Waterfront: The Decline and Rebirth of Manhattan's Western Shore*. New York: Fordham University Press, 2007.

Sember, Robert. "In the Shadow of the Object: Sexual Memory in the AIDS Epidemic." *Space & Culture* 6, no. 3 (August 2003).

Shepard, Benjamin. "Sylvia and Sylvia's Children: A Battle for a Queer Public Space." In *That's Revolting! Queer Strategies for Resisting Assimilation*, ed. Sycamore [Mattilda Bernstein]. New York: Soft Skull, 2004.

Shepard, Benjamin, and Greg Smithsimon. *The Beach beneath the Streets: Contesting New York City's Public Spaces*. New York: State University of New York Press, 2011.

Smith, Neil. *The New Urban Frontier: Gentrification and the Revanchist City*. London: Routledge, 1996.

Smithson, Robert. *Robert Smithson: The Collected Writings*. Edited by Jack Flam. Berkeley: University of California Press, 1996.

Stosuy, Brandon, ed. *Up Is Up, but So Is Down: New York's Downtown Literary Scene 1974–1992*. New York: New York University Press, 2006.

*Street Transvestite Action Revolutionaries: Survival, Revolt, and Queer Antagonist Struggle*. New York: Untorelli Press, 2013.

Sugano, Marian Zwerling. *The Poetics of the Occasion: Mallarmé and the Poetry of Circumstance*. Stanford, CA: Stanford University Press, 1992.

Tattelman, Ira. "Staging Sex and Masculinity at the Mineshaft." *Men and Masculinities* 7, no. 3 (January 2005): 300–309.

Taylor, Marvin, ed. *The Downtown Book: The New York Art Scene 1974–1984*. Princeton, NJ: Princeton University Press, 2006.

Torres, Mario Garcia. *9 at Leo Castelli*. San Juan, PR: Instituto de Cultura Puertorriqueña, 2009.

Trask, Michael. *Cruising Modernism: Class and Sexuality in American Literature and Social Thought*. Ithaca, NY: Cornell University Press, 2003.

Treichler, Paula. *How to Have Theory in an Epidemic: Cultural Chronicles of AIDS*. Durham, NC: Duke University Press, 1999.

Turner, Mark W. *Backward Glances: Cruising Queer Streets in London and New York*. London: Reaktion, 2003.

Wagner, Robert F., Jr. "New York City Waterfront: Changing Land Use and Prospects for Redevelopment." In *Urban Waterfront Lands*. Washington, DC: National Academy of Sciences, 1980.

Ward, Nathan. *Dark Harbor: The War for the New York Waterfront*. New York: Farrar, Straus and Giroux, 2010.

———. "Take Me to the River, Finally." *New York Times*, July 4, 2010.

White, Edmund. *City Boy: My Life in New York during the 1960s and '70s*. London: Bloomsbury, 2011.

———. *Nocturnes for the King of Naples*. London: Picador, 1984.

———. *States of Desire: Travels in Gay America*. London: Pan Books, 1986.

Whitman, Walt. *Complete Poems*. London: Penguin, 2004.

Williams, Linda. *The Erotic Thriller in Contemporary Cinema*. Bloomington: Indiana University Press, 2005.

Williams, Richard J. *After Modern Sculpture*. Manchester: Manchester University Press, 2000.

Wines, James (SITE). *De-Architecture*. New York: Rizzoli, 1987.

Wojnarowicz, David. *Close to the Knives: A Memoir of Disintegration*. New York: Vintage, 1991.

———. *Memories That Smell Like Gasoline*. New York: Artspace Books, 1992.

Wojnarowicz, David, with James Romberger and Marguerite van Cook. *Seven Miles a Second*. New York: DC Comics, 1996.

Wolfe, Tom. "Radical Chic: That Party at Lenny's." *New York*, June 8, 1970.

Young, Allen. "Interview with Allen Ginsberg." In *Gay Sunshine Interviews*, vol. 1, ed. Winston Leyland. San Francisco: Gay Sunshine Press, 1974.

# Index